Developmental Parenting

Developmental Parenting

A Guide for
Early Childhood Practitioners

by

Lori A. Roggman, Ph.D.

Lisa K. Boyce, Ph.D.

and

Mark S. Innocenti, Ph.D.

Utah State University
Logan

·P·A·U·L·H·
BROOKES
PUBLISHING C?®

Baltimore • London • Sydney

Paul H. Brookes Publishing Co.
Post Office Box 10624
Baltimore, Maryland 21285-0624
USA

www.brookespublishing.com

Typeset by Integrated Publishing Solutions, Grand Rapids, Michigan.
Manufactured in the United States of America by
Versa Press, Inc., East Peoria, Illinois.

The individuals described in this book are composites or real people
whose situations are masked and are based on the authors' actual
experiences. Real names and identifying details are used by permission.

Library of Congress Cataloging-in-Publication Data

Roggman, Lori A.
  Developmental parenting : a guide for early childhood practitioners / by Lori A.
Roggman, Lisa K. Boyce, and Mark S. Innocenti.
     p.   cm.
  Includes bibliographical references and index.
  ISBN-13: 978-1-55766-976-6 (pbk.)
  ISBN-10: 1-55766-976-7 (pbk.)
  1. Home-based family services—United States.   2. Parents—Services for—United
States.   3. Child development—Study and teaching—United States.   4. Parenting—
Study and teaching—United States.   I. Boyce, Lisa K.   II. Innocenti, Mark S.
III. Title.
  HV699.R65 2008
  362.82'86—dc22   2008027176

British Library Cataloguing in Publication data are available
from the British Library.

2025 2024 2023 2022 2021
10   9   8   7

Contents

About the Authors

Lori A. Roggman, Ph.D., Professor, Department of Family, Consumer, and Human Development, Utah State University, Logan, Utah 84322

Dr. Roggman began her career as a Head Start home visitor and subsequently provided training to home visitors in the western United States for several years. Since the mid-1980s, she has been involved in research with several early childhood and infant/toddler home visiting programs, including research funded by the Administration on Children, Youth and Families. Her approach to research integrates theory-based inquiry with practical questions and program evaluation in longitudinal and intervention research. Her research interests focus on early development, in multiple domains, in relation to parenting by both mothers and fathers. She has studied various aspects of practices used in home visiting programs, the impacts of parenting support programs on children's cognitive, language, and social-emotional development, and the relation of specific parenting behaviors to children's developmental outcomes. With her colleagues, she has developed several tools for improving practices for working with parents, including an observational measure of developmental parenting and a measure of home visiting practices.

Lisa K. Boyce, Ph.D., Research Assistant Professor, Department of Family, Consumer, and Human Development; Research Scientist, Emma Eccles Jones Center for Early Childhood Education and Early Intervention Research Institute, Utah State University, Logan, Utah 84322

Dr. Boyce currently teaches child development and child guidance courses at Utah State University. She has conducted numerous assessments with children with disabilities and those who are at risk for disabilities. She has also provided parenting support to families with children with disabilities through home visits and parenting groups. Her research has focused on facilitating children's language and emergent literacy development through everyday parent–child conversations, self-regulation and development through parenting and preschool practices, and the creation and use of meaningful literacy materials. This work has been funded for Migrant Head Start families by the Administration on Children, Youth and Families and for young children with disabilities and their families through the Office of Special Education Programs.

Mark S. Innocenti, Ph.D., Associate Director, Early Intervention Research Institute, Center for Persons with Disabilities; Research Associate Professor of Psychology, Utah State University, Logan, Utah 84322

Dr. Innocenti has more than 25 years of experience working with infants and young children at-risk of having or with disabilities and their families through multiple research, training, and model demonstration projects. He has served as Principal Investigator on a number of research projects including the Longitudinal Institute on the Effects and Costs of Early Intervention for Children with Disabilities and the Bilingual Early Language and Literacy Support (BELLS) Project. Other research projects have examined various aspects of intervention and outcomes for families and children in early intervention, in Head Start, and in at-risk environments. Dr. Innocenti has experience in projects that have examined areas such as social interaction, child transition, naturalistic intervention, parent–child interaction, and service systems. His recent work has focused on implementing the practices described in *Developmental Parenting: A Guide for Early Childhood Practitioners* in home visiting and preschool programs.

Foreword

I was excited to read *Developmental Parenting: A Guide for Early Childhood Practitioners,* and I am delighted to be invited to write the foreword. The authors and I have come full circle on this topic. I first "met" the lead author, Lori Roggman, when I visited Bear River Head Start in Logan, Utah, on a pre-award site visit for the first wave of Early Head Start programs in 1995. Lori and I talked by phone (ironically, I was the one in Logan, as she was out of town due to a family emergency). She shared her perception about the work of the program and the likelihood of success of what we referred to then as their "home visiting" model. Lori had begun her career in early childhood education as a home visitor some decades earlier; in fact, the beginning of her professional career as a home visitor is delightfully portrayed in the final chapter of *Developmental Parenting.* After this visit, Lori subsequently partnered with the Early Head Start program to apply for a research grant, and that partnership was selected to participate in the Early Head Start Research Consortium. Through these local and national partnerships, she grew further in her understanding of how home visiting works, from the inside out, from the visitor through the parent to the child. There is no one I trust more to understand home visiting than Lori Roggman, together with her outstanding coauthors Lisa Boyce and Mark Innocenti. Mark was one of the reviewers in the first years of Early Head Start grants, and Lisa later joined the Early Head Start Utah State University research team.

At a time when it seems that what is written about home visiting is repetitious and often polemic, *Developmental Parenting* provides a fresh view. In some ways, Roggman, Boyce, and Innocenti have turned the concept of home visiting on end, and in so doing, have opened the door for a new era of home visitation-related thinking.

First, the authors have used the term *developmental parenting* to move the focus for home visitation from a delivery system with widely varying strategies to a particular type of program that directly supports parenting "on the living room floor"—or wherever parents and children interact. Developmental parenting, as the authors define it in Chapter 1, "is the kind of parenting that values a child's development, supports a child's development, and changes along with a child's development. Developmental parenting is warm, responsive, encouraging, and communicative. It is the kind of parenting that many programs serving infants and young children, especially home-based programs, hope to increase through home visits or other parenting support services" (p. 1).

Second, their approach leads us to reflect more carefully on the purposes for home visitation. The authors, drawing on their years of providing and researching home visitation, present attitudes, behaviors, and content for a particular form of home visitation—one that specifically facilitates parenting and thereby empowers parents to more effectively support the development of their children. To move into a new era, it is time for home visitation as a field and for specific home visiting programs to convey their theories of change about how each program is expected to work. This book does a good job of explaining how to do that.

Third, their model is compatible with newer conceptualizations of home visitation that emphasize a triadic model, in which the home visitor skillfully engages with parent and child in a three-way relationship. This triadic model represents a more sophisticated approach than earlier models that emphasized the home visitor's relationship to the child or the home visitor's relationship to the parent alone. With the triadic emphasis, the authors seek a respectful and supportive way to help parents provide more effective support for their children's early (birth to kindergarten) development, and they contrast that with "show-and-tell" approaches that use demonstration and/or didactic information. This model also is compatible with an emerging literature on coaching that fully elaborates on the skills and roles of the coach—who performs many of the functions identified by the facilitative home visitor in this book—building on strengths of children and parents, observing and co-creating plans and goals with children and parents to determine where the emphases are best placed during home visits and between sessions, and offering new information in the context of interaction rather than through handouts or from a script. The information provided in *Developmental Parenting* will enable home visitors to continue to refine and develop the concepts and techniques for expert guidance of parents in this more subtle way.

Fourth, *Developmental Parenting* is very specific about the attitudes, behaviors, and even the content of home visits that support parents so that they can support children's development. The authors are to be commended for linking the theory and research to specific aims and behaviors right down to the dialogues used during the home visit. In fact, a real joy of this book is the large array of sample dialogues that home visitors who adopt the assumptions of the authors can consult. In no way do these examples detract from the creativity assumed for the *Developmental Parenting* home visitor. However, there are enough examples that the reader can truly contrast them to ways of talking and interacting with parents under a different set of assumptions. These frequent examples do two things very well. First, the examples help to meet the authors' objective of providing practitioners with concrete ways to start putting developmental parenting ideas into practice. Second, the examples also illustrate the clear links to research in the tables so that the book can be used as a textbook for undergraduate parenting classes that cover parenting support programs or for special education or early childhood methods courses that cover approaches to involving and working with parents.

Developmental Parenting, in my opinion, comes at home visiting about 1,000 feet up but then zooms down for a closer look through the many excellent examples. This perspective makes it perfect for Early Head Start home visiting programs that may be in search of specifics to enhance their selected approaches. Practitioners in programs that already may follow a more specified protocol, such as Nurse-Family Partnership or Parent-Child Home, can read the book to sharpen their focus, to determine how what they do is the same and different from what is advanced here.

The National Home Visiting Forum promoted the need for understanding similarities and differences—sharpening focus—among programs. This forum was initiated in 1998, following on a seminal article by Deanna Gomby, then with the Packard Foundation, who suggested that evidence for positive impacts from home visiting was meager. Subsequently, the National Academy of Sciences convened a meeting of scientists and practitioners, and then Packard and the E.W. Kauffman Foundations funded the forum to examine more closely practices and rigor of U.S. home visiting programs. The six largest home visiting programs in the United States participated in this forum—Early Head Start, Nurse-Family Partnership, Parents as Teachers, HIPPY, Healthy Families America, and the Parent-Child Home Program. The National Home Visiting Forum provided an arena for home visiting programs to share and clarify their theories of change. The process made apparent that some programs are more specific than others but that most aim to influence children through parenting and most are not dissimilar from the Early

Head Start model, which allows some latitude in how to support parenting. Thus, *Developmental Parenting* is likely to be useful to practitioners across many different programs and is truly a book for the post Home Visiting Forum era, marked by a greater awareness of how program intentions may more effectively reach their mark of enhancing parenting and ultimately children's development.

Helen H. Raikes, Ph.D.
Professor, Department of Child, Youth, and
Family Studies, and Associate, Center
on Children, Families, and the Law
University of Nebraska–Lincoln

Preface

This book is written for those who work with parents of infants and toddlers, on an individual basis, to improve children's developmental outcomes. These practitioners of child development, psychology, social work, nursing, or other disciplines may meet with parents in various locations, but a common setting is the family's home. Practitioners who work with parents in the parent's home are often called home visitors. We use both terms, *practitioner* and *home visitor*, in this book. Nevertheless, a wide variety of job titles and job responsibilities may involve the basic approach of working with individual parents to help them promote their children's development. We believe this book will have useful ideas for any of them.

Similarly, the ideas in this book are likely to be useful for those who work with other caregivers of infants and toddlers, not just parents. We use the phrase *developmental parenting* to refer to valuing, supporting, and adapting to children's development, but it is not only parents who do these things. Many caregivers in child care centers, family child care homes, nursery schools, and preschools also value children's early development, support it, and adapt to the challenges it presents. Those who supervise, train, and support these nonparental caregivers are also likely to find the ideas in this book useful in their work.

We use two terms throughout this book that can use some clarification: *developmental* and *facilitative*. We use the word *developmental* to refer to children's predictable changes over time that lead to positive outcomes in social-emotional, cognitive, and language domains. *Developmental* also describes the kinds of parenting behaviors, parent–child interactions, experiences, opportunities, and environments that support children's development. In addition, *developmental* describes types of programs and services that are designed to promote early development. The word *facilitative* describes a specific kind of program model or approach. *Facilitative* refers to the kinds of attitudes, behaviors, content, practices, relationships, and even supervision and management that are effective in programs that foster developmental parenting.

We are grateful for our
opportunities over the years to
learn from practitioners, parents, and children
in many programs aiming to help parents support their
children's early development. We dedicate this book to them.

1

What Is Developmental Parenting?

Developmental parenting is what parents do to support their children's learning and development. It is what parents are doing when they clap their hands for their baby's first steps, soothe their frustrated toddler, encourage their preschool child to sing a song, or ask their first-grade child what happened at school. It is the kind of parenting that values a child's development, supports a child's development, and changes along with a child's development. Developmental parenting is warm, responsive, encouraging, and communicative. It is the kind of parenting that many programs serving infants or young children, especially home-based programs, hope to increase through home visits or other parenting support services.

VALUING DEVELOPMENT

Valuing development does not mean that everyone values the same aspects of development equally. Almost all parents value many of the new skills and ideas children acquire in the early years—from a baby's first smile and first words to a young child's first bicycle ride—but not every parent values a child's first "No" or first "Why?" or first "Why not?", although these, too, are important milestones of development in the early years. Not all parents are aware of the many small steps children have to take in acquiring the skills of exploration or communication that are needed before they begin to walk and talk. In fact, some parents need help noticing some of these small steps of development and supporting them. Even in the best of circumstances, it is often hard for a parent to notice all of the small steps of a child's development. For some parents, life can be too hectic, stressful, or chaotic to take note of something as significant as a child's newly acquired ability to climb until they see their child someplace unexpected. But noticing the small steps of development is essential for supporting it. It is only by noticing a child's development that a parent can respond to it and thereby support the young child's further development.

Not all parents value the same aspects of development. One parent may be more concerned about raising a smart child while another may be more concerned about raising a polite child. Most parents want many good outcomes, such as a child who grows into a happy, healthy adult with a good education, a steady job, close relationships, and a clean record of no criminal behavior. There are many ways parents can respond to their children's development in the early years to help make these and many other positive outcomes more likely.

SUPPORTING DEVELOPMENT

Supporting development first requires the major job of keeping children safe and healthy. In addition, research shows that parents make a difference in their children's success in life by being *warm, responsive, encouraging,* and *conversational.* These developmental parenting behaviors are linked in study after study to three important outcomes in children's early development—*attachment, exploration,* and *communication.*

The parent–child relationship provides a major context for much of early development. The interactions between parents and children promote development in children's social behaviors, their language, and their thinking. When the parent–child relationship is positive, children develop a sense of security, explore with confidence, and learn to communicate effectively. These three outcomes—secure attachment, confident exploration, and effective communication—are the foundations of social-emotional, cognitive, and language development. These are, in turn, the foundations of the outcomes that parents dream of for their children, because all three of these domains of development support school readiness, academic success, social competence, and mental health (see Table 1.1).

Parents express their love and affection for their children in many kinds of ways, but however parents show affection, children benefit from that sense of closeness and connectedness. When children feel close and connected to their parents, they benefit by being more likely to be compliant and less likely to have tantrums and misbehave. From a parent's responsiveness, an infant learns to trust and forms a secure attachment to the parent, which provides a sense of security about

Table 1.1. What is the scientific evidence for developmental parenting?

Early developmental supports	Research findings	References
General parent–child interactions	Parent–child interactions influence child development in social-emotional, language, and cognitive domains that are of central importance to children's later school success.	Culp et al., 2001, Estrada et al., 1987; Fewell & Deutscher, 2002; Gardner et al., 2003; Hubbs-Tait et al., 2002; Lee et al., 2002; Shonkoff & Phillips, 2000
Specific kinds of parenting interactions	Social-emotional, language, and cognitive development are all linked with parent–child interactions characterized by the parent supporting, nurturing, and engaging in play and conversation.	Bornstein et al., 1992; Bornstein & Tamis-LeMonda, 1989; Estrada et al., 1987; Harnish et al., 1995; Hart & Risley, 1995; Kelly et al., 1996; NICHD Early Child Care Research Network, 1999
Warm, loving interactions	Warmth, including physical closeness and positive expressions, is related to less antisocial behavior, better adjustment, more compliance, and better school readiness.	Caspi et al., 2004 ; Dodici et al., 2003; Estrada et al.,1987; MacDonald,1992; Petrill et al., 2004; Sroufe et al.,1990
Responsive interactions	Responsive interactions are important both directly and indirectly because they foster secure attachment between parent and child, which leads to the child's continuing social, cognitive, and language development.	Booth et al., 1994; Bornstein & Tamis-LeMonda, 1989; De Wolff & van Ijzendoorn, 1997; Easterbrooks et al., 2000; Goldberg, 1977; Kochanska, 1995; Londerville & Main, 1981; Roggman et al., 1987; Slade, 1987; Sroufe, 1983; Suess et al., 1992; Tamis-LeMonda & Bornstein, 1989; van den Boom, 1994; Youngblade et al., 1993
Interactions that encourage exploration through play	Playing together increases children's initiative, curiosity, creativity in their play, and their developing social and cognitive skills.	Bakeman & Adamson, 1984; Hunter et al., 1987; Landry et al., 1996; Roggman et al., 2004; Smith et al., 1996; Spencer & Meadow-Orlans, 1996
Teaching and talking; interactions that encourage conversation	Conversations with adults and exposure to many words help children learn language sooner and better.	Bornstein et al., 1998; Hart & Risley, 1995; Snow, 1983
Other regular home experiences	Reading books, telling stories, and sharing family routines support language and early literacy.	DeTemple, 1999; Dickinson et al., 1999; Lyon, 1999; Snow, 1983; Snow & the RAND Reading Study Group, 2002

being cared for and protected and establishes the foundation of social-emotional development. Infants who are securely attached, compared with those who are not, grow up to be more sociable, better able to handle stress, better able to maintain close relationships, and more likely to become good parents themselves. In the early years of life, a parent often responds not only to a child's physical distress in the context of caregiving—by picking up a crying infant, feeding a hungry toddler—but also to the child's actions and expressions in the context of interacting and conversing, such as by taking an offered toy or answering the child's questions. When a toddler offers a parent a toy or reaches for something he or she cannot quite grasp, for example, the parent's response can create an opportunity for the child to explore objects and how they work in the world, providing the foundation for cognitive development. Similarly, when a young child asks, "Why?" the parent's answer offers the child an opportunity to use communication to learn, which provides the foundation for language development and the motivation for future learning. When a parent provides encouragement and play, a toddler learns to explore, try new things, and acquire new skills. When a parent asks questions, provides information, and has a conversation with a child, the child not only practices communication skills but also learns new words and ideas. These parenting behaviors support the fundamental foundations of child development.

Confident and curious children who explore new things and have the language to communicate and ask questions are more likely to enter school ready to learn academic skills and succeed in school. Children who start school insecure and anxious, wary of new situations, and with limited language skills are simply not prepared to learn and succeed in school. But those who are prepared to succeed in school will be less likely to face problems of unemployment and poverty later in life.

CHANGING WITH DEVELOPMENT

In developmental parenting, a parent's behavior changes over the course of time in response to a child's changing developmental needs. This doesn't mean that the parent should stop doing one kind of behavior, such as showing warmth and affection, and start doing another kind of behavior, such as teaching and talking, when the child reaches a certain age or developmental milestone. It does mean, however, that how the parent shows affection or what the parent talks about with the child will change as the child grows and changes. Few parents would play Peekaboo with a 4-year-old, recognizing that most 4-year-olds have moved beyond this type of play, but a parent may not notice when a child is ready to put on his or her own clothes or choose what to have on a sandwich. Teaching parents how to notice developmental changes and read emotional cues from their children will help parents learn to develop and adapt their parenting skills to support their children's development at any age.

FACILITATING DEVELOPMENTAL PARENTING

If developmental parenting is so important for children, how can we make it easier for all parents to do? To *facilitate* something is to *make it easier*. How can we facilitate developmental parenting? Developmental parenting may be easy for many parents, but it is hard for some. Even for parents who find developmental parenting easy, some additional encouragement and ideas can help them do even more to support their children's development. Parents who are living in tough economic circumstances, trying to adapt to a new culture, or struggling to survive past trauma or abuse are often too stressed or distressed to notice their children's everyday developmental needs, to see ways to incorporate play and talk in family routines, or to think about how their parenting may need to change as their children get older. Although many parents will find a way to comfort and interact positively with their children even in extremely difficult circumstances, other parents in stressed circumstances need even more help to make developmental parenting easier. They need encouragement, guidance, and support to focus on their parenting. Yet, practitioners working in parenting programs sometimes find it particularly challenging to focus on parenting with the parents who need the most help.

What about Parents in Crisis?

For a parent worried about finding food and shelter or who needs mental health or substance abuse intervention or treatment, those services need to be provided immediately. A parent in crisis is unlikely to show much developmental parenting. For a parent in extremely difficult situations, who is homeless or hungry or severely depressed, developmental parenting is not just hard but is next to impossible. A child, however, is still developing and still has developmental needs. The child's development will not wait while the parent finds shelter, food, and relief. If a traumatic situation interferes with parenting, then it is likely to be even more traumatic for a very young child who is easily stressed and has only a child's resources for coping. Moreover, when a child is not learning to trust, play, and talk, that child is more likely to be learning to be insecure, anxious, and timid.

Consider, for example, a family who has survived a natural disaster such as a major flood, hurricane, tsunami, or earthquake. For the parents, there may be urgent and frightening challenges to take care of—dealing with injuries, finding shelter, obtaining food and water, or coping with the loss of their home or other family members. Having a 2-year-old to take care of at the same time only increases the stress. For the child, the challenge of getting comfort and care when everything is strange and frightening can be completely overwhelming. A child's main source of comfort is from the mother or father. When that comfort is not available, the grief, fear, and sense of loss can leave some children seriously disturbed for long periods of time. They may have recurrent problems sleeping and eating or controlling their emotions and behavior. For most families the situation is never so extreme, but the chaotic and stressful situations faced by some families can get in the way of their parenting, and their children often suffer for it.

Recommendations for parents and other adults who care for children in crisis situations typically include taking time to reassure and respond to the children and finding at least a few minutes to play and talk. In other words, the best way to help children in a crisis situation is through developmental parenting. Parents can benefit from support and encouragement to provide developmental parenting for their children in ways that are realistic and comfortable for their families. By facilitating developmental parenting, practitioners can help parents, even in difficult situations, keep their children learning, growing, and developing. If practitioners can help parents develop secure relationships with their children, then even in chaotic circumstances, their attachment to each other will help to sustain the parents and children, now and in the future.

Focus on Parenting

Various programs for infants and young children aim to increase developmental parenting. Some of these programs send practitioners (often called *home visitors,* but sometimes called *family educators, home educators, parent educators,* or *parenting facilitators*) into homes to work with parents and their children. The practitioners may include educators, disability specialists, therapists, social workers, nurses, or other kinds of practitioners. While the term *home visitor* may be the most common and easily understood title, it is also one that offers little description of what happens on home visits. Most programs intend for the home visitor to do more than visit and do not restrict the visits to occur only in homes. Practitioners could also meet with parents at a center or anywhere else in the community where parents go with their young children. The as-

Figure 1.1. Models of home visiting.

sumption, however, is that these practitioners work with parents and children together, in homes or elsewhere.

When practitioners in programs for infants and young children work with parents, they typically use one of two basic models: child-focused or parent-focused models. *Child-focused* models provide direct services to the child. *Parent-focused* models offer services to the parent. A growing number of programs, however, use a *parenting-focused* model, sometimes called an *interaction-focused model* or a *relationship-focused model* (see Figure 1.1), which focuses on both the parent and child in interaction with each other. A parenting-focused model is different in four ways from the other two models. First, it provides indirect child development services through the parent to the child. Second, it emphasizes developmental parenting as a primary outcome of the program. Third, it addresses broad foundational areas of early development across a wide age range rather than specific milestones at only one age. Fourth, as indicated by the double-ended arrows in Figure 1.1, in a parenting-focused model, the practitioner follows a parent's lead by observing and responding to the parent's values, existing skills, and resources. The model guides the parent to follow the child's lead by noticing and responding to the child's emotions, interests, and emerging skills.

Child-Focused Model In a child-focused model, a practitioner plans and provides specific child learning activities, similar to the kinds of developmental learning activities that would be offered in an enriched, center-based classroom environment. The practitioner then does these activities directly with the child (see Figure 1.2). In this model, the role of the parent is typically that of an observer who is expected to learn through imitation and, later, to do a similar activity with

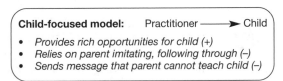

Figure 1.2. The child-focused model.

the child. Although there are advantages to the child-focused model, there are disadvantages as well.

An advantage of working directly with a child is that someone with expertise in child development can provide rich and varied experiences that nurture development and provide a good example for the parent to imitate. In a child-focused model, a practitioner typically models or demonstrates developmental learning activities for a parent to observe and then encourages the parent to do the activity several times before the next home visit. The activity may be scripted for the parent, may involve materials left for the family, and may require the parent to make notes. This model can be effective with some parents, and it is easy for a practitioner with a child development background to implement with limited training.

A disadvantage of this model is that if the parent does not imitate the practitioner, the opportunity for the child to engage in the learning activities occurs only when the practitioner is present. If the parent does not work with the child between visits, then the learning activities happen only when the practitioner can interact with the child and are not likely to have much impact on development. For many families, this model does not work well. Some parents do not have time to do structured learning activities with their children or do not like doing them.

A more serious disadvantage of the child-focused model is that even though it can show the parent a good model for fostering development, it can undermine the role of the parent. A child-focused model often sends an implicit message, whether intended or not, that compared with the expert practitioner, the parent is inadequate at promoting the child's development. For some parents, this implicit message actually discourages them from trying to do similar activities or any other learning activities with their children. In home visiting programs that use this model, parents sometimes have gone to another room to do household chores or take a break on their own, leaving the visiting practitioners and children to interact alone! A practitioner sometimes provides activities for a child, fearing that no one else will. Either way, the potential impact of the program is limited. When the practitioner is not present, the learning activities and support for development are over, thereby limiting both the intensity and the long-term effects of the program.

Parent-Focused Model   A parent-focused model, in contrast, focuses on helping the parents (see Figure 1.3). This may involve making referrals to help get families' basic needs met, obtaining community resources for housing, food, education, or employment, and providing emotional support for distress resulting from parents' problems in life.

Parent-focused model: Practitioner ⎯⎯⎯➤ Parent
- *Provides referrals, information, and support to parent (+)*
- *Relies on parent using child development information (–)*
- *Sends message that life problems can interfere with parenting (–)*

Figure 1.3.   The parent-focused model.

It may also involve a practitioner providing information about child development or making suggestions for learning activities that a parent can do with the child. Often, the practitioner provides and discusses written materials with the parent, such as pamphlets or informational handouts on topics related to the parent's concerns and problems. In addition, the practitioner typically spends a lot of time listening to the parent, building a relationship, and providing emotional support. An advantage of this model is that it can provide effective case management for families in crisis while still providing some supplemental information about child development and parenting.

For parents with multiple needs, it may seem much more important to get food rather than play games with children! It is true that a hungry child is not a playful child. Basic needs do come first. A depressed and anxious mother is not likely to be a responsive parent without some essential emotional support that can, in turn, help her attend to the needs of her child. As discussed earlier in the chapter, however, a child's development does not stop while his or her parent focuses on solving family and personal problems. A disadvantage of the parent-focused model is that it is unlikely to help parents observe, support, or adapt to their children's development. Information may be provided about child development, but parents are not necessarily helped to put the information into practice. The implicit message is that the parents' problems interfere with responding to their children, so it might be hopeless to try. Troubled parents are then even less likely to respond to their children's developmental needs.

Parenting-Focused Model   A parenting-focused model is different from the other two models because it emphasizes parents' support of their children's development. Using this model, the practitioner focuses neither directly on the child nor on the parent but rather on the parent–child interactions that support child development (see Figure 1.4). The practitioner may bring some materials to do a planned activity, but the family's available household materials often are used. Activities often are based on regular family routines that can support the child's development, and the activities are usually planned ahead of

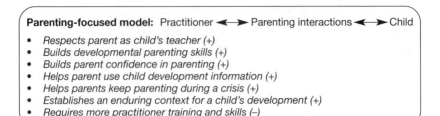

Parenting-focused model: Practitioner ◄─► Parenting interactions ◄─► Child

- *Respects parent as child's teacher (+)*
- *Builds developmental parenting skills (+)*
- *Builds parent confidence in parenting (+)*
- *Helps parent use child development information (+)*
- *Helps parents keep parenting during a crisis (+)*
- *Establishes an enduring context for a child's development (+)*
- *Requires more practitioner training and skills (–)*

Figure 1.4.   The parenting-focused model.

time so the parent can prepare. The practitioner helps the parent identify ways to enjoy the activity with the child and to use developmental parenting behaviors he or she already does to promote the child's development. The practitioner also helps guide the parent to observe and interpret the child's cues and respond to the child's needs, interests, and emerging developmental skills.

The parenting-focused model has multiple advantages. It sends an implicit message of respect for the role of the parent as someone who can provide good developmental experiences for the child, even in difficult times. Parent–child interactions during everyday activities are central to both early and later development. The research literature clearly shows that supportive parent–child interactions contribute to children's social-emotional, cognitive, and language development. These developmental domains are of central importance to children's later academic and social success. Parents often need information and encouragement to increase the amount of supportive developmental interactions they have with their children. In a parenting-focused model, the practitioner serves as a consultant to provide that information combined with direct help and encouragement to put the information into practice.

In addition to needing information, help, and encouragement to provide good developmental experiences for their young children, parents often first need confidence about their ability to provide those experiences. By focusing on the parent as the person best able to support the child's development, and by building on the parent's strengths and sharing expertise collaboratively, a parenting-focused model increases the parent's confidence, knowledge, and motivation. An additional advantage of the parenting-focused model is that as parents develop skills for providing developmental opportunities for their children, they can more readily incorporate these opportunities into their everyday family routines.

By helping parents use daily activities to provide developmental opportunities, a parenting-focused model ensures that supportive interactions and activities are likely to continue on a regular basis even after the parenting program has ended. The parent–child relationship is likely to be an enduring one, the best and primary context for development, whereas the practitioner–child relationship is likely to be only a temporary one.

The parenting-focused model does have some disadvantages. Practitioners need a higher level of skill and cannot follow a tightly scripted curriculum. The practitioner responds to each parent's values, interests, and parenting skills while encouraging the parent to respond to the child's emotions, interests, and developmental skills. This model, in which practitioners work with parents to provide child development services in the context of everyday interactions and activities, requires knowledge and skills related not only to child development but also to parenting and adult development. It also requires sensitivity and responsiveness to each family's values, goals, and culture.

Using a Parenting-Focused Model with the Facilitative Approach

Parenting-focused models require a *facilitative* approach to effectively promote developmental parenting that supports early child development. Parenting-focused models, therefore, do the following:

1. Deliver services from practitioner to parent, and then through parenting to the child

2. Help parents observe, support, and adapt to their children's development

3. Address foundations of social-emotional, cognitive, and language development

What Is a Facilitative Approach? A facilitative approach makes developmental parenting easier by emphasizing child development and the parenting behaviors that support it, focusing on parent–child interaction and building on family strengths. A facilitative approach could be applied to various services, but when applied to a parenting-focused model, it means that practitioners deliver child development services by helping parents use their own skills and resources to support their children's development. How is a parenting-focused model implemented with a facilitative approach?

1. The emphasis is on child development.

2. The focus is on parent–child interactions that support development.

3. Strategies are used to assess and expand on family strengths to support early development.

4. The emphasis, focus, and strategies make developmental parenting easier.

Both of the following vignettes describe a home visit using a parenting-focused model. Only one of them uses a facilitative approach. Look for the differences.

A Traditional Approach

Amy: Hi, come on in. Sorry about the mess.

Lauren [*while giving a quick hug to Jacob, Amy's son who is almost 2 years old*]: No problem. How have you been?

Jacob [*jumping around while singing Lauren's name and reaching for her bag*]: Lauwen, Lauwen, whatcha got? Whatcha got?

Lauren [*with smile and a wink*]: Be patient, Jacob—you just have to wait a minute.

Lauren [*turning to Amy*]: Any progress on solving the conflicts with your park manager?

Amy: Well, we can stay here for now.

Lauren: Good news! I bet that's a relief for you, Amy. I know you were really worried about moving. How did the reading time with Jacob go this week?

Amy [*after hesitating*]: Well, things were pretty hectic. We didn't get much of that done.

Lauren: Maybe next week will be better now that you don't have to worry about where you'll be living!

Lauren [*while pulling a book out of her bag*]: Jacob, can you tell me what's on the front of this book?

Jacob [*excitedly*]: El-phent! El-phent!

Lauren [*to Amy*]: I noticed last week that he was really interested in the elephant puzzle so I brought a book with an elephant this time. Would you like to read it to him?

Amy: No thanks, you go ahead. I'm so tired.

Lauren: Are you sure? Well, okay. Here Jacob, let's look at this book. What do you think it's about?

Jacob: El-phents!

Lauren: That's right, it is about an elephant, a special elephant named Edgar who can't find his shoes. Where are your shoes? [*Jacob points to his shoes.*] That's right. Show your mom your shoes, Jacob.

Jacob: Ma, my choos!

Amy: Good boy!

Lauren: He's saying so much more now than even a few weeks ago, Amy.

Lauren reads the book to Jacob, stopping often to ask questions about the book and about Jacob's experiences related to what is in the book.

Lauren: Do you ever lose your shoes, Jacob?

Jacob: My choos!

Amy: He lost a shoe last week and I still can't find it.

Lauren [to Jacob]: Did you lose a shoe?

Jacob: Choo gone.

Lauren: Well, Edgar lost both of his shoes! Let's see if he can find them.

After finishing the book, Lauren pulls out and opens a small container.

Lauren [*to Jacob*]: Here's some playdough for you to play with, Jacob, while I talk to your mom. See? You can roll it into balls.

(continued)

(continued)

While Jacob squeezes the playdough, Lauren goes over several handouts with Amy, one on easy snacks for toddlers, another on preventing colds, one with rhyming finger-plays, and one with a recipe for making playdough.

Lauren [*to Amy*]: You can make some this week and try it out.

Lauren [*to Jacob*]: Would you like Mama to make you some playdough, Jacob?

Jacob: Pa-do ma!

Amy [*with little enthusiasm*]: We can probably do that . . .

A Facilitative Approach

Lauren parks alongside the old mobile home in the trailer park on the outskirts of town. She goes up to the trailer door and knocks. Amy opens the door.

Amy: Hi, come on in. Sorry about the mess.

Lauren [*while giving a quick hug to Jacob, Amy's son, who is almost 2 years old*]: No problem. How have you been?

Jacob [*jumping around while singing Lauren's name and reaching for her bag*]: Lauwen, Lauwen, whatcha got? Whatcha got?

Lauren [*with smile and a wink*]: Jacob, Jacob!

Lauren [*turning to Amy*]: Any progress on solving the conflicts with your park manager?

Amy: Well, we can stay here for now.

Lauren: Good news! I bet that's a relief for you, Amy. You were concerned about how Jacob would take the move.

Amy: I was. He seems so attached to his blanket and bear and routines, it was hard to imagine how he'd cope with moving in with my mom and not having a real place to live for a while.

Lauren: Well, blankets and bears can be carried along with you and that often helps kids, but you're right that moving is hard on kids this age. So, what have you and Jacob been up to this week?

Amy [*after hesitating*]: Well, he had a pretty good week. He had a friend over and they were "building things." That was fun, huh Jacob?

Lauren: Wow, tell me more about that—were they pretending?

Amy: Oh, they were mostly just stacking blocks and knocking them over, but they said they were buildings.

Jacob: Bidding crash!

Amy [*to Jacob*]: Go get your blocks from under your bed to show Lauren.

Lauren [*to Amy*]: That's pretty cool! Using blocks like a real building is a kind of pretending that's a big part of cognitive development and language development, too.

Amy [*after a pause]:* I like that it's good for him to play with blocks. He sure can spend a lot of time just stacking them up and knocking them down, so it's good to know it's good for something.

Lauren: Blocks are great for pretending because they can be so many things—they could be cars, the sides of a road, or even people. We could play with the blocks next time and come up with even more games like that if you like.

Amy [*with some enthusiasm*]: Oh, he'd love that. It would be fun.

Lauren [*after pausing and glancing out the window*]: Actually, rather than going to the park for our visit like we planned, we could just play with blocks now because it's looking like rain.

Amy [*to Lauren*]: Sure, if that's okay. You know, these blocks are actually ends of wooden boards that his dad brought home and sanded smooth, but they're easy for him to stack.

(continued)

(continued)

Lauren: That's wonderful that he made these blocks that Jacob can play and pretend with. They are great educational toys for talking about and pretending with, and they're the right size for small hands.

Amy [*laughing*]: Well, the price was right! They were just throwing the ends away where he was working, so he brought a bunch home for free.

Lauren: I wonder what Jacob wants to do with them today.

Amy [*to Jacob*]: What do you want to build? Let's build a tall skyscraper.

Jacob looks quizzically at his mom.

Lauren: Does he know that word?

Amy [*to Lauren*]: Maybe not.

Amy [*to Jacob*]: Jacob, let's build a really, really tall building. That's called a skyscraper.

Jacob [*squealing*]: A sty-staper!

Amy [*frowning*]: He doesn't pronounce some things right.

Lauren: Many kids this age don't combine sounds very well, but it's more important that he is learning a lot of words and that you can understand them.

Amy: Well, I can understand a lot of what he's saying, and that's a lot better than it used to be.

Lauren [*nodding*]: I remember that he wasn't talking this much even just a couple months ago and he was hard to understand.

Amy: I know; he's saying a lot more words now.

Lauren: So he's probably more interested in new words too. What new words have you noticed this week?

Amy: Oh my gosh; he's been saying so many new words. He asked for 'ice-keem' and said 'socks,' where before he had been saying 'choos' for both shoes and socks, and he said something about the 'ba-tub' too.

> **Lauren:** That's great; he's been taking off in his language and you've been paying attention!
>
> *Jacob interrupts with a word Lauren doesn't understand.*
>
> **Lauren** [*to Amy*]: What's he saying?
>
> **Amy** [*laughing*]: I think he's saying this is a road, only without the *r*.
>
> **Amy** [*to Jacob*]: Is this your road, honey?
>
> **Jacob:** Oad!
>
> *The conversation continues.*

The two approaches are similar in some ways. In both vignettes, the interactions between the home visitor and family are warm and positive, and the child is happy to see the visitor. However, the two approaches differ in many ways, as well. See Table 1.2 for descriptions of how a facilitative approach differs from a traditional approach.

The differences between the two vignettes are primarily in the roles of the practitioner and the mother. In the facilitative model, more of the direction for activities is left up to the parent who knows what her child likes, what the family has, and what she is comfortable with herself.

Characteristics of the Facilitative Approach Following are several important characteristics of the facilitative approach that we recommend to best promote developmental parenting.

- *A facilitative approach emphasizes child development and the parenting behaviors that promote it.* A facilitative approach maintains an emphasis on the kinds of parenting behaviors, knowledge, and attitudes that support a child's development. Parenting includes what the parent does with a child but also what the parent knows about the child, the parent's goals for the child, the values he or she wants to teach the child, and the home environment that the parent shares with the child. In a parenting-focused program using a facilitative approach, services always include the parent. For example, if the child's parent (or caregiver) can't be there for a home visit, there is no reason for the visit. There can be no service delivery of a parenting-focused child development program if the parent is not there, because the services are supposed to be delivered through the parent to the child. Table 1.3 shows examples of what a facilitative approach emphasizing child development is like and what it is not like.

- *A facilitative approach focuses on parent–child interaction.* To facilitate developmental parenting, the practitioner engages both parent and child together whenever possible (i.e., whenever the child is awake and present). The focus is on parent–child interaction, so both parent and child are involved with each other for as much of the home visit time as possible. One home visiting program sets a standard of

Table 1.2. How does the facilitative approach differ from a traditional approach?

A facilitative approach sounds more like this . . .	And less like this . . .
Practitioner helps the family think about whatever materials they have available to use for the child's learning activities, and encourages use of available materials.	Practitioner brings all of the materials used for the learning activities during the home visit. The child reaches for the materials the practitioner brings; practitioner controls when materials are available and makes suggestions to the child about how to use them.
Conversation about family problem emphasizes the child's feelings, the mother's concerns about the child, and the mother's insights about the child.	Conversation about family problem mentions only the mother's feelings.
Practitioner asks open-ended questions about what the parent and child did together during the week.	Practitioner asks whether or not an assigned activity was done, encourages better follow through next week.
Practitioner suggests doing an activity for the visit that is something the family is already doing. Original activity parent and practitioner planned together won't work because of rain, so practitioner listens for alternative ideas.	Practitioner does activities the practitioner planned using materials the practitioner brought to the visit.
Practitioner supports parents using recommended practices, for example, cueing parent to explain a new word.	Practitioner uses recommended practices, for example, asking the child questions about a book, referring to the child's experiences and encouraging the child to talk.
Practitioner asks parent about child's signs of development, such as pretend play, and encourages parent's observations of child's new skills, such as use of new words.	Practitioner tells mother about child's developmental progress and tells child to show skills to mother.
Practitioner helps parent understand development in context of what is happening with the child now and the parent's concerns about the child's development.	Practitioner gives mother several written documents relevant to her child's health and development.
Practitioner encourages parent to use materials the family already has and activities the parent and child already enjoy as resources for learning.	Practitioner suggests activity for mother and child to do during the week that family has not done before that will require some time for preparation, and about which the mother shows little enthusiasm.

Table 1.3. Examples of facilitative approach emphasizing child development

An approach emphasizing child development sounds more like this . . .	And less like this . . .
"We ask the parent what the child is like, what the child can do, and what she wants the child to be able to do."	"We test the child's developmental level so we can bring activities to the home to teach what the child needs for school success."
"We help the parent find his own comfortable style of helping the child learn because we want the parent to know he will be able to keep supporting his child's development."	"We do activities with the child to provide a good model for the parent."
"We encourage the parent to do activities she already does with the child because that is what they are most likely to keep doing in the future."	"We start out doing activities with the child and then try to bring in the parent."
"We find 'learning activities' in what the parent already does so he will be able to keep finding new activities to support their child's development."	"We do learning activities with the child because otherwise no one else does."
"We help the parent take whatever steps needed to better support the child's development."	"We help parents get resources for their personal problems before we try to get them interested in child development."

at least two thirds of the home visit time involving both parent and child together. Activities to facilitate developmental parenting should be scheduled when a child is awake and rested. When the child is sleepy or not feeling well, for example, the parent–child interaction may happen for only a brief part of the time. For most of the time, the parent and child should be involved jointly. Table 1.4 provides examples of statements that do and do not focus on parent–child interaction.

Table 1.4. Examples of facilitative approach focusing on parent–child interaction

An approach focusing on parent–child interactions sounds more like this . . .	And less like this . . .
"We encourage whatever positive interactions the mother has with her child because the child's development can't wait."	"We have to help the mother before she can interact well with her child."
"We build a partnership with the parent by working together to support the child's development."	"We establish a good relationship with the parent before working with the child."
"We start working with every family as they are, helping parents enjoy whatever interactions they have with their child."	"The parent/family/home is so depressed/dysfunctional/chaotic, we have to get things settled down before we can get the child and parent involved in activities together."

- *A facilitative approach uses strategies that build on family strengths.* Developmental parenting involves activities parents and children do together in their everyday lives, using materials they already have. A facilitative approach therefore shows respect for what the parents already know, already do, and already have. Family strengths include the knowledge, people, routines, and resources of each family. Practitioners show respect for family strengths when they ask what parents know, plan activities together with parents as collaborators, remember what parents tell them, and offer resources or information that parents really want (not necessarily what the practitioner thinks they need). Building on family strengths involves the use of family routines, activities, and resources to promote early development. Table 1.5 includes examples of statements that may or may not reflect how a facilitative approach builds on family strengths.

- *A facilitative approach includes content that addresses broad foundations of development.* A facilitative approach emphasizes activities that help parents promote their children's security, exploration, and communication because these are the foundations of social-emotional, cognitive, and language development. Facilitative practitioners keep the focus on these basic areas of development because children who are secure, motivated to learn, and able to communicate will develop every day as they play, explore, and interact with the world. By helping parents focus on these basic foundations, practitioners can

Table 1.5.   Examples of facilitative approach building on family strengths

An approach building on family strengths sounds more like this . . .	And less like this . . .
"We find out what a parent already knows about the child and talk about how to use this knowledge to support the child's development."	"We go over lots of wonderful handouts of information they need to know."
"We encourage families to use what they already have because they are likely to still have it in the future."	"We bring in high-quality educational equipment the family can't afford to buy."
"We schedule home visits to include everyone in the family because parents don't parent their children separately."	"We schedule half the home visit for the 1-year-old and the other half for the 2-year-old."
"We guide parents to use the unique resources they have in their own homes to enrich their children's development."	"We bring the program to the home by planning the same kinds of activities children would get at the center."
"We help parents identify whatever strengths they already have."	"We recognize that some families are so dysfunctional that they need a lot of help to build any strengths at all."

Table 1.6.   Examples of a facilitative approach addressing broad foundations of development

An approach addressing broad foundations of development sounds more like this . . .	And less like this . . .
"We help parents notice their children's development and find ways to support development in lots of areas."	"We assess each child's developmental milestones and then teach the next step in the normal developmental sequence."
"We help parents teach their children lots of words and concepts, recognizing that all language development helps prepare children for school."	"We help parents teach specific school readiness concepts like colors and shapes to their children."
"We emphasize children's social–emotional development, cognitive development, and language development so they are ready to learn more in all areas."	"We emphasize phonological awareness and knowing 10 letters so they can learn to read."

keep the message simple while making the long-term impact stronger. Table 1.6 shows examples of how a facilitative approach addresses broad foundations of development rather than specific skills.

CONCLUSION

Developmental parenting supports children's development in the early years. Without it, children will struggle in school and face compounded risks often into adulthood. By facilitating developmental parenting, a parenting-focused model will have a long-term impact on children's development. Maintaining a focus on parenting, emphasizing parent–child interaction, and building on family strengths are often complex tasks for practitioners taking a facilitative approach to working with parents and their children. Thus, practitioners need to learn the fundamentals of the facilitative approach, which include a combination of a parenting-focused program model and facilitative attitudes, behaviors, and content (or ABCs), described in later chapters.

2

Building a Facilitative Developmental Parenting Program

What kind of program best facilitates developmental parenting? A developmental parenting program could be set up in several different kinds of ways. Parents could meet with practitioners in their own homes, at a child care center, in a community center, at a school, or in an office building. In many of these settings, parents could meet with practitioners either individually or in groups. Although any of these possibilities could work, we recommend a program in which practitioners meet individually with families in their own homes.

WHY AN IN-HOME PROGRAM?

In-home developmental parenting programs help parents support their children's early development at home and around their community during their everyday lives. Home is where young children, even those in regular child care, spend most of their time with their parents. Parents are usually the most long-term caregivers and teachers that children will ever have. Parents have an enduring relationship with their children, so a program that increases parents' support of their children's development can have a lifelong impact. Also, all families who would benefit from a parenting program, even those with limited transportation, can participate in a developmental parenting program at home.

Regular activities and routines in the home offer easy and, therefore, efficient situations for parents to promote their children's early

23

development and continued learning. Because home-visiting services are delivered to families in their homes, often in kitchens or living rooms, they offer opportunities to support good parenting practices that are already happening and improve the home environment for learning and development. By working with parents in their own homes, practitioners who are knowledgeable about child development and parenting can help parents find ways to use their family's home activities and routines to promote their children's development. By working with one family at a time, practitioners can identify unique opportunities to individualize their program to meet the specific needs and build on the strengths of each child and each family. By working individually with parents and children in their homes, practitioners can tailor the program to parents with children of any age or to families with diverse needs.

Home means more than only a family's living space where they sleep, however. Home also means neighborhoods and communities— wherever parents and children spend time together. Parents spend time with their children in a variety of places—hanging out at home, shopping at the grocery store, going to the park, doing errands at the bank or post office, washing clothes at a laundromat, or going other places. Those are the times and places when parents and children can be building their relationship, exploring the world together, and communicating with each other—sharing the experiences that support early development. By working with parents in the places where they spend time with their children, programs can increase developmental parenting in families' everyday lives.

A disadvantage of in-home services is that families can remain isolated if they do not go to a center where they can interact with other parents and children. Practitioners can feel isolated, too. Providing in-home services can be stressful for practitioners who may work on their own for days at a time visiting individual family homes, often in stressful or chaotic circumstances. It is challenging for supervisors to have practitioners working out in the community away from a central location because they often have infrequent opportunities for supervision and support. The biggest disadvantage of in-home services is that the home visiting approach for delivering services has been questioned in the research literature. Several studies have questioned the efficacy of home visiting to make lasting changes in children's lives.

Research on Home Visiting

Some studies comparing home visiting with other service-delivery strategies or with no service delivery have shown only weak or no effects of home visiting on children's early development. In a 1999 issue of *The*

Future of Children, Deanna Gomby summarized the methods used in several studies questioning the effectiveness of home visiting programs. The primary limitation of these studies is that few of them tested any variations of home visiting *within* the programs. Therefore, little was learned about how home visiting quality affects the outcomes of programs that use home visiting as their service delivery strategy.

A 2004 meta-analysis, or study of studies, of home visiting by Monica Sweet and Mark Applebaum was more positive about the outcomes of home visiting, reporting overall impacts on children's social and cognitive development and on parents' behaviors and attitudes. Other research shows the importance of variations in the quality of home visits and the responses of families to home visiting. For example, our study of home visiting, published in 2001, investigated variations in the quality of interactions during home visits in an infant–toddler program that aimed to promote positive parent–child interaction. What we learned was that when home visitors were observed effectively engaging parents and involving parents and children together, the families were rated as improving the most. This means that getting parents involved in the home visit and getting them interacting positively with their children at home are important elements for an effective home-visiting program. These strategies were part of that program's overall design and integrated into the specific approaches used by participating home visitors. The effectiveness of these strategies for any particular developmental parenting program depends on how the program is planned, what the practitioners do with each family, and how well the practitioners are trained and supervised.

For many programs, the advantages of home visiting outweigh the disadvantages. It is the quality of the home visiting that becomes critical for the success of the program. What makes high-quality home visiting? High-quality home visiting is described here as *facilitative* because it facilitates, or paves the way, for positive parent–child interaction and parenting behaviors that support children's early development.

What Is Facilitative Home Visiting?

Facilitative home visiting refers to an individualized approach to service delivery in families' homes that effectively promotes early development by facilitating parents in supporting their own children's development. When practitioners provide guidance, information, and encouragement to parents, it facilitates (or "makes easier") the parents' job of supporting their children's early development.

Practitioners effectively facilitate developmental parenting when they help parents focus on parenting, observe their children's behavior, and support their children's development as part of their everyday lives. In turn, good supervision and management help practitioners use effective strategies and resources. Based on information from research, experience, and many conversations with home visitors and their supervisors, we have learned that to do all this effectively, developmental parenting programs require

1. Thoughtful planning

2. Good practices with good tools

3. Ongoing program improvement

Thoughtful Planning   Thoughtful planning first requires being clear about what a program is trying to do. A developmental parenting program is most likely to be successful when everyone in the program is clear about the program's goals and how the program's strategies will enable the program to reach those goals. In other words, both the staff members who work directly with families and other program staff members need to know their program's *theory of change.*

Theory of Change   What is a theory of change? It is a series of clear statements or a diagrammed model of what changes the program is trying to make happen, what the program is doing to make those changes, how the changes happen, and what additional factors can help or hinder change. For a developmental parenting program to be successful, the people working there must be clear in their minds about how home visiting fits in with their program's theory of change.

Why does a practitioner in a developmental parenting program need to know about the program's theory of change? Programs expect practitioners to do things based on philosophies or theories about how to make changes in the lives of families and children, whether a theory of change is clearly articulated or not. If practitioners are going to do a good job or even just do what they are supposed to do, they need to understand the strategies and expected outcomes of their program's theory of change.

To be successful, a program's theory of change describes the expected outcomes and the strategies planned for making those outcomes happen. A good theory of change also specifies how the process should occur and why it is effective or what the pathways are for change. In addition, a good theory says what other factors influence the success of the program for each family, or what works best for whom. In other words, the theory describes the pathways from strategies to outcomes—from what practitioners do to how parents and children change. It should be clear from a program's theory of change why practitioners make home visits and what they are expected to do to make changes happen for parents and children.

We developed a theory of change for developmental parenting programs. Figure 2.1 shows a diagram of a theory of change for developmental parenting programs. This is the theory of change used for this book. Having a clear theory of change benefits a developmental parenting program in several ways. First, it makes practitioners who work directly with families more aware of the purpose and reasons for a program's strategies, including home visiting. Second, it helps practitioners plan activities and select materials that are consistent with the strategies and processes described in the theory of change. Third and finally, when something unexpected happens, a theory of change offers a guide to practitioners for problem solving "on their feet" when they are out making a home visit often miles away from supervisors or other program support staff.

A program's theory of change may incorporate home visiting for several reasons. One program may believe that home visits are appropriate because they make it easier to individualize services to families with children at particular points in development or in particular family situations. Another program may believe home visits are appropriate because effective changes in a parent's behavior toward one child can benefit other children in the family and persist through later years after the end of the intervention program. Whatever a program's reasons are for selecting home visiting as a primary service delivery strategy, practitioners who make home visits are better able to deliver services successfully when they understand their program's theory of change. If program staff members are aware of the goals of the program and the strategies planned for reaching those goals, they will be better prepared to implement the strategies successfully.

Although a program's theory of change often develops out of practitioners' direct experience and intuition, it may also be grounded in more formal human development theories. For example, Urie Bronfenbrenner's ecological model of human development, described in articles published in 1978 and 1986, has influenced many early intervention programs since it was first developed. Bronfenbrenner's model puts a child and family at the center of a set of concentric circles that represent the increasingly wider worlds of the child's life: neighborhood, community, and society. This model suggests that early development occurs in the context of relationships children have with their parents and other caregivers and that these relationships interact with the larger contexts of neighborhood, community, and society. One of these contexts could be a developmental parenting program.

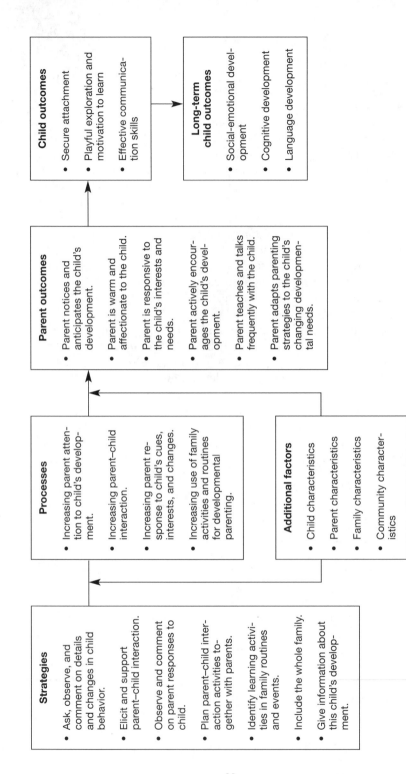

Figure 2.1. A diagram of a theory of change for developmental parenting programs.

Strategies

- Ask, observe, and comment on details and changes in child behavior.
- Elicit and support parent–child interaction.
- Observe and comment on parent responses to child.
- Plan parent–child interaction activities together with parents.
- Identify learning activities in family routines and events.
- Include the whole family.
- Give information about this child's development.

Processes

- Increasing parent attention to child's development.
- Increasing parent–child interaction.
- Increasing parent response to child's cues, interests, and changes.
- Increasing use of family activities and routines for developmental parenting.

Additional factors

- Child characteristics
- Parent characteristics
- Family characteristics
- Community characteristics

Parent outcomes

- Parent notices and anticipates the child's development.
- Parent is warm and affectionate to the child.
- Parent is responsive to the child's interests and needs.
- Parent actively encourages the child's development.
- Parent teaches and talks frequently with the child.
- Parent adapts parenting strategies to the child's changing developmental needs.

Child outcomes

- Secure attachment
- Playful exploration and motivation to learn
- Effective communication skills

Long-term child outcomes

- Social-emotional development
- Cognitive development
- Language development

Bronfenbrenner's model points to the importance of relationships between parents and children, between practitioners and parents, between homes and program, and between program and community. Building relationships with families is essential for effective home visiting. Thoughtful planning, therefore, includes consideration of the role of relationships in a facilitative developmental parenting program.

Mutual Competence   Relationship building is essential for facilitative home visiting. An approach of *mutual competence* fosters relationships between parents and children and between parents and practitioners. This approach was developed by Victor Bernstein at the University of Chicago and was described in articles by him and his colleagues in 1991 and 2001. A mutual competence approach is based on recognition and support of each other's strengths and each other's competence. Parents recognize and support their children's emerging strengths and skills, and practitioners recognize and support parents' strengths and values.

A mutual-competence approach to working with families makes the social-emotional health of the parent–child relationship the first priority for practitioners. Practitioners using a mutual competence approach focus on increasing positive parent–child interactions in which both parent and child learn together and feel secure, valued, successful, happy, and understood. The approach acknowledges the importance of everyday family activities for learning and builds on strengths in the parent–child relationship.

Facilitative practitioners take a mutual competence approach by

1. Supporting strong relationships between parents and children

2. Building collaborative partnerships with parents

3. Encouraging parents to use daily activities and routines to promote development

4. Increasing parents' self-confidence in building strong relationships with their children

5. Observing with parents what is going well in the parent–child relationship

6. Enhancing parent awareness of the impact of stress and negative events and thereby preparing the parent–child relationship to endure in times of stress

A mutual-competence approach is appropriate for home visitors to use when covering a wide variety of areas and activities with parents and children. For example, practitioners could emphasize nutrition, language development, or any other area of health and development within a mutually competent framework. However, the focus always remains on the importance of parent–child interaction and building on the strengths of the parent–child relationship.

Cultural respect is part of all of the strategies, processes, practices, and tools of a program using a mutual competence approach. Parents' values and beliefs are respected and supported in the context of their culture and community. Using a mutual competence approach is not a passive process, however, in which the practitioner merely does whatever a parent wants. Practitioners bring their own strengths, expertise, and resources to contribute to the process.

Whether a family receives only 2 visits or more than 150 visits, practitioner–family relationships remain central to how effectively the program facilitates developmental parenting. When practitioners know the theory of change for their program and use a mutual competence approach to build relationships with families, they are able to effectively use the strategies and resources that make up good practices for home visiting.

Good Practices with Good Tools   Effective practices are often called *best practices,* but because even the very "best" practices may not work for everyone, a set of "good" practices is needed that can be adapted to individual families, situations, and home visitors. Good practices for a developmental parenting program are consistent with the program's theory of change and are faithful to a mutual-competence approach to relationship building with families. From both research and practical experience, the following are characteristics of good practice in facilitative home visiting:

1. Responsiveness to individual families

2. Flexibility to meet when and where families are comfortable

3. Emphasis on parent–child interaction and developmental parenting

4. Collaborative partnerships between practitioners and parent(s)

5. Involvement of additional family members, especially fathers and siblings

6. Encouragement of everyday family activities as learning opportunities

7. Information provided to parents as needed and wanted, to support developmental parenting

8. Guidance for parents to plan activities to promote their children's early development

9. Family friendly assessments and curriculum materials

These characteristics of facilitative practices will be described in more detail in later chapters. Incorporating these characteristics takes planning, time, and practice. What really helps practitioners, though, is supportive supervision. And what really helps a program is regular feedback.

Good practitioners need supportive supervision. Practitioners who provide in-home services typically work alone and travel from home to home, sometimes driving their own cars in rural areas or using complex public transportation systems in urban areas, and they must carry with them whatever materials they need. They typically serve diverse families and often need additional guidance from supervisors to identify strategies to effectively support developmental parenting for each family. Supportive supervision, like other aspects of a facilitative program, uses a mutual competence framework in which both supervisors and practitioners recognize and support each other's strengths and competence. Effective working partnerships between practitioners and their supervisors parallel the mutual competence partnerships that work so well between parents and practitioners. Supervisor–practitioner partnerships should be similarly responsive, flexible, supportive, and collaborative. Supervision to support practitioners as they develop and improve their skills requires regular meetings that are efficient, supportive, and stimulating. The advantage of regular and effective meetings for supervisors and practitioners is that they

1. Give practitioners a place and time to meet and work together

2. Provide practitioners with access to their supervisor

3. Help build relationships that are positive, facilitative, and respectful

4. Offer an opportunity for frequent and regular feedback to practitioners

5. Help practitioners share ideas and solve problems with each other and their supervisor

6. Ensure that everyone knows what the program is about

7. Establish respect for families, cultures, and privacy

8. Allow open discussion of "red flags"

9. Promote readiness to change or improve as needed

Ongoing Program Improvement   How do you know if your program is working well? A program is likely to be most successful when the people who work for the program get ongoing feedback about how it is working. With a clear theory of change in mind, and with supportive supervision in place, practitioners and other program staff can take a look at what strategies are actually being used and how well they match the program's theory of change. Together, they can then plan ways to make the program more effective.

Earlier evaluations of in-home programs have shown that how well a home visiting program is implemented affects the outcomes of the program. For example, when Anne Duggan and her colleagues evaluated Hawaii's Healthy Start home visiting program, they found that benefits to families depended on which of several agencies administered the program. These findings led to increased efforts by the agencies to monitor evaluation data to be regularly returned to the program for improvement, a process called *continuous program improvement*. Data on the practices and outcomes of home visiting can be used not only to meet program requirements but also to assess program quality and make improvements to the program.

Many sources of information can be used to provide feedback to practitioners and help programs make improvements to the home visiting process. The most valuable sources of feedback are videotaped observations of home visits because they allow both practitioners and their supervisors to observe directly what really happens during home visits with individual families. Additional sources of information include observation notes, program records, staff reports and discussions, and descriptions or ratings by practitioners and parents. All of these sources of information can be used to examine the match between a program's theory of change and what the program's practitioners actually do. Based on that information, program staff can plan ways to improve the program.

CONCLUSION

Together, the approaches described in this book facilitate developmental parenting. The essential components of thoughtful planning, good practice with good tools, and ongoing program improvement are interrelated and linked together to make a developmental parenting program successful. The approaches, strategies, and examples in this book will be helpful, but it is also necessary for practitioners to make adaptations to their own programs and the families they serve. The basic concept of developmental parenting is wide reaching, but the specific ways it will happen may be different in one family compared with another. Likewise, the best ways to support developmental parenting may differ both by family and by program. The task of practitioners working with parents is also developmental. To be effective at promoting the development of parents, practitioners need to be aware of parents' development—value it, support it, and change along with it.

3

A Is for
Approach and Attitudes

The ABCs of good practice, which we consider to be *approach and attitudes, behavior,* and *content,* are quality indicators for programs using a parenting-focused model. They are also the fundamentals of practice for practitioners who *facilitate* developmental parenting in parenting-focused programs. These ABCs are designed for child development programs in which trained practitioners work with individual parents, typically in the parents' homes, to help support their children's development. Parenting-focused models provide services through parents to support early child development, but not all parenting-focused models use a facilitative approach that incorporates these ABCs to focus on developmental parenting, engage parents and children together, and build on family strengths.

The ABCs of facilitative practice have a foundation in research and experience and are associated with effective programs that use home visiting or other individualized parenting-focused strategies to deliver child development services. Like any set of guidelines for practice, however, there may be some occasions when one or more of these practices is not effective with a particular family at a particular time. A child with a disability, for example, may need targeted practice on a particular developmental milestone in motor development in addition to the broad developmental foundations of attachment, exploration, and communication we recommend. A teen mother in a large, chaotic, extended family household may benefit from having a home visit involving only her and her infant and not the whole family. The flexibility to adapt the program to individual and family needs is essential.

The authors of this book have had more than 40 years of combined research experience with parenting-focused programs and more than 10 years of combined practical experience as practitioners working with parents and children in their homes. From this extensive base of experience, we have learned that a facilitative approach requires these three major components:

1. *Approach and attitudes:* Beliefs and feelings based on the assumption that every family has strengths that can be increased through responsiveness, flexibility, and supportiveness

2. *Behaviors:* Specific techniques to use during home visits to engage parents in parenting, to elicit parent–infant interaction, and to collaborate with parents to support their children's development during family activities

3. *Content:* Appropriate information and activities to help parents promote their children's early social-emotional, cognitive, and language development

Facilitative attitudes lay the groundwork for facilitative behaviors and content. These attitudes are important not just for the practitioners who work directly with parents but also for their supervisors and the support staff in their programs. If all the staff members working in a parenting-focused program have facilitative attitudes, then practitioners working directly with families will be better able to engage in facilitative behaviors and provide facilitative content.

For example, when supervisors and other program support staff are responsive to family needs and flexible about activities and content they expect in home visits, practitioners can more easily be responsive and flexible. And a practitioner who is responsive to a family and flexible about home-visit activities can more easily help the family plan activities they will enjoy doing with the child and will do again later. This chapter describes a facilitative approach and facilitative attitudes; the next two chapters describe facilitative behaviors and content.

A FACILITATIVE APPROACH

A practitioner using a facilitative approach promotes developmental parenting by emphasizing parent–child interaction and building on family strengths. The first priority for those working with parents, then, is to increase positive parent–child interactions in which both parent and child are learning and feeling secure and successful. The things that families already do well or resources they already have are strengths that can serve as starting points for building further strengths and addressing challenges families might face.

Rather than simply telling a parent what to do with a child, a tactic that often works poorly, a practitioner using a facilitative approach observes what the parent already does with the child and encourages the parent to use those interactions to support the child's development. By starting with something the parent already does, it becomes easier to then identify ways to provide the assistance he or she needs, either with parenting or family problems. The facilitative approach we recommend includes the strengths-based approach recommended in 2002 by ZERO TO THREE: "A strengths-based approach recognizes and encourages parents' capacities and provides needed assistance in coping with difficulty."

Practitioners may know about child development, but parents know their children. Both practitioners and parents, then, have their own source of competence. This mutual-competence perspective emphasizes family strengths in several ways. Practitioners take a mutual-competence perspective when they recognize and value family strengths, acknowledge that both they and the parents have areas of competence, and work together in partnerships with parents to promote children's development. Practitioners use this perspective not only when they respond to parents' interests and ideas first but also when they contribute their own strengths, expertise, and resources in response to information from parents to select the best ways to help individual parents support their children's development. For example, it may be very important to one mother to teach beginning sports skills to her young child, and the mother may have many of those skills herself. The practitioner working with this family may or may not put the same emphasis on sports skills but can share more general ideas about teaching new skills to the young child, such as starting with very simple steps, using skills the child already has, and keeping the activity fun.

When interactions, either between parent and child or between parent and practitioner, are mutually competent, both people enjoy learning together and feel secure, valued, understood, successful, and happy. Mutually competent parent–child interactions support a child's development and increase a parent's self-confidence in being able to support the child's development. In this way, a facilitative approach based on mutual competence builds strong relationships between parents and practitioners, supports parents in building strong relationships with their children, and increases parents' awareness of child development by helping them understand their children's experience.

Practitioners can establish mutually competent relationships with parents in several ways. First, during the initial meeting with a family, the practitioner can be clear about the program's goals, expectations, and boundaries so the parents understand the purpose of the program and its parenting focus. Second, during every interaction, the practitioner can show acceptance of the parents' reasons and parenting methods—even if the practitioner does not agree—to build trust and openness for the future. Third, the practitioner can show respect for the parents' strengths by taking time to understand each parent's perspective first before sharing his or her own expertise. Fourth, the practitioner can open the door for more communication by keeping discussions focused on behaviors rather than perceptions. Fifth, the practitioner can support collaboration by planning activities and interventions based on what both parent and practitioner agree on. Sixth, the practitioner can maintain accountability in his or her partnership with the parents by reviewing activities in terms of how well they went and whether the activities accomplished the intended goals.

Our facilitative approach uses a mutual competence framework to

1. Stay focused on parenting, parent–child interaction, and a strong parent–child relationship (in contrast to modeling the "right" way to teach a child)

2. Establish a working partnership between the parent and the practitioner (in contrast to the practitioner acting as a teacher of the child or the case manager for the family)

3. Help the parent understand the child's developmental experiences in the context of everyday family activities (in contrast to teaching developmental milestones)

4. Build parent self-confidence by supporting the parent's relationship with the child (in contrast to an emphasis on parent training)

5. Create opportunities for parents and practitioner to observe and discuss what is "going right" in the parent–child relationship (in contrast to discussions of what is going wrong)

6. Help the parent see the impact of stressful events and family crises on their children, thereby strengthening the parent–child relationship in times of stress (in contrast to waiting until problems are solved before addressing child development)

7. Respect and support the parent's values and beliefs in the context of the family's culture and community (in contrast to assuming a common set of values)

8. Use a parallel approach for many different program activities and topics, such as supervision and program planning (in contrast to using it only for working with parents on child development)

Our facilitative approach, based on a mutual competence perspective, is compatible with approaches referred to as *strengths-based, family-centered,* or *relationship-focused.* These approaches represent an emerging consensus about the most effective practices for working with parents and children together to promote children's development. When practitioners have a mutual competence perspective, they can make effective use of the attitudes, behaviors, and content that form good practice. Table 3.1 includes practice recommendations from the field that support a facilitative approach.

FACILITATIVE ATTITUDES

Two major attitudes are essential to facilitate developmental parenting: *responsiveness* to family resources, needs, values, and culture; and *flexibility* in helping families use their resources to meet their needs consistent with their values and culture. Responsiveness is perhaps the most essential, but it is not sufficient without flexibility. With these attitudes it becomes easier for practitioners to be supportive and accepting in relationships. Finally, to promote developmental parenting, practitioners need to stay focused on child development. Practitioners express these essential attitudes in many ways in parenting-focused programs through the emotional climate, setting, and timing of their meetings with parents and children.

Table 3.1. What recommendations support a facilitative approach?

Consensus-based recommendations	Rationale	References
Be responsive to family strengths and culture.	Responsiveness to family strengths and culture opens opportunities to increase positive aspects of parenting and family functioning to support a child's development.	Bernstein et al., 1991; Brorson, 2005; Caldwell et al., 1994; Daro & Harding, 1999; Lanzi et al., 1999; Slaughter-Defoe, 1993; Smith, 1995; Trivette & Dunst, 1986
Be flexible in strategies and activities.	Flexibility enables providers to individualize to each family and to respond to changing needs of families over time.	Daro et al., 1993; Daro & McCurdy, 1994; Donnelly, 1992; Gomby et al., 1999; Lanzi et al., 1999; Olds & Kitzman, 1993; Weiss, 1993
Be supportive and accepting in relationships.	Positive relationships between practitioners and family members promote trust and responsive parenting.	Barnard et al., 1993; Bernstein et al., 1991, 2001; Emde et al., 2000; Roggman et al., 2001

Practitioners show *facilitative attitudes* when they are

- Responsive to family strengths and culture
- Flexible in strategies and activities
- Supportive and accepting in relationships with the family

Responsiveness to Family Strengths

Responsiveness to family strengths and culture is essential because each family is unique and each child is unique. Although some developmental needs apply to all children, the timing of those needs varies by individual child, and the resources for meeting those needs vary by individual family. A facilitative parenting-focused practitioner helps parents identify their children's developmental needs and the family's mix of resources available to meet those needs. A responsive practitioner asks about family strengths, notices and comments on them, and helps the family find ways to use their strengths to meet their children's developmental needs. A responsive practitioner also asks about the family's cultural traditions, values, and expectations as a source of family strengths. Responsiveness is more than tolerance and more than acceptance. Responsiveness requires actively learning about each family, expressing appreciation for their strengths and unique characteristics, considering those characteristics when planning program activities, and helping parents see their families' routines, traditions, and idiosyncrasies as resources for supporting their children's development. Responsiveness is the core attitude of a strengths-based approach to help parents support their children's development.

Parents vary in their previous experience with infants and children. Some parents have a lot of experience with infants and toddlers either because they have older children or because they had previous experience with children in their family or work life. Other parents have limited experience with infants before having one of their own and may find it more challenging to be relaxed and comfortable interacting and playing with their infant. Similarly, one parent may have extensive knowledge about child development and primarily need support and encouragement, while another parent may have very little knowledge about development and want more information about what to expect as the child grows. Using a facilitative approach involves responding to these varying needs and adapting information and activities in response to parents' varying backgrounds, knowledge, and experience.

It is sometimes more difficult than it sounds to observe and comment on parent–child interactions from a strengths-based perspective.

Families, parents, and children vary widely, and practitioners do not always know what child behaviors parents consider important, and they are sometimes unfamiliar with cultural expectations. For example, in one family, a mother may sing songs with her children, an activity known to support language development and other aspects of cognitive and emotional development. Increasing the frequency and variety of these interactions is an appropriate, strengths-based way for a practitioner to have an impact on targeted child outcomes. In another family, however, the same activity may be so unlikely to happen that it would be pointless to recommend it—because the parent hates to sing, or finds it silly or embarrassing, or for any other reason. Other activities that are more enjoyable and come more naturally to the family are then more appropriate.

Responsiveness is called for when parents initiate discussions or have ideas for activities to do with their children as part of home visits or other aspects of a parenting program. One of the goals of a facilitative approach is to engage parents in planning collaboratively for the activities of each subsequent home visit. Some parents are more ready than others to engage in collaborative planning, and they easily think of ideas for activities and discussion topics extending from the basic information provided by a practitioner. Other parents, who may have little experience in planning activities for their children or little confidence about promoting their children's development, have few ideas about activities or topics or are reluctant to make any suggestions. Particularly with these parents, a responsive practitioner listens carefully for indications of parents' interests and ideas and responds positively to them. In the same way that parents are encouraged to "follow the child's lead" when engaging in play interactions, practitioners are encouraged to follow the parent's lead when engaging in discussions and when planning activities to do and topics to discuss during home visits or other program events. A practitioner who is responsive to each family is flexible about how they deliver services through the parent to the child, maintain an emphasis on parent–child interaction, and build on family strengths. (See Table 3.2 for examples of strategies that show responsive attitudes.)

Flexibility in Strategies and Activities

Flexibility in thinking is essential for facilitating developmental parenting for two main reasons. First, a practitioner who is flexible can individualize the program to fit each parent and child. There is no one-size-fits-all procedure that works with all families or even with both parents and all children in the same family! What works for any given parent and child depends on where the child is developmentally, what the

Table 3.2. Strategies showing responsive attitudes

Strategies	Examples
Ask about family strengths.	"What are some things your family especially enjoys doing together?"
Observe and comment on family strengths.	"I see you have a garden—what a great place for your child to learn about plants!"
Ask about past experiences with children.	"What kinds of experiences did you have with children before you had your own?"
Observe and comment on parent experience.	"That sounds interesting, what did you enjoy about that babysitting experience?"
Ask about parent knowledge of child development.	"What have you noticed about your child's language development?"
Observe and comment on parent knowledge.	"It's interesting that you notice your child putting words together because that is an important change in language development."
Ask about what parent wants in child's development.	"How do you feel about how your child is developing? What do you think is the most important thing for her to learn?"
Observe and comment on parenting values.	"I like how you redirected him from hitting his brother; it seems important to you that they learn to get along well with each other."
Ask about what parent does to help child's development.	"What other things do you do to help them learn to get along?"
Observe and comment on parenting strategies.	"I notice that you smiled at both of your children when they were playing together so they know you like it when they do that."
Ask what parent enjoys doing with the child.	"What's fun for you to do with your kids?"
Observe and comment on parent's interests and ideas.	"I notice that you enjoy cooking. Have you tried doing cooking activities with your child?"

child is like temperamentally, what the parent and child do when they are together, what the parent knows, how the parent feels, what kinds of values the parent holds, what kinds of family backgrounds influence the parent's expectations, what the culture and social group are for that family, where they live, how they live, who lives there, and more. In other words, it is not likely that even the best of plans for meeting the needs of one parent and child will work for other families the same way.

Second, a practitioner who is flexible can show respect for each individual family by adapting program activities to each family's unique situation. Everyone has values that they believe are important (otherwise they would not be called *values*). People vary, however, in what childrearing values they hold and which ones have priority. A parent's values and priorities will affect what the parent wants and needs from a parenting program. Parenting activities and information, even if developmentally appropriate for both parent and child, will not be appropriate at all if they are in conflict with a family's values.

For example, parents vary widely, both across and within cultures, in how much they talk to their children and how much they expect their children to talk to them. Practitioners who help parents promote their children's early language development are likely to suggest a lot of adult–child conversation, but this suggestion may be received differently by families with different childrearing values. In Family A, the mother and father feel that it is more important for children to be respectful and quiet with adults than for them to be talkative. In Family B, the opposite is true—the children are actively encouraged to talk with visitors to the home and to "show off" what they know. To expect the parents in Family A to be comfortable encouraging their child to be talkative with visitors would be as disrespectful of their values as would expecting the parents in Family B to be comfortable shushing their child's conversations with visitors. Nevertheless, participating in conversations is important for children's language development, so some flexibility is needed to help the parents in Family A figure out how to encourage their child's conversational skills in ways that are consistent with their family's values. In Family A, the practitioner helps parents think of times when they have enjoyed a give-and-take conversation with their child, perhaps when there were no other adults around, and also helps them think of ways to make those times happen more often. In Family B, the practitioner simply responds positively to the child's talkativeness and also lets the parent know how these conversational opportunities promote their child's language development.

Flexibility helps practitioners adapt the *location* of activities. The location of home visit activities depends on where families are comfortable. Although parent–child interactions are easier to elicit when they are at the same level, for example, while playing on the living room floor, some families are more comfortable with activities at the kitchen table. Some activities may occur in one area and other activities in a different area of the home or even the front porch or backyard. In some situations, it may help to suggest a blanket for floor activities that can be used as a play space for a child between visits. Some activities may not happen in a home at all. When practitioners are flexible, home visits can include any routine activity in or out of the home (e.g., meal table, bath time, shopping). Some "home visits" are scheduled in alternative locations such as a program center classroom, a restaurant, or a park. Some "home visits" are more like family field trips to places families often go, such as grocery stores, laundromats, post offices, or health clinics. In such excursions, practitioners can help parents find ways to make the experience positive and interesting for the child. Practitioners and parents together can decide the best places for the program's activities.

Flexibility is especially needed in some homes where stressful circumstances make life so difficult that families and their households become disorganized and chaotic. When many people live in a small amount of space or must cope with multiple sources of stress, such as poverty, family conflict, and mental illness, they may not keep up with cleaning or organizing the household. The idea of planning space for home visit activities at a table or on the floor may be impractical because there is no empty space at the table or no table at all or no empty floor space to sit on. This is when a balance of planning ahead and being adaptable is particularly important.

With flexibility, a practitioner can help a family find a place to do activities with children by asking them to help plan the activities. It may be that for some families, the best activities will be those that require very little space, so a table or floor space is not needed. For other families, it may be okay to meet in one room but not another. Practitioners who are open to unexpected alternatives can find what works best for each individual family by working together to plan activities ahead of time. Flexibility helps practitioners show respect for each family and acceptance of their current situation while helping parents find good areas for activities to promote their children's learning.

Flexibility also helps practitioners adapt the *schedule* for activities. Facilitative home visits are scheduled, as much as possible, when they will be effective and responsive to family needs. For some families, daytime visits are convenient if a parent is home and not at work or school, and should be scheduled when the child is usually rested and awake. For other families, evening or weekend visits are better because a parent works during weekday daytime hours. To involve both mothers and fathers, home visits need to be scheduled to accommodate both parents' work schedules. Programs intending to support parenting among working parents may need to recruit and hire practitioners who are able and willing to work during evenings, weekends, or early morning hours. Not every visit has to happen on the same day and time every week. Sometimes, a practitioner may want to schedule a home visit at a certain time in order to observe a family routine, or a mother may want some advice on what to do with her child during bath time or dinnertime. These situations offer opportunities to support developmental parenting.

Adapting the schedule of activities may also mean that visits to some families occur less often or more often than the standard schedule for the program. The first author, along with several other Early Head Start researchers, reported in 2008 that families were more likely to drop out of home visiting programs when their home visits were shorter and more frequent, so having longer visits less often may provide a good alternative for programs that offer more than a year of services. Some parents, though, are quite comfortable with visits lasting 45 minutes to an hour because they do not have time for a longer visit or because other problems or a family crisis sometimes make a longer visit impossible. Parents who are in a crisis situation may require even more flexibility on time and place. Even in a time of crisis, however, parents often need support to keep parenting in ways that support children's development. It is especially at those times when a practitioner's responsiveness, flexibility, respect, and adaptability will make a difference.

Constraints imposed by funding agencies may limit flexibility. For example, policy standards for Head Start and Early Head Start home-based programs recommend home visits every week for an hour and a half. Even in these programs, however, flexible scheduling is important to accommodate the needs of individual families who work unusual hours or have other time demands that make it difficult to have home visits during weekdays or at the same time every week. (See Table 3.3 for examples of strategies showing flexible strategies.)

Supportive and Accepting Relationships with the Family

When practitioners meet with families, they begin to build relationships. When relationships between families and practitioners are friendly, supportive, and accepting, parents are more likely to be comfortable with activities planned to promote developmental parenting. A positive practitioner–parent relationship will help them work together to form a partnership in planning activities to support the child's development. When parents feel supported and accepted, they can respond more positively to ideas and feedback from the practitioner without feeling suspicious or defensive. A parent who feels judged or disrespected is not likely to engage in the process at all. The positive responsiveness and acceptance of every family as it is provides a foundation for a relationship between practitioner and parent that fosters trust and mutual respect. The support and acceptance the practitioner conveys often help the parent feel more at ease in interacting with the child, which, in turn, helps build a more supportive parent–child relationship. The relationships between practitioner and family members will grow and develop over time, but from the beginning, these relationships are the context for the program's entry into the family to facilitate developmental parenting that supports child development. Starting on a positive note will begin the relationship-building process.

A practitioner's positive attitude and enthusiasm for the family helps build relationships with the family whether the purpose is to

Table 3.3.   Strategies showing flexible attitudes

Strategies	Examples
Adapt to the family's situation.	"You say it's very hard for you to be living with your parents now. Do you want to have the visits here or would you like to meet someplace else for our visits?"
Adapt to what the parent already knows.	"I noticed that you know a lot of songs that you sing with your daughter. Teach me and let's sing together with her!"
Adapt to what the parent already does.	"You have a lot of photographs of your children. Let's use those to get them talking."
Adapt to what the parent wants to learn and do.	"If you want to work on toilet training, then let's work on that first."
Adapt to what the parent cares about and values.	"I know you want your children to be polite, so let's think of some activities to teach 'magic words.'"
Adapt activities so that they happen where the family is comfortable.	"Where do you think it would be best to do this activity?" "Where in the house do you and your child play together most often?"
Adapt to the family's living space.	"Maybe we'd have a little more room on the floor if we moved this basket over there. Would that be okay?" "Maybe we could have our next visit in the kitchen?"
Adapt activities so that they can happen in other outdoor places.	"Would you like to go to the park for our next visit?" "Several families are interested in going to the zoo, so we're meeting there on Saturday morning if you'd like to come."
Adapt to the family schedule.	"What time of day do you spend time with your child? Do you have one-to-one time then?" "If you work nights, is it better to have a visit when you are getting off work or before you go to work?"
Adapt special visits for other family members, such as father, siblings, or grandparent.	"Who else in your family would enjoy that activity? Could we have a visit when they could join us?"
Be clear about what flexibility is possible, given program policies.	"Here is a page that describes the home visits our program provides and our policies and requirements. Let's talk about it."

provide support for developmental parenting of young children, as parenting-focused programs are designed to do, or to help families obtain needed community resources as case management is designed to do. A positive atmosphere is particularly important for facilitating developmental parenting because if parents and children experience the activities positively, then they will be more likely to repeat the activities in the future. Regardless of the goals of the program or the challenges of any particular family, positive interactions between program staff and families are more likely than negative interactions to facilitate developmental parenting.

When program services are delivered in home visits, practitioners should consider how a guest should behave. In a home visiting program, a practitioner is a guest in a family's home and should behave as a good guest does—with warmth, acceptance, respect, and courtesy. Every culture has expectations about the role of guest and host. So when a family invites someone into their home, the nature of these roles involves personal greetings and expressions to each family member. Some cultures and families have other expectations of guests that help establish a positive atmosphere and build good relationships. For example, in their role as host to a visitor to their home, a family member may offer the visitor a food or beverage. Although it is not required to accept these offerings, accepting food can help build a positive relationship if the ritual of eating together is an expectation of the host. An acceptable alternative may be to ask for a glass of water or a cup of tea.

In parenting programs that deliver services during home visits, the roles of guest and host sometimes present a challenge for delivering developmental parenting support or other program services. The family hosts the home visit, and the practitioner arrives as a guest, but this guest sometimes has plans for activities to be done in the family's home. For example, as part of the developmental services a program provides, a practitioner may suggest developmental learning activities that are best done on the floor or at a table. It is not the role of the guest, however, to determine where activities take place. If a parent is uncomfortable being on the floor or physically unable to get on the floor, then flexibility will be required to adapt the activity so the parent is comfortable. When practitioners and parents plan future home visit activities together, the host or parent can plan the kind of space that is needed for the activities.

Sometimes during early home visits, a family is concerned about the appearance of the home and may work to clean an area for the home visit. If that area was the living room and the practitioner suggests meeting at the kitchen table, then the parent may feel disappointed because the carefully prepared living room was ignored or the parent may feel embarrassed because the kitchen was not cleaned. Planning ahead together with the parent can help avoid such a problem. Being clear about the goals and purposes of each home visit with no hidden agenda will also help avoid problems. During each home visit, the practitioner and parent can discuss activities for the next visit so that the parent can prepare and make any necessary arrangements. Interactions are more likely to be positive when the practitioner is flexible about where activities take place because flexibility shows respect for the needs of the family. (See Table 3.4 for strategies showing supportive and accepting attitudes.)

Table 3.4.   Strategies showing supportive and accepting attitudes

Strategies	Examples
Greet each family member in a friendly, positive way.	"Hi Jennie, how are you doing? And how is baby Joshua doing today?"
Focus on family strengths.	"I know you've had a hard week so it's really great that you can take some time to hold your baby."
Show warmth and acceptance.	"I appreciate that you have your own way of interacting with your baby."
Show respect and courtesy.	"Would it be all right with you if we sit on the floor for this activity?"
Be clear about goals and purposes of the program.	"The purpose of this program is to provide support for you to help your child's development."
Plan activities to involve the child.	"Let's decide what to do next week. What has your child been especially interested in lately?"

CONCLUSION

A practitioner with the right attitudes is better prepared to do the behaviors discussed in the next chapter that facilitate developmental parenting. When all the staff members of a parenting-focused program share these attitudes, the practitioners who work directly with families can get the support and supervision they need to implement the behaviors and provide the content that make up developmental parenting-focused programs.

4

B Is for Behavior

What behaviors facilitate developmental parenting? What do practitioners actually do when they are facilitating developmental parenting? In a parenting-focused model, the practitioner delivers child development services through the parent to the child by facilitating parent–child interaction during most of their time together. A facilitative approach emphasizes parenting, elicits parent–child interaction, supports developmental parenting behaviors, establishes partnerships, involves the whole family, and uses family activities. This chapter will describe many specific strategies to accomplish these things.

FACILITATIVE BEHAVIORS

What a practitioner actually does with parents and children and the kinds of activities that are planned will make a difference in the effectiveness of a parenting program. The program is likely to be effective if the practitioner focuses on parenting, gets parents and children doing things together, works in partnership with parents, encourages parenting behaviors that support child development, gets other family members involved, and uses family activities and routines as learning opportunities. The program is less likely to be effective if the practitioner focuses mostly on the parent or mostly on the child, plans all of the activities, brings all of the materials, and ignores other family members.

Beware of Red Flags—Signs of Ineffectiveness

The following are some red flags that practitioners should watch for that are signs that the home visitor is *not* effectively facilitating parent–child interactions that support children's early development:

- The parent leaves the room or is in and out during a home visit.

- The child races to greet the home visitor and wants to rummage through the bag of materials, ignoring his mother.

- The practitioner spends a lot of time dealing with a family crisis, "putting out fires," and not focusing on child development.

- The practitioner does not expect to get much accomplished when other family members are present during a meeting because they are such a distraction.

- The practitioner would like to visit the family's home more often, because it seems like it is the only time that the child gets any attention.

- The parent makes excuses for not doing the "assignments" of activities to do with the child between visits.

- The parent often says to the home visitor, "You are so good with children!"

If you are a practitioner reading this book, and you are seeing red flags in your home visits, you are like many in your field who have had these experiences. Parents sometimes get confused about the purpose of the program, or they want something special for their child and hope the practitioner can provide it, or they expect a child care provider or a shoulder to cry on or someone to rescue them. These hopes and expectations can be overwhelming to practitioners, especially those who are inexperienced or confused themselves about their roles when they work with parents in their homes. A practitioner may feel like he or she has to be a social worker, psychologist, nurse, teacher, and friend all rolled into one. That is why the strategies described in this chapter can be useful for keeping the parent focused on parenting and the practitioner focused on facilitating developmental parenting.

Parenting-focused programs are more likely to increase developmental parenting if practitioners do things to directly facilitate it. Fortunately, studies of home visiting programs suggest ideas for how in-home parenting programs can be effective. What may seem like good strategies—describing developmental parenting, demonstrating how to do it, and telling parents to do it—do not actually work that well. More effective strategies are evident in the conversations, interaction patterns, planning process, people involved, and activities done during home visits. The practitioner's role, in a developmental parenting program, is to follow the practices shown to have positive impacts on parenting and on children's development. A number of research studies have provided evidence that particular practices in home-based intervention programs are more likely to be effective than others. These studies provide a basis for evidence-based practice in home visiting programs. See Table 4.1 for evidence-based practices for working with parents of young children.

These behaviors are known to be effective in parenting programs. The research evidence is from many different kinds of in-home parenting support interventions. What the evidence shows is that home vis-

Table 4.1. What are evidence-based practices for working with parents of young children?

Evidence-based practice	Rationale	References
Emphasize parenting and child development.	Having an impact on parenting makes it more likely that a program will then have an impact on children. A parenting program's primary purpose is to promote parenting that fosters children's early development.	ACYF, 2002; Bernstein et al., 1991; Daro & Harding, 1999; Gomby, 1999; Guralnick, 1998; Smith, 1995; van den Boom, 1995; Weiss, 1993
Engage parent and child together.	Facilitating parent-child interaction is related to more family improvement.	Mahoney et al., 1998; Roggman et al., 2001
Directly support parent warmth, responsiveness, encouragement, and conversation.	Directly encouraging parents to teach, talk, and interact responsively and warmly with children can be effective and help parents improve child outcomes.	Hebbeler & Gerlach-Downie, 2002; Guralnick, 1989; Mahoney et al., 1998; Mahoney & Perales, 2005; Pfannenstiel & Seltzer, 1989; Roggman et al., 2001
Collaborate with parents.	Working together with parents to plan, implement, and review activities increases parent capacity to support development and increases program capacity to have more lasting impact.	Dunst, Trivette, & Hamby, 2006; Hebbler & Gerlach-Downie, 2002
Involve other family members.	Interacting with fathers and siblings helps children learn more vocabulary and language skills.	Azmitia & Hesser, 1993; Oshima-Takane et al., 1996; Perez-Granados & Callanan, 1997; Roggman et al., 2004
Build on family activities.	Incorporating learning into everyday family routines and other regular activities increases the number of opportunities for parents to support their children's development.	Dunst et al., 2006; Guralnick, 1989; Woods et al., 2004

iting interventions are most likely to be effective at promoting positive parenting and child development when practitioners put an emphasis on parenting and child development and elicit parent–child interaction during the visits. Furthermore, programs are more effective when practitioners establish collaborative partnerships with parents and build on family strengths. These are the key practitioner behaviors that facilitate developmental parenting.

Characteristics of Facilitative Behaviors

Practitioners show *facilitative behaviors* when they

- Focus parents on child development

- Elicit parent–child interaction

- Support developmental parenting behaviors

- Establish a collaborative partnership with parents

- Involve other family members

- Use family activities as learning opportunities

Focus Parents on Child Development   Practitioners who facilitate developmental parenting spend most of their time with families focused on parenting and child development. Although there may be competing family demands, personal problems, or other distractions, the primary purpose of meeting in the family's home is to support parenting, so most of the time should be spent on parenting. Sometimes these distractions are formidable barriers for parents. For example, a mother who cannot afford the next month's rent and fears getting evicted with no place else to go is unlikely to participate enthusiastically in an activity such as finger painting, and it would be unrealistic to expect her to do so. This is a time, however, when she especially needs help and guidance to keep parenting and supporting her child's development. It may take months to solve the rent problem, and it may involve the upheaval of moving more than once, but meanwhile her child is still developing. A child's development during the early years is on a fast timetable and can be derailed by the stress and anxiety of neglect. In other words, it is when family problems are most severe that parenting may matter most to a child's development. It is also a time when parents often need the most help to focus on their children.

The general strategies offered here include various ways a practitioner can keep the focus on parenting the young child regardless of the content or topic of a particular home visit. These strategies can be used equally well with mothers, fathers, siblings, and anyone else who plays with or helps take care of the child in the home. By using these strategies with everyone present for the home visit, the practitioner will encourage everyone in the family to provide opportunities for the child to explore and communicate. Strategies that encourage a parent to stay focused on parenting and child development include commenting on observations of the child's behavior or development, asking for information about the child's behavior, development, and interests, and offering information and materials related to child development.

"Say what you see" is a key strategy and an easily remembered guideline for commenting on observations. For example, a practitioner could say, "I see that your child is often asking you, 'What's that?' She seems interested in learning lots of new words." A practitioner can be a careful observer of a child's behavior and can then describe the child's emerging skills to the parent to provide feedback that increases the parent's awareness of the child's development. By commenting on observations, the practitioner directs the focus of attention toward the child and toward parent–child interactions. Descriptions that include concrete details of the child's behaviors help a parent learn to pay more attention to details and help him or her remember things to look for in the future.

"Ask about what you don't see" is another useful strategy. For example, a practitioner could ask, "How does he do at bedtime? What's it like when he's getting ready to go to bed?" Asking for information about a child's typical behavior, interests, or feelings is another strategy that encourages the parent to become a better observer of the child. Ask a parent questions about how the child responds to various things, what skills the child is learning, what the child likes to look at, what toys the child especially enjoys playing with, when the child most wants to be held, what the daily patterns and routines are like for the parent and child, what the parent does to entertain or quiet the child, and how the child communicates his or her needs. By asking these kinds of questions, the practitioner keeps the focus on parenting and encourages the parent as a good observer and provider of appropriate developmental opportunities for the child.

Parents know their own children better than a practitioner does, but sometimes parents are not fully aware of their knowledge until someone else asks a question or offers an observation that triggers more conscious thoughts about the children. A simple question such as, "Does he get used to new things easily or does it take him a while?" helps a parent reflect on a child's temperament. Other questions help parents focus on their children's developmental progress or the kinds of activities the children like and dislike, such as, "Does she like to try to feed herself?" A practitioner can also ask a parent questions about interactions with the child, such as, "Why do you sit him in that position?" Sometimes a practitioner can best make a point about parenting and child development by focusing more on the child's behavior and less on the parent's behavior. Practitioners can avoid making assumptions based only on their own experiences by asking parents for more information about their children and about why parents do things the way they do.

Two strategies are effective in helping to keep a parent's focus on parenting and child development. One is to offer resources such as information or materials for developmental learning activities. This could involve giving lists of developmental stages to parents or leaving a book on a certain topic. The other strategy is to provide information related to recent parent–child interactions or in response to a parent's questions or requests. Responding to parent requests makes information more relevant, meaningful, and memorable to parents, so it is a more facilitative strategy for supporting developmental parenting than giving information that parents did not request.

Information is retained better if it is in context. Therefore, information is more likely to be meaningful and memorable to parents when it is related to their children's current behavior, recent parent–child interactions, or questions the parents ask. For example, information about language development will make more sense when a parent and child are engaged in language activities such as sharing books or singing, or when a parent has taken notice of the child's emerging language skills. Parents may need additional ideas or background information on a particular topic and may ask for accurate information. Parents may express interest in other materials the program could provide, such as basic art materials or books. If information is offered at a relevant moment or a parent has requested the information, then the parent will be more likely to use the information than if it comes in a stack of handouts sent from the program, whether the parent wants them or not, on everything from baby food recipes to job training opportunities.

Some parents lead the home visit in a direction away from parenting and child development when they have many needs of their own that they want to talk about. A home visit can be diverted from its developmental purpose by a parent's mental health or survival needs. It is important to help parents find resources for addressing critical needs, but the focus of developmental home visits needs to remain on parent–child interaction. The primary purpose of a developmental parenting program is for children's development. Children will keep developing, for better or for worse, no matter what happens to their parents or families. Children's developmental needs do not wait for practitioners and parents to build their relationships or for families to solve their problems.

No matter what challenges a family is facing, it is essential for parent–child interaction to continue and for a parent to see the child's developmental needs. When family problems divert the focus away from the child, the practitioner can ask about the family's resources for meeting parent and family needs, offer more information about community resources, and then shift the focus back to parent–child interaction by asking questions about the child and the child's responses. To shift the focus to the child's responses, shine the light on the child by saying, for example, "How do you think what has been happening in your family affects your child?" Often this shift back to a focus on the child's development takes more than one question: "How have you been different with her?" "How has he been sleeping?" "Are you still doing the same bedtime routine?"

The amount of time spent on child development topics during home visits is critical for better outcomes for both parents and children. In the national Early Head Start Research and Evaluation Project, home visitors recorded the percentage of each visit they spent on child development topics, family concerns, and relationship building between visitor and parent. Helen Raikes, a professor at the University of Nebraska and a consultant to the U.S. Department of Health and Human Services, collaborated with several other researchers studying the impact of Early Head Start home visiting to examine these percentages of time on child development, family issues, and relationship building in relation to parent and child outcomes. They reported, in 2006, that the greater the percentage of time spent on child development during home visits, the better were the home learning environment, the parents' support for language and learning, and the children's cognitive and language development scores when the children were 3 years old. This research shows that practitioners working with families in their homes need to keep the focus on child development in order to make a difference in children's development and in how parents support their children's development. (See Table 4.2 for strategies.)

Elicit Parent–Child Interaction to Keep the "Action" Between Parent and Child   A parent will remain in a child's life long after the developmental parenting program ends, so establishing or enhancing parent–child interaction as a rich context for development has the potential to foster child development for many years. If a primary purpose of a developmental program is to support parents in their role as early educators, then the behaviors of practitioners in the program should encourage a lot of parent–child interaction. In a home visiting program, for example, most of the interactions during a home visit should involve both parent and child together. Some interactions can

Table 4.2. Strategies to focus parents on child development

Strategies	Examples
Make clear statements about the parent's role.	"Parents are a child's most important teachers."
	"You are an important teacher because you are the one who will be in her life the longest."
	"You'll be able to help him learn and develop now and when he's in school, too."
Observe and comment on the child's development.	"I notice he's starting to put words together; he said, 'Book mine.'"
	"She's pretending her bucket is a chef's hat."
Offer information about development in the context of children's behavior.	"Crying is his way of letting you know he wants something. It will get easier when he starts pointing and using words."
	"See how she's holding the marker? Kids usually do it like that before they can hold it like we do."
	"You're right; he's saying more new words, which means he'll put together two-word sentences soon!"
Offer materials to read or use when they are relevant or requested.	"Would you like a chart of language development?"
	"Our program has extra drawing paper. Let me know if you'd like some."
	"We could check out a puzzle from our toy library if you'd like to try it with her."
Shift focus by asking how family needs affect the child.	"How is she affected by what has been happening with your family?"
	"Did you notice how he looked when you were talking about that? Do you think he might be worried, too?"
	"How has she been this week when these things have been going on? What do you think would help her feel more relaxed?"
For other family needs, ask about resources for meeting those needs.	"What have you done when this happened before? Where did you get help?"
	"Is there someone you know who could help you figure it out?"
Provide information about community resources for meeting family needs.	"Here's a list of places in town where you can go for help with that." "Here's a phone number for the food bank."
Be clear about roles of different staff members regarding social services.	"Here's the number to call our social services coordinator, who has a lot more information about this kind of thing."

involve the practitioner with the parent or both the practitioner and parent with the child. Very few interactions should involve only the practitioner and child.

One easy and practical way for practitioners to keep the action between parent and child is to hand all materials for learning activities directly to the parent, not the child. This is a simple behavior, but a powerful one. The best materials for learning activities in the home are usually materials the family already has, but sometimes practitioners will bring materials provided by the program. By always handing such materials to the parent, the practitioner is sending a message to both the parent and the child that the parent is the one in charge of these activities, not the practitioner. This behavior keeps the parent in the role of the real "teacher," while the practitioner remains in a consultant role of offering information, support, and encouragement to the parent while not taking over the parenting or teaching role with the child. Handing materials to the parent also sends a message to the child that it is the parent who does the fun, stimulating activities. This simple action, repeated many times, establishes parent–child interaction as the context for fun and learning.

"Say what you see" and "Ask what you don't see" strategies are particularly useful for eliciting parent–child interaction. Observations of the child's responses to the parent along with the parent's response to the child are important to observe and describe well. By saying what is seen in parent–child interactions, the practitioner helps parents become more aware of these interactions and better self-observers. By sticking to observations, you can avoid making assumptions about why parents do what they do, what they think, or what they want. Rather than make assumptions about what the parent is doing, ask for more information if you do not understand the reason for what you see. For example: "I see that you raise your voice when you say certain words. Why do you do that?" This prevents you from making assumptions based on your own perspective that may not fit with the parent's perspective.

It is sometimes difficult for practitioners to just sit back, be quiet, and observe without jumping in with a quick comment or question. Waiting for the parent and child to keep interacting and giving time for them to pause and then continue allows for a richer observation of the child's development and the parent's support of it. Asking questions about what the child can do or what the child likes often encourages the parent to try something new with the child and enriches their interactions.

Although it is sometimes tempting for a practitioner to be the "star" of the home visit, or the center of attention, the purpose of facilitative home visiting is to encourage parent–child interaction and thereby support the parent–child relationship, not the practitioner–child relationship. Parent–child interactions should be the real "star" of a facilitative home visit. If a practitioner arrives at a family's home, and the young child eagerly approaches in anticipation of fun activities, it is a good sign because it indicates that the visits have been a positive experience for the child. If the child expects the practitioner to be the one

providing the fun, however, it is not a good sign because it indicates
that the practitioner has not been helping the parent become the one
to provide the fun. The arrival of the practitioner to the home should
signal to both child and parent that they will have a good time but that
the good time will happen mostly between parent and child. (See Table
4.3 for strategies for eliciting parent–child interaction.)

Directly Support Developmental Parenting Behaviors

Key behaviors of developmental parenting are important for practitioners to support and encourage. These are the parent's *warmth* expressed toward the child, the parent's *responsiveness* to the child's cues,
the parent's *encouragement* provided to the child, and the *conversation* be-

Table 4.3. Strategies to elicit parent–child interaction

Strategies	Examples
Hand materials to the parent rather than to the child.	"Here, see if he likes this toy!"
	"Here are the markers I said I'd bring so you could use them with her."
Observe and comment on parent–child interaction.	"I could tell from how he looked at you that he enjoys it when you laugh!"
	"I noticed that you tapped his hand and then he looked at you—does that usually get him to pay attention?"
Observe and comment on the child's response to the mother.	"Oh, she watches you so carefully when you talk to her. She moves her eyes as your head moves."
	"When you asked about that puzzle, she looked at it and smiled so it looks like she enjoyed it."
Observe and comment on the mother's response to the child.	"You noticed his change in attention right away and asked him what he was looking at."
	"When she got frustrated trying to string the beads, you patted her back and then she could start over."
Ask about the child's response.	"Does she usually like new things or is she a little wary at first?"
	"When you asked him about his binky, he put his hand over his mouth. What do you think he was telling you?"
Ask what the child can do.	"Does he take his shoes off by himself?"
	"Can she reach the sink to turn the water on and off?"
	"Does he make marks with a crayon?"
Ask about the child's interests.	"What kinds of toys does she like best?"
	"Does he like to be outdoors?"
Ask about the difference between when things work and when they do not.	"He seems to pay attention more some times than others. What are you doing when he pays attention compared to when he's not?"

tween parent and child. Parent–child interactions that are warm, responsive, encouraging, and conversational promote children's social-emotional, cognitive, and language development. Facilitative home visiting emphasizes these aspects of parent–child interactions as a major program strategy for promoting children's early development. These parenting behaviors are important and are supported by research on early development. (See Table 4.4 to see the parenting behaviors supported by research.)

"Say what you see" and "Ask about what you don't see" remain key strategies when practitioners directly support specific developmen-

Table 4.4. What parenting behaviors does research support?

Developmental parenting behavior	Evidence of outcomes	References
Warmth	Showing love, physical closeness, and positive expressions toward the child helps the child feel close and connected in ways that support positive behavior outcomes including more compliance, less aggression, and eventually more school readiness.	Carton & Carton, 1998; Caspi et al., 2004, Dodici et al. 2003; Estrada et al., 1987; MacDonald, 1992; Petrill et al., 2004; and Sroufe et al., 1990
Responsiveness	Responding sensitively to the child's cues and expressions of needs or interests is related to more secure attachment, better cognitive development, better social development, better language development, fewer behavior problems, better emotion regulation and empathy.	Bornstein & Tamis-LeMonda, 1989; Davidov & Grusec, 2006; Landry et al., 2001; Spencer & Meadow-Orlans, 1996; Mahoney & Perales, 2005; Tamis-LeMonda et al., 2001; Volker et al., 1999, Wakschlag & Hans, 1999.
Encouragement	Encouraging children's interests and self-direction and not being too restrictive or intrusive is related to greater independence, less negativity, more willingness to try challenging tasks, better cognitive and social development, better language development.	Frodi et al., 1985; Hart & Risley, 1995; Ispa et al., 2004; Kelly et al., 2000; Landry et al., 1997
Conversation	Having verbal interactions with children helps them practice their emerging language skills, exposes them to more words, and is related to better language and literacy development.	Baumwell et al., 1997 ; Bornstein et al., 1998; Hart & Risley, 1995; Hubbs-Tait et al., 2002; Snow, 2001; Snow, et al., 1998; Tamis-LeMonda et al., 2005.

tal parenting behaviors. The facilitative practitioner supports a parent's warmth, responsiveness, encouragement, and conversations with the child by noticing the parent's positive behaviors, commenting on them, asking the parent about the child as they do these behaviors, and offering information or materials that the parent may need. All of these specific strategies can be used throughout every home visit to support parenting interactions that promote early development.

Warmth is an important developmental parenting behavior because it provides a young child with a sense of being loved and cared for. The resulting sense of closeness and connectedness between the parent and child lays a foundation for a positive relationship that can be sustained for the child's lifetime. Warm interactions and the sense of connectedness that results from those interactions are both important for establishing the kind of parent–child relationships that continue to support children's development from early in life into adulthood. In fact, it is the sense of closeness and connectedness that often sustains parent–child relationships later through the sometimes tumultuous years of adolescence.

Frequent and consistent parenting interactions that are warm and affectionate lead to children being more compliant and less likely to use misbehavior to get attention or control. Most children will have temper tantrums and misbehave at times. However, when a child feels connected and loved, it is less likely that the child will feel the sadness and anger that often lead to tantrums and misbehavior. Thus it is in the context of a close relationship with the parent that the child develops the self-regulation needed for behaving appropriately in a variety of situations. Also, when the child has a close relationship with a parent, the child is more willing to express feelings, communicate about needs, try new skills, and attempt new ways of communicating. These efforts contribute to the kind of parent–child relationships that support children's development in all domains.

Facilitative practitioners encourage parental warmth by observing and commenting on the various ways parents express their love. Because warmth can be expressed in many ways, it is important to watch carefully to see how each parent expresses warmth—some with physical closeness, some with positive expressions, and some in other ways. Some parents often come right out and say, "I love you" to their children and combine the words with displays of physical affection such as hugs, kisses, or tickles. Some parents show their warmth in less obvious ways that still clearly build a connection with their children. For example, warmth can be expressed by a positive tone of voice, positive statements about a child or what the child does, and a willingness to be fully engaged in interactions with the child. By commenting on expressions of warmth when they see them, practitioners can promote more parental warmth in parent–child interactions. Practitioners can also promote parental warmth by helping parents observe their children's reactions to affection and by offering parents information about how warmth supports early development. (See Table 4.5 for examples of facilitative strategies for supporting parent warmth.)

Responsiveness is a key developmental parenting behavior that is important for early development. Responsive interactions are essential to secure attachment, the foundation for early social development. Responsive interactions and the security of attachment that follows are both important to a child's continuing social, cognitive, and language development.

The kinds of parent–child interactions that support a child's secure attachment are often the same interactions that support the development of exploration and communication, other essential developmental foundations. Responsiveness is valuable for children's developing cognitive competence because when parents are responsive to children's cues, children are more likely to engage in interactions that help them do things they may not be able to do on their own. Secure children are also more likely to maintain their interest in challenging tasks. In addition, when parents are responsive, children are more likely to engage in interactions that involve language so they hear words describing what they are doing and the things around them.

Facilitative practitioners encourage responsiveness by commenting on it when they see it. They observe and comment on a parent's responses to a child's cues, expressions, vocalizations, and beginning words. Because responsiveness occurs in many ways, it is important to watch carefully the ways in which a parent can respond to a child. A parent is responsive by talking about what the child seems to be "saying," whether or not it is verbal. A parent is responsive by doing something to increase the child's comfort when the child is expressing some distress or frustration. Responsiveness also means that the parent follows the child's "lead" in play and gets involved in what the child is doing, not by taking over the activity but by participating in it. For example, a

Table 4.5. Strategies to support parent warmth

Strategies	Examples
Observe and comment on warmth.	"You speak to him in a very sweet voice."
Prompt the parent to express his or her warmth.	"How do you show her you love her?"
Ask about the child's response.	"How does she react when you smile at him?"
Offer information about child development.	"Toddlers often stay calmer if you stay nearby."

parent can participate in play by accepting pretend food or taking a turn with a toy the child offers. A responsive parent also pays attention to what the child's interests are by talking about things the child looks at or describing things when a child seems curious. All of these behaviors are easily observed and can be commented on by a facilitative practitioner. (See Table 4.6 for strategies for supporting parent responsiveness.)

Encouragement is another key aspect of developmental parenting that supports a child's early development. Encouragement involves letting the child explore, make choices, and use the beginning abilities of self-control. It includes praising the child's emerging skills, supporting efforts to do things independently, and not intruding on or directing the child's play. These parenting behaviors encourage the child's autonomy. Parents encourage autonomy when they help children learn to take care of themselves. A busy or distracted parent may benefit from concrete ideas for helping a child learn to get dressed or use the toilet. Home visit activities can include the things young children typically learn to do to help take care of themselves: feeding themselves, washing their hands and face, and getting dressed. Activities can also include simple household chores like dusting, wiping the table, or putting away toys.

Parents encourage autonomy when they play together with children and toys. By being a playmate, a parent can encourage the child to "lead" the play activities. Sharing toys is related initially to children's developing social skills and then increasingly to their developing cognitive skills. Not only do children learn to share their toys but also they begin to pay attention to the words their parents use to describe the toys and begin to try harder to do new things with the toys. A parent can slightly increase the challenge of these activities as he or she observes a child's comfort levels and introduce new ideas or activities as the child is ready. For example, the parent may see that the child puts one block on top of another, so the parent can then hold the bottom block steady to help the child build a taller tower. When parents get in-

Table 4.6.   Strategies to support parent responsiveness

Strategies	Examples
Observe and comment on responsiveness.	"You saw right away that she was getting frustrated and helped her do it another way."
Prompt the parent to respond.	"What do you think he's asking for?" "See what happens if you imitate him."
Ask questions about the child's cues.	"What does he want when he makes that sound?"
Ask questions about what the child is feeling.	"Does he sound tired or hungry to you?"
Offer information about the child's cues.	"Hungry cries often have a steady rhythm."

volved in play and pay attention to their children's interests, they encourage initiative, curiosity, and creativity in their children's play, important foundations for cognitive development. When practitioners ask questions, observe, and comment on these developmental parenting behaviors, they support parents' encouragement of their children.

Encouragement is especially important when children are trying new tasks or coping with new or frustrating situations. By asking parents when children may get frustrated or bored, practitioners can then help them think of ways to encourage their children to better cope with those situations. A practitioner may ask parents how their children are likely to react when running errands or having relatives visit, and then help think of ways to better prepare their children (or themselves) for these experiences. For example, if a parent complains that the child whines too much in public, the practitioner can ask about when the child whines and help the parent predict those occasions. For one child, whining may be a sign of being hungry, and the practitioner can help the parent think of easy snacks to take along while running errands. For another child, whining may be a sign of boredom, and the practitioner can help the parent think of ways to keep the child engaged and interested in what they are doing by talking more about where they are going and what they are seeing.

Parents often need and ask for specific suggestions for problems that arise as they encourage their children's emerging skills. Practitioners can help a parent solve a problem first by asking questions, then by asking what else has worked or helped with the child in the past, before giving suggestions. The goal is to use questions to lead parents to their own solutions. However, some parents need suggestions at times, even if offered sparingly, so facilitative practitioners benefit from good training in child development and caregiving practices. Practitioners need that background information to help parents solve problems.

Even more important, practitioners need strategies to help parents learn effective problem-solving techniques. When practitioners ask about a child's cues, difficult situations, past solutions, and other possibilities, a parent often thinks of more things to try. Having many possible solutions helps a parent find a solution to try while still having alternative solutions to fall back on if the first idea does not solve the problem. Suggestions from the practitioner can help the parent consider the child's development and temperament in the context of the current situation to evaluate possible solutions. Parents' concerns about their children are opportunities for practitioners to use these "teaching moments" to teach parents more about developmental parenting. Guided by parents' interests and concerns and by children's unique developmental pathways, practitioners can design the content of home visit information and materials to support developmental parenting while addressing parents' current concerns, such as mealtime behavior, bedtime routines, or sibling conflicts. (See Table 4.7 for strategies for supporting parent encouragement rather than focusing on the negative.)

Conversation is another key developmental parenting behavior. Early on, parent–child conversations may seem a little one-sided, as parents chat with babies who look interested but may not even make speech sounds yet. But by using many words and many different words, parents can help children learn language sooner and better. Children's early language development is influenced both by how much parents talk to them and by the number of different words parents use. Early conversations involve paying attention to where a child is looking and talking about what the child sees. Later conversations involve asking questions, answering questions, explaining things, telling stories, and talking about books. When a parent shares a child's attention, by looking where an infant is watching a dog walk by outside or talking about a toy a toddler is playing with, for example, the parent not only encourages the developing child's interests and curiosity but also provides language labels even before the child starts speaking any words.

Parent–child conversations promote children's developing language and their later literacy skills. During typical early conversations, a parent exposes an infant to the speech sounds and words of their language and provides labels for the objects, animals, and people in the child's world. By asking a lot of questions, the parent provides opportunities for the child to practice using emerging language skills, especially when the parent asks "wh" questions beginning with *why, where, how,* and *who.* The parent then helps the child learn more about using language when expanding on what the child says by repeating it and adding more words. Other parent–child language interactions, such as reading books, telling stories, playing together, and sharing family rou-

Table 4.7. Strategies to support parent encouragement

Strategies	Examples
Observe and comment on encouragement.	"When you smiled and told her to keep trying, it helped her figure it out herself."
Ask about what the child can do.	"Can he put on his shirt?"
Ask about the child's interests.	"What does she like to do at the park?"
Offer information about development.	"One sign of being ready for toilet training is staying dry for several hours at a time. Is he starting to do that?"
Offer suggestions for preventive discipline.	"Maybe you could play a game of finding red things or round things at the store."

tines support language and also the early beginnings of literacy. (See Table 4.8 for strategies to support parent–child conversations.)

Establish a Collaborative Partnership with Parents

In facilitative parenting-focused home visits, the parent and practitioner take on different roles than in child-focused or parent-focused visits. In a parent-focused visit, the practitioner is often in a problem-solving or counseling role, talking mostly about family problems and a parent's personal needs. In some child-focused visits, the practitioner is in a teacher role, talking more about child development, while the parent is in a learner role. In other child-focused visits, the practitioner is in an expert role demonstrating or modeling the right way to do activities with the child while the parent is in an observer role, if present at all. In a parenting-focused home visit, in contrast, the parent is in a teaching role doing developmental parenting with the child: showing warmth toward the child, responding to the child, encouraging the child, and having conversations with the child. So what is the practitioner's role?

In a facilitative home visit, a practitioner can be effective as an interested observer, commenting on positive aspects of parent–child interactions. The practitioner's role can expand from there to act as a supportive consultant. A supportive consultant offers needed background information, makes specific suggestions, provides detailed observational feedback, and uses motivating encouragement. The roles of parent and

Table 4.8. Strategies to support parent–child conversations

Strategies	Examples
Observe and comment on conversation.	"He really had a lot to say when you started asking him questions about his toy cars." "That expansion of what she said will help her learn more words."
Prompt the parent to ask the child questions.	"Does he know what that is?" "Ask if she remembers what happened at the park."
Ask about the child's verbalizations.	"What is he saying?"
Help plan activities that involve conversation.	"When does she talk the most? Let's do that on our next visit."
Suggest using community resources.	"On our next visit we could go to the thrift store that has lots of children's books."
Offer information about development.	"Asking him about his own experiences helps him relate the book to his own life. That will help him think about what he is reading when he gets to school."
Offer materials to read or use.	"I could bring some materials to make your own book for her."

practitioner form a collaborative partnership in which the goal of promoting early development in the child is explicit, the expertise is shared from both sides, and plans are made together.

By using the mutual-competence approach, based on recognition and support of family strengths and values, a practitioner establishes a balanced partnership with parents and makes the social-emotional health of the parent–child relationship the first priority for home visits. To keep the parent in the parenting role, it is not only necessary for a practitioner to stay out of that role, but it is also necessary to provide support and encouragement for the parent to stay and grow in that role. Practitioners who facilitate developmental parenting aim to ultimately "work themselves out of a job" by helping parents learn to provide a rich environment for early development on their own. Unfortunately, some programs lack an explicit plan for when and how parents will take over the job. By establishing collaboration from the beginning, practitioners keep parents in their job as the main promoters of early development with home visits as a resource for information, problem solving, support, and encouragement.

A specific strategy for establishing a collaborative partnership is to begin planning together for the activities of the second home visit during the first home visit. A practitioner may be able to select or design an activity perfectly matched to the developmental level and needs of an infant or toddler. But even a perfectly selected activity will have little long-term impact if it does not engage both parent and child. Developmental activities planned for a home visit are intended to engage parent and child together in experiences that support the child's development. When the parent is involved in planning activities, it becomes easier to identify activities that the parent will enjoy because the practitioner can just ask.

Sometimes a parent is too depressed or withdrawn or even hostile to say more than "I don't know" or "I don't care." Although parents vary widely on how prepared they are to plan activities to do with their child, practitioners can adapt their role gradually to shift more of the activity planning to the parents gradually over time. On the first visit, a parent may be prepared to simply choose from two or three simple, everyday activities to do on the next home visit. Several visits later, the parent may easily think of activities to do, materials that will be needed, and related topics to discuss. Another parent may be more enthusiastic about planning together from the beginning, and yet another may have specific plans for something, such as teaching her 2–year-old to read, a not-quite-yet developmentally appropriate activity. Practitioners who establish partnerships to facilitate developmental parenting begin "where the parent is," offering simple choices to some, matching the enthusiasm of others, and guiding developmental parenting for each of them.

A practitioner can begin to plan with a parent by asking about activities the parent and child do every day as part of their daily routines, such as eating, bathing, doing chores, playing, or reading books. Routine activities also usually include errands and events outside the home, such as shopping or going to the park. The practitioner and parent can then select one of the family's routine activities to do for the next home visit. By asking about what the child does and likes during those routines, the practitioner can use the information with the parent to generate ideas for using the routine to develop the child's skills and knowledge. During the activities, the practitioner can provide further positive feedback about the child's behavior and the parent's warmth, responsiveness, encouragement, and conversation. As practitioners ask questions and provide feedback during the home visit activities, parents will become increasingly aware of learning opportunities during the activities they do with their child and how to take advantage of those opportunities. The practitioner and parent can then consider similar activities to plan for future home visits. By enhancing and enriching the kinds of interactions parents already have with their children, practitioners encourage more frequent positive interactions that parents and children are truly likely to do after the home visits. The interactions parents and children enjoy and the interactions that occur as part of regular routines are the ones most likely to offer ongoing opportunities to support children's development. (See Table 4.9 for strategies for establishing collaborative partnerships.)

Involve Other Family Members in Home Visit Activities   In
families with multiple children or more than one adult, home visits are typically enriched by including everyone who is home. Home visits that include only one parent and one child may set up artificial expectations that development can be fostered only if the parent and child can find some time alone for one-to-one interaction. Although one-to-one time is valuable for parent–child relationships, it is sometimes available only for short periods of time. Children in large families with siblings and extended family members usually develop positive relationships with their parents even without much one-to-one interaction time. Parents may want help learning to find a little more of that valuable one-to-one-time, but they are likely to need as much or more help finding ways to involve other family members in activities that are good for the development of all the children in the family. What's more, the involvement of more family members is likely to be fun and to continue contributing to children's development over long periods

Table 4.9.   Strategies to establish a collaborative partnership

Strategies	Examples
Say what the program goal is.	"Most of the visit time will involve both you and your child interacting together. I'll be here to help, offer suggestions, give feedback, and answer your questions."
Ask what the parent knows.	"What is your child just starting to learn to do?" "What do you think she'll start to do soon?"
Ask about possible activities for visits.	"What things do you especially enjoy together?" "When during the day do you interact most with him?"
Ask about family routines.	"What things do you do together every day?" "What happens with her when your family is all together?"
Help the parent choose activities.	"Do you and your child enjoy being more active or more snuggly?"
Offer background information.	"Not all babies crawl first. Some pull themselves up and start walking without ever crawling."
Make specific suggestions.	"Maybe you could try putting the couch cushions on the floor for him to climb over."
Provide detailed feedback.	"When you were singing that song, she was staring at your mouth and moving her mouth."
Use motivating encouragement.	"Wow! He just loves it when you imitate his sounds! He will want to play this game more with you!"
Plan together what will occur between visits.	"What activities will you focus on with your child this week?" "What is your goal for conversations with your child this week?"
Check on the plan when you come for the next visit and use as a learning opportunity.	"Were you able to meet the goal you set for yourself at our last visit?" "Which things worked best and which were hard to do?"

of time. This does not mean that a home visit with only a mother and a child is not beneficial. Sometimes, a parent needs to get comfortable interacting with the child in new ways before becoming comfortable having those interactions in the presence of other family members. Nevertheless, if there are other people in the child's family, practitioners can facilitate activities that engage those family members with the child in ways that support child development.

Infants, toddlers, and young children learn a lot from their mothers and also from other people who are important to them. Children learn from their fathers and siblings, if they have them, and from other people who are part of their family household. For parents to provide a rich environment for supporting the development of their children, they need to be able to do it wherever they are with whoever is there. In other words, if the family home includes several children along with two or more adults, all of them are part of the environment in which the parent is promoting the youngest child's development. The people who interact most with the child are part of the child's developmental environment. When those people are involved in positive interactions with the youngest children in the family, parents can more easily provide a supportive environment for their children's development. When everyone in the home is invited to participate in the home visit activities, the message is that everyone in the home can help support the early development of the youngest children in the family. Their involvement may include simply having fun with the children in the home visit activities, but it can also include learning more about how to help the children develop and stay safe and healthy.

There are many benefits to sibling interactions that should be encouraged. Douglas Downey and Dennis Condron at Ohio State University examined the benefits of having siblings in a large study of 20,000 kindergarten children. They found, as they reported in 2004, that children with at least one sibling, compared with children without siblings, were better able to

1.   Make friends and maintain the friendships

2.   Get along with children who were different from themselves

3.   Help others

4.   Express their feelings in positive ways

5.   Respond sensitively to others' feelings

These benefits are important social skills that come from repeated interactions requiring resolving conflict, sharing, talking, working, and playing together. Supporting parents in interacting with all of the interested children may make home visits more meaningful because these interactions are closer to the day-to-day interactions families will continue to have between home visits and after the home visiting program has ended.

When home visits are set up by their timing and planning to involve fathers, the message is that fathers contribute to children's very early development. Mothers are the typical "target parent" of many home-visiting programs, but involving fathers can be valuable for children's development because fathers often interact with their children differently from how mothers do and sometimes in more exciting ways. Home visiting activities that engage fathers, when they are available, are important for enhancing children's early development. Father involvement not only benefits children's development but also provides support to mothers in their mothering roles. (See Table 4.10 for research evidence on why it is important to involve fathers.)

Some mothers may feel uneasy about involving fathers if there is marital conflict or if the mother has personal concerns to discuss. Practitioners should ask the primary caregiver, usually but not always the mother, about other family members and be sensitive to individual family situations, but if acceptable, they can offer an invitation of involvement to all family members beginning with the first home visit. (See Table 4.11 for strategies for involving other family members.)

Table 4.10. Why is it important to involve fathers?

Benefits of father involvement	Research findings	References
Father involvement and engagement	Fathers' involvement with their children enhances the children's early development in cognitive and social domains.	Grossman et al., 2002; Nugent, 1991; Pettit, Brown, Mize, & Lindsey, 1998; Roberts, 1998; Wachs, Uzgiris, & Hunt, 1971; Yogman, Kindlon, & Earls, 1995
Father–child play	Play, in general, is associated with better peer relations and emotional regulation.	Pettit, Brown, Mize, & Lindsey, 1998; Roberts, 1998
Father–child toy play	More complex father–child toy play with 2-year-olds is associated with increased cognitive development, language development, and emotion regulation.	Roggman, Boyce, Cook, Christiansen, & Jones, 2004
Father support of child play	Support of toddler exploratory play promotes attachment security through childhood.	Grossman et al., 2002
Father caregiving	Involvement in caregiving may buffer the effects of an unresponsive or depressed mother or enhance the effects of a responsive mother.	Feldman, Greenbaum, Mayes, & Erlich, 1997; Field, 1998
Father involvement over time	Involvement over time has beneficial effects during the transition to adulthood on educational and economic attainment, delinquency, and psychological well-being.	Harris, Furstenberg, & Marmer, 1998

Table 4.11.   Strategies to involve other family members

Strategies	Examples
Involve whichever family members are there to participate.	"Hi, Dad! Come and join us." "Is your sister here often? Would she like to be involved with us?"
Identify the child's "family."	"Who else plays with him or helps take care of him?"
Schedule home visits to include other family members.	"We could set up a time to meet when your other children can join us."
Bring enough materials for everyone.	"I have enough chalk for everyone to draw on the sidewalk."
Provide information about other family relationships.	"Babies learn a lot from their older brothers and sisters."
Ask questions about how the infant responds.	"Does she play any differently with Dad than with Mom?"
Make suggestions to other family members.	"You can help by singing to your baby brother."

Use Family Activities as Learning Opportunities for Both Parents and Children   Facilitative home visiting includes the family in activities that the family already does: routines, chores, celebrations, hobbies, and leisure activities. Facilitative home visiting also uses what the family already has: household materials, books and other things in print, recyclable stuff, and family hobby materials. These are the resources the family is likely to continue to have after the home visit is over and after the program has ended.

Home visits with multiple family members need to include activities that are fun for all ages because those are the activities most likely to be repeated after the home visit is over. Practitioners typically have training and experience to select developmentally appropriate activities for an infant or young child, but may struggle to think of activities a whole family can enjoy. An activity one family finds fun and engaging may seem boring to another family. A practitioner can learn quickly what kinds of activities will be engaging for a particular family by asking them what they already enjoy doing together. By beginning with what a family enjoys together, the practitioner can be fairly sure it will be a successful home visit activity. The parents, in turn, can be fairly sure they are capable of providing appropriate developmental activities for their children because the activities they already enjoy together can be used to support their children's development. It can be hard, however, to engage infants and toddlers in some family activities because very young children rarely stay engaged in the same thing for very long. Engagement need not be long for a child to get a lot out of an ac-

A Good Tip!

Some strategies in this chapter may come easily to practitioners
making home visits. Others may take some practice and attention. One way to for practitioners to learn these strategies is to
videotape a parent interacting with his or her child. Practitioners
and supervisors can then meet and watch the videotape together
to observe, comment, and ask about the interactions. The practitioner who works with that family will be prepared to watch the
videotape with the parent on the next visit and use the strategies
in this chapter to focus on parent strengths. This videotaping
technique can also help the parent become a better observer
of his or her children.

tivity, but when planning together, practitioners can help parents think
about how long their children will want to be involved in an activity
and how they can keep their children happy and comfortable.

Everyday chores are family activities that don't always seem fun,
but they can be especially valuable sources of learning opportunities for
children. While eating, bathing, getting dressed and undressed, or just
watching other family members doing chores, young children are learning a lot about who they are, about their family, the words for things
they want or do not want, and how their physical world works. Although some parents may think that involving a very young child in
household chores will take too much time, it often takes less time than
trying to do the chore while being interrupted by a toddler's need for attention or stimulation. To help parents increase the enjoyment of everyday chores, facilitative practitioners can make specific suggestions for
keeping a child engaged; finding ways even a young toddler can help
with a task; or making unexpected, playful changes in the routine such
as doing things out of their usual sequence.

Anything families do together can be included in home visits.
Making food, going for a walk, and drawing pictures are all open-ended
activities that invite a variety of kinds and levels of involvement. Open-
ended activities with multiple ways of being involved are often the
most easily adapted to a variety of ages and a variety of families. For example, a young child may make simple marks with chalk on an outdoor
sidewalk, whereas older children and adults may make more complex
drawings or designs, everyone working together or separately at vari-

Table 4.12. Strategies to use family activities as learning opportunities

Strategies	Examples
Ask about family activities and routines.	"What do you all enjoy doing with the baby?" "Tell me what happens in your child's day?" "What things does your family do every day?"
Plan family activities for home visits.	"Could we do laundry on our next visit?" "We could do a 'field trip' to the grocery store."
Ask how family activity time can be increased.	"When else could you do this activity?"
Suggest ways to make family routines fun.	"Maybe you could sing songs during bath time."
Suggest ways to involve a child in helping during family routines.	"How could he help with his bath—could he put his bath toys in a basket or hang up a towel?"
Suggest funny changes in routines.	"Would he laugh if you put his socks on his hands?"

ous developmental levels. For a young child these activities offer experience with sensory materials, motor skill practice (sometimes more small motor skills, sometimes more large motor skills), language labels for objects and properties (color, size, texture), and practice using words to make choices and plans. Even more important, each of these activities offers opportunities for warm and responsive parent–child interaction and parent encouragement of playful exploration and communication.

The activities families already do offer a great starting point, but for some families, activities that involve infants or very young children do not happen often. By encouraging parents to do activities that involve their children more often, practitioners can help increase the frequency of opportunities for parents to promote early development. For example, by helping a parent find ways to involve a young child in meal preparation more frequently, a practitioner helps the parent provide more opportunities to enrich the child's language environment by talking about a topic (food) that is familiar and important to the child. (See Table 4.12 for strategies for using family activities as learning opportunities.)

CONCLUSION

Facilitative behaviors are strategies for delivering effective developmental services from practitioners through parents to children. By focusing on parent–child interaction as a context for development, facilitative home visiting behaviors help parents establish a pattern with their children that can continue to support early development for several years. Because many parents need information and ideas to provide a rich environment for their children's early development, the content of facilitative home visits provides additional resources. By using facilitative behaviors from this chapter, facilitative content described in Chapter 5 can be delivered through parents to children.

5

C Is for Content

What is the content of a developmental parenting program? What kinds of information does a practitioner provide? What do the parent and practitioner talk about? What are the activities of the home visit? Is there a lesson plan? Many answers to these questions have been provided in earlier chapters. The content is about developmental parenting. The information is about the foundations of early child development and the parenting behaviors that support early development. The activities are things families can do together that support the development of the youngest children in the family. The lesson plan is whatever the parent and practitioner planned together.

FACILITATIVE CONTENT

Facilitative practitioners use appropriate content materials that are useful for parents, with sensitivity to their concerns, values, and culture. Content is facilitative when it is immediately relevant to a child's behavior or a family's concerns or when a parent specifically requests it. Content is facilitative when it is a good fit with the goals of the parent and family. To support developmental parenting, the "curriculum" needs to be as much about parenting as about children's development.

Parents need and want to learn about their children's development as part of parenting. They want information that will continue to be useful and appropriate as their children grow and develop. Facilitative practitioners help parents select topics to discuss in home visits that are interesting and relevant to the parents. Most parents are interested mostly in information relevant to the age and development of their own children right now, but also want to know what to expect as their

children get older. In addition, parents often want information to help
them solve everyday or more serious problems with their children. The
content of facilitative home visits is thus guided by topics relevant to
parenting, planned collaboratively with parents to provide what the
children need, based on family friendly tools, and supplemented with
community resources.

Characteristics of Facilitative Content

Practitioners provide *facilitative content* when they

- Provide information parents want and need now
- Emphasize broad developmental foundations
- Plan a "curriculum" on developmental parenting
- Help parents plan child development activities
- Get information about community resources

Provide Information Parents Need and Want for Parenting

Sometimes, all that a parent really needs in order to promote a child's
early development is some basic information about development and
what promotes it. Practitioners in home visiting programs often provide a great deal of written and verbal information to parents about
child development, but the amount of information can be overwhelming for some parents. Information is unlikely to be used if it comes in a
stack of printed handouts to a parent with limited literacy skills or in a
verbal stream that sounds like a lecture to the parent. The parent is unlikely to read or absorb the information if there is too much of it. In
some home visits, the number of handouts to go over and the number
of forms to fill out take up so much of the visit that there is little time
left over for activities that encourage positive parent–child interaction.
The home visit then becomes little more than an expensive information delivery system that could be implemented by mailing handouts
and forms directly to the parent.

Materials should be selected very carefully to provide only as much
information as parents really need and want. A way to do this is to ask
parents ahead of time what information they want and then individualize the information to their interests, their children, and their families.
Some parents may have no idea what information they want or need
in order to support their children's early development and may benefit
from practioners' suggestions about what they should get first. Others
may have specific questions that require practitioners to do some research and find the information that the parents are requesting.

By having a list of possible handouts and other informational materials the program has available, chunks of information can be offered in menu format from which parents can select the information they want and need. Programs often develop printed materials for parents written by support staff or copied from other materials directed at parents of young children. Practitioners can use information from these materials to cut and paste into handouts for parents who read well or into guides for discussing the topics directly with parents during a home visit.

Whatever strategies a program uses for developing informational materials, appropriate materials have several characteristics. Good informational materials are

1. *Short*: Parents of young children are often very busy and have little time to read a long message that could be written in many fewer words. Home visit time is valuable, and although practitioner–parent discussions are an essential component of facilitative home visits, parent–child interaction is an even more essential component that should not be sacrificed to allow more time for adult discussion.

2. *Clear*: The materials should clearly state what parents should do with the information. Specific, real-life examples should be provided to make it easier to understand general ideas.

3. *Relevant*: The information should be linked directly to a parent's needs and the child's needs at a particular time. Any informational materials that are broadly distributed to parents in a home visiting program should be broadly applicable to all families, regardless of family composition, culture, or individual situations. Otherwise, the materials should be individualized to each family's needs and interests.

4. *In the parents' language*: For non–English-speaking parents, a translation in their language is essential. When a translation into the parents' speaking language is impossible, use simple words, few words, and simple grammar in English. Even for very good readers, information is understood more easily when the writing is simple.

5. *Individualized*: There will always be variations in the information needed by families. Programs providing facilitative home visiting need a file of informational materials on specific topics that are unlikely to be needed by all parents but likely to be needed by some parents, such as bottle feeding, impacts of divorce, or care of an uncircumcised penis.

Emphasize Broad Developmental Foundations   Curriculum materials for infants and toddlers often target specific developmental milestones in the early months and years of development. It may be interesting for a mother to know that if her 8-month-old is now using his fingers to "rake" small objects into his hand, he'll soon start using a pincer grasp to pick up those small objects with his thumb and forefinger. It is more useful and important, however, to know that his sudden "fits" when dropped off at the new baby sitter are actually a good sign of developing secure attachment, not a sign of a spoiled baby just trying to get his way.

Using the previous example, a facilitative practitioner may tell parents what a pincer grasp is, but will spend more time helping parents observe and support the broader foundations of early development: security, exploration, and communication. These three foundations are emphasized because their early development is a basis for continuing development in all domains. By learning about how their children are developing security, curiosity, and communication skills now, parents learn how to continue to support their children's development with warmth, responsiveness, encouragement, and conversation. These parenting behaviors and the development they support can be part of many different kinds of activities.

In facilitative home visits, the same activity can be used to help parents learn a wide variety of ways to support different skills at different ages in different developmental domains. For example, an infant development curriculum could suggest a particular activity of rolling a ball back and forth. One parent may play this game to help a 6-month-old child learn to reach for a moving object, but it could also be used to help a 2-year-old learn to take turns. The ultimate goal of the activity is less to promote a particular skill in a child and more to promote broad developmental goals and provide opportunities for parents to be warm, responsive, encouraging, and communicative with their children.

The simple game of rolling a ball back and forth can support the development of secure attachment, playful exploration, or good communication skills. The ball game will support secure attachment if a parent shows enjoyment of the game and is responsive to the child's cues of interest or frustration during the game. It will support playful exploration if the parent is open to changing the ball game in new ways that the child "invents." It will support good communication skills if the parent talks about what they are doing and elicits responses from the child during the ball game, "Your turn! Catch it! What do you want?" As key developmental foundations of security, exploration, and communication are developing, the child will readily acquire more specific developmental skills, such as reaching for objects or taking turns. In other words, a secure, playful, communicative child will generally achieve developmental milestones without necessarily needing targeted teaching activities for each milestone. (See Table 5.1 for research evidence for these broad foundations of development.)

Table 5.1.   What are the broad foundations of development?

Developmental foundations	Outcomes	References
Secure attachment	Secure mother–child attachment leads to positive child development, especially in social-emotional domains.	Kochanska, 1995, 2001; Laible & Thompson, 2000; Roggman et al., 1987; Slade, 1987; Sroufe, 1983
	Social-emotional competence is critical for children's school success and is often a goal of school readiness programs.	Arnold et al., 1999; Hinshaw, 1992; Kupersmidt & Coie, 1990; Ladd et al., 1997, 1999; McClelland et al., 2000; Raver, & Zigler, 1997; Wentzel & Asher, 1995
Playful exploration	Infant–toddler play shows increasing levels of cognitive complexity and skill that increase when parents encourage and engage in play.	Belsky & Most, 1981; Bornstein et al., 1996; Hrncir et al., 1985; Landry et al., 1996; Smith et al., 1996; Spencer & Meadow-Orlans, 1996
	In parent–toddler play, toddlers share focus and experience, important for language and cognitive development, and initiate interaction and take turns, important for communication and appropriate social interaction.	Bakeman & Adamson, 1984; Charman et al., 2001; Diener et al., 2003; Goldfield, 1987; Laasko et al., 1999; Mundy et al., 1992; Newland et al., 2001; Roggman et al., 2004; Saxon et al., 2000
Good communication skills	Infants perceive all human speech sounds, but the more different words they hear, the more language they learn.	Bornstein et al., 1998; David et al., 2003; Hart & Risley, 1995; Kuhl, 2000, 2004; Snow, 1983
	Telling stories, reading stories, and having conversations support expressive language, listening comprehension, and the beginnings of literacy.	Hart & Risley, 1995; Leseman & de Jong, 1998; Lyon, 1998; RAND, 2002; Sénéchal, 1997; Snow, 1983
	A child's ability to express and understand language supports later reading and writing.	Catts et al., 1999; Dickinson et al., 2003; Dickinson & Tabors, 2001; Neuman & Dickinson, 2001; Poe et al., 2004; Snow, Burns, & Griffin, 1998; Snow, 2001

Secure attachment is the developmental foundation for strong social-emotional development. Security contributes to a child's development both during infancy and in the years beyond. Because some parenting programs are intended to promote later school readiness, they sometimes strongly emphasize cognitive development, but social-emotional development is just as important for a child's school success. An administrator of a home visiting program said, "We are being pushed into more and more literacy and math . . . but the social-emotional stuff is still key." Indeed, because children's social-emotional competence is critical for their school success, fostering social-emotional development has been a goal of programs that emphasize school readiness, such as Head Start. As parents learn about developing secure attachment and the importance of their own warmth and responsiveness for supporting their children's security, they will be learning to promote their children's social emotional development.

Playful exploration is a developmental foundation for cognitive development. Playful exploration supports learning at any age, but it is especially important for infants and toddlers. Because children play in ways that are consistent with their developmental level, playful exploration provides experiences that are a good fit for their development. In fact, children's early play behavior is so closely related to their early cognitive development that it is like a window into their minds that lets us see their emerging thinking abilities.

As toddlers begin to pretend and create complex sequences, play with toys such as dolls and toy cars reveals their increasing levels of cognitive skills with symbols and ideas. When parents join in on the play, children often play at a more complex cognitive level than when they are playing alone. When parents are responsive and let their children take the lead in play, they encourage their children's exploration and initiative. When parents support their children's play by encouraging it and engaging in it, they are supporting several aspects of their children's development. During play, a parent and child share an experience and take turns, both of which are essential experiences for social development and language development. Play offers a rich context for communication, another key foundation of development. As parents learn about the importance of play for development and about ways to encourage it, they will be supporting their children's cognitive development.

Good communication skills are the developmental foundation for language development. Communication skills allow infants and toddlers to survive and to thrive. Language development is absolutely essential to later academic and life success, but it has simple beginnings in the earliest communication between parents and their infants. As infants start learning to communicate with their parents, they are acquiring the beginnings of the skills they will need to succeed in school. Young infants learn to hear the sounds of their own language from hearing people around them speaking, and they learn words from the words they are exposed to by their parents and other caregivers. As parents learn about their children's developing communication skills and begin exposing them to more words and more different kinds of words, they are supporting their children's language development.

Storytelling and playing together support communication, language and, in addition, the beginnings of literacy. When parents read stories and talk about them with their infants and toddlers, they are supporting their children's listening comprehension and language skills. Conversations between parents and their toddlers, whatever they are about, help children learn to express themselves with words. By helping children learn to understand and express language, parents are promoting skills that will help their children learn to read and write later.

These three broad foundations—attachment, exploration, and communication—are, therefore, the emphasis of programs that facilitate developmental parenting. As parents expand the frequency of interactions that promote these foundations, they increase their support of the early development of their children in all domains. With a good developmental start in these broad foundations, the small steps of specific developmental skills will be easier for children to learn because they will have the security needed to explore and question, the motivation needed to learn about the world, and the language abilities to learn from others.

> "Language will never be acquired without engagement in a world of persons, objects, and events—the world that language is about and in which language is used."
> —Lois Bloom (1998, p. 1276)

Plan a "Curriculum" on Developmental Parenting   The basic program of content, or "developmental parenting curriculum," includes experiences and information that help parents learn more about supporting child development. Parents do not need to become experts in child development; they just need to become experts in the development of their own children. The aims of a developmental parenting curriculum are to increase parents' basic knowledge of their children's development, to expand their use of available resources to support their children's development, and to help them prevent problems for their children later. A curriculum on developmental parenting emphasizes the broad foundations of early development: secure attachment, playful exploration, and good communication.

A "curriculum" on developmental parenting is not really a curriculum at all. Basic child development information may be included in the content, but more time should be spent on helping parents identify their own resources for developmental parenting and think through ideas to solve or prevent problems. The basic content needed for a parenting curriculum, therefore, includes child development information, guidance on using the family's own resources for supporting child development, and ideas for solving and preventing problems.

Child development information is about what develops, when it develops, and how it develops. The most useful child development information for parents is about what their particular children are developing now, especially about what their children's development now means for their children's later school success and social well-being. By learning some basics about each foundational area of development—secure attachment, playful exploration, and good communication skills—parents learn what to look for. They also learn about ways to support their children's development during interactions with their children. The three foundational areas of development are linked to the fundamental parenting skills—warmth, responsiveness, encouragement, and conversation.

Warmth and responsiveness promote secure attachment; encouragement promotes playful exploration; and conversation promotes communication. It is not this simple, of course, because each of these types of parenting interaction contributes to other foundational areas of child development, too. Responsiveness, for example, also fosters exploration and communication. These developmental parenting behaviors are the strongest predictors of the developmental areas we view as foundational in children's early development.

Available resources in every home are valuable for developmental parenting. The developmental parenting curriculum itself doesn't provide the resources parents need to support their children's development. But the curriculum can help parents discover the resources they have. Topics and activities in a developmental parenting program help parents identify the resources they have for fostering their children's development. Perhaps the most valuable resource is in the everyday routines of the family. Regular everyday family routines are a major source of developmental opportunities for young children. By helping parents discover ways to use routines such as cooking, cleaning, and shopping to foster development, facilitative practitioners help parents take advantage of frequent, easy, and available opportunities to promote the early development of their young children.

Other sources of developmental opportunities are offered by seasonal changes where the family lives and by special events or holidays celebrated by the family. Playing outside in water in the summer or in the snow in the winter, for example, offer rich opportunities for building the parent–child relationships and for encouraging children's exploration and communication. Planning for family get-togethers at holidays offers opportunities for parents to respond to children's needs and build security. Neighborhood and community events offer multiple opportunities for learning activities for young children. A public playground or a children's museum, for example, offer opportunities for various kinds of exploration and communication.

Problem prevention and problem solutions are important to parents. Ideas for preventing and solving problems are therefore an important part of a developmental parenting curriculum. When parents learn about ways to help children sleep, eat, use the toilet, and get along with others, they prevent many behavior problems. Learning about infant–toddler health and safety helps parents prevent illness, injury, and other health problems. Parents also need to know about ways to keep supporting their children's development, even during times of crisis.

The information and activities of a developmental parenting curriculum will help parents prevent many problems. Some problems, however, seem to defy prevention, such as when a child who has been cheerfully eating healthy finger foods suddenly starts refusing to eat anything but bananas. What should the parent do? The solution is not always easy, but a facilitative practitioner can help the parent solve a problem by guiding him or her through a typical problem-solving sequence with questions:

- "What exactly is the problem? Tell me more about the problem."

- "What do you want to change? How do want your child to behave differently?"

- "What has worked in the past with similar problems?"

- "What are other possibilities for solving the problem? What else?"

- "How might each of the possible solutions work?"

- "What do you want to try first? How will you know if it's working?"

Help Parents Plan Activities for Promoting Child Development

If parents are to serve in the role of the primary teachers of very young children, parents may need assistance in planning the "child curriculum" for their infants and toddlers. A formal curriculum is unlikely to be appropriate for most families, but the various activities parents plan to do with their infants and toddlers provide an informal curriculum for early development.

Some parents may be ready to play responsively with their children without planning any particular activities; some may already know a lot about development and be prepared to plan specific activities to foster their children's development. Most parents, however, will need and want ideas for good developmental learning activities. Fortunately, everyday family activities can be used as developmental learning activities. Practitioners typically have a lot of ideas for good learning activities, but a facilitative practitioner provides only as much information as the parent is ready to use.

One way to provide parents with information about development specific to their own children's particular stage of development is to help parents use an easy developmental assessment tool, such as *Ages & Stages Questionnaires® (ASQ): A Parent-Completed, Child-Monitoring System* (2nd ed.) developed by Diane Bricker and Jane Squires at the University of Oregon (Paul H. Brookes Publishing Co., 1999). Regular developmental assessments every couple of months can help parents keep realistic expectations. Some parents expect too much of their children, thinking they should be learning to read or to ride a bike when they are only 2 years old. Other parents may not notice that their children are lagging behind developmentally, not saying any words when most children are starting to combine words. By doing a simple developmental assessment, parents can see where their children are in an expected developmental sequence.

When parents do developmental assessments, it takes the mystery out of "testing." It keeps the process more open and the information accessible. When parents do the assessments, they see what skills their children have and can use that information to look for skills that are likely to be emerging in the near future. This process keeps information about their children's development from being secret or mysterious. By assessing their own children's development regularly, parents learn that development progresses in small steps. They become better observers of their children and more aware of multiple domains of development. They can then make better use of ongoing family activities to encourage their children to practice emerging skills or to explore new things. They can use words to describe their children's behavior and abilities that encourage the children's motivation to master new skills. In these ways, parents can provide a developmental curriculum perfectly individualized to each of their own children.

In reaction to the changing developmental needs of their own children, parents can emphasize different kinds of interactions, experiences, and activities at different ages. Certain kinds of parent–child interactive behaviors at certain times contribute best to a child's development. Many lists are available on important interactions by child age. Using parent-administered developmental assessments every few months provides a great way to make this information meaningful for the parent. Table 5.2 includes some information to answer the question, "What should parents do, when?"

Identify Available Community Resources for Other Needed Services   Some families need resources in the community that a developmental parenting program does not offer. Programs sometimes have case managers or social service workers as part of the services they provide. These experts in community resources can help parents find the help their family needs if it is available. Some programs do not provide these services, but parents may still need help. If a mother is anxious about having a place to live or food for the family, then she is unlikely to be able to generate much concern about her toddler's playful exploration or secure attachment. Practitioners can help parents shift their focus from basic survival to their children's early development by

Table 5.2.   What should parents do, when?

Age ranges	Important interactions	References
0–6 months	Coordination of social attention in face-to-face play, mutual gaze, mother's initiations of interaction and play	Baldwin, 1991; Stern, 1977
6–12 months	Recognizable games and predictable routines, infant's active involvement, mother's predictability in interactions	Rome-Flanders, Cossette, Ricard, & De'carie, 1995
1–2 years	Child's initiation of interactions, mother's response to initiations, joint attention to objects, exchange of objects, interactive pretending	Dunham & Dunham, 1992; Gustafson et al., 1979; Ross & Kay, 1980; Tamis-LeMonda & Bornstein, 1990, 1994; Tomasello, 1990
2–3 years	Interactive roles, extended pretense, frequent complex verbal exchanges or conversations between parent and child, teaching interactions, responsiveness to child's conversations and stories	Hart & Risley, 1995; Kelly, Morisset, Barnard, Hammond, & Booth, 1996; NICHD, 1999; Ross & Kay, 1980; Saxon, Frick, & Columbo, 1996
All 3 years	Mutual positive affect, because it is a valuable indicator of the quality of the mother–infant relationship linked to positive outcomes for children	Grusec & Goodnow, 1994; Lay, Waters, & Park, 1989; Londerville & Main, 1981

having information readily available about resources that can help families provide food, shelter, and health care for their children.

Community collaborations are an important part of any developmental parenting program. Parents may have basic survival or mental health needs that are beyond the capacity of the program to provide. Nevertheless, these needs must be met in order for a parent to comfortably focus on parenting his or her young child. By establishing partnerships with other community resources, a developmental parenting program can make prompt and appropriate referrals to help families get basic needs met so that they can more easily provide a supportive developmental environment for the children in the family.

A facilitative practitioner knows the community well. Where do you go to get food stamps? Where do you apply for health insurance for uninsured children? How are all of the employment offices in the community different? Are there English classes available nearby? What kinds of classes does the community education program offer? Who is the best person to contact for services for immigrant families? What is fun for toddlers to do at the county fair? Are there swimming classes for toddlers in the community? Who can a parent call for emergency child care? Does the health department still loan out infant car seats? These are all questions that parents may be asking the home visitor. Although it is always appropriate to say, "I don't know, but I'll find out," it is helpful to be familiar with local community resources and opportunities that are available for families with infants and toddlers. A facilitative home visiting program may need to provide training for practitioners about community resources for families and for children. "Field trips" to community agencies or meetings that invite community partners to meet together with program staff members can help put faces with names and places. This level of partnership in the community helps support family needs so that parents can focus on their children's needs.

One of the most important community resources that parents may need is child care. For many families, child care is often needed so that parents can be employed or so that parents can get the education and training they need in order to be employed. The quality of that child care, however, will make a big difference in a child's early development. Practitioners need to provide information to parents that can help them select high-quality child care, establish good communication with other caregivers, and help their children with the transitions and separations involved in having multiple caregivers. The quality indicators of early child care include small group sizes, a small number of children per caregiver, good training for caregivers, and low turnover of caregivers.

The National Association of Child Care Research and Referral Agencies provides free brochures listing observable child care quality indicators. A summary of these indicators is listed in Figure 5.1. Practi-

Questions to Ask about Child Care

_____ Are children watched at all times, including when they are sleeping?

_____ Are caregivers warm and welcoming?

_____ Do caregivers pay individual attention to each child?

_____ Do caregivers avoid yelling, spanking, and other negative punishments?

_____ Are caregiver/teacher-to-child ratios appropriate (1 adult per 3–4 infants, 4–6 toddlers, 6–9 preschoolers)?

_____ Do the caregivers have credentials or specific training on child development?

_____ Do caregivers have current CPR and first aid training?

_____ Are there age-appropriate toys in an organized play space?

_____ Are there daily or weekly activity plans available?

_____ Do the caregivers regularly engage children in conversation and read to them?

_____ Do caregivers and children wash hands after using the bathroom/changing diapers and before eating?

_____ Do all of the children enrolled have the required immunizations?

_____ Are all poisonous materials locked and out of children's reach?

_____ Are first aid kits readily available?

_____ Is there a plan for responding to disasters (e.g., fire, flood)?

_____ Have all caregivers passed a criminal history background check?

_____ Is the outdoor play area safe (age appropriate equipment in good condition with soft surface underneath)?

_____ Are group sizes appropriate (6–8 infants, 6–12 toddlers, 12–20 preschoolers)?

_____ Is the program well-managed and regularly evaluated?

_____ Does the program work with parents?

Figure 5.1. A summary of indicators of quality child care. (*From* National Association of Child Care Resource and Referral Agencies. [2006]. *Is this the right place for my child? 38 research-based indicators of high-quality child-care.* Copyright © 2006, National Association of Child Care Resource and Referral Agencies, http://www.naccrra.org/; adapted by permission.)

tioners can use these or similar resources to help parents consider the child care that will be best for their children and their family. When parents have confidence in their child care providers, they are better able to support their children's adjustment to a child care setting and better able to establish good communication with child care providers who care for their children. Parents may also need additional guidance about preparing their children for a transition to child care, such as beginning with short visits together. Parents also need to establish positive relationships and communication with other caregivers, such as determining the best times to get updates from the other caregiver, either when children are dropped off or picked up.

CONCLUSION

All of these aspects of facilitative content help support developmental parenting. By providing information that parents want and need and emphasizing broad foundations of development, a "parenting curriculum" promotes the development of parents as experts on their children's development. Practitioners aiming to support developmental parenting will provide ideas for appropriate developmental activities for children and they will become familiar with community resources for families. Facilitative content delivers the information and experiences that parents need, when they need it, to support the early development of their own children. Additional content comes from specific curriculum resources that programs may use, which is discussed in Chapter 7. The facilitative attitudes, behaviors, and content of a developmental parenting program are sometimes challenging. Chapter 6 offers a guide to putting the ABCs into practice.

6

Putting It into Practice

What does a facilitative approach look like in practice? How do the attitudes, behaviors, and content all come together in what a practitioner says and does with parents? Understanding the attitudes, behaviors, and content that facilitate developmental parenting is an important first step. Implementing a facilitative approach with a wide range of families and situations can be challenging, however, and requires extensive planning and often some good problem-solving skills. Planning is important to make sure each family gets the support they need to promote early development. Problem solving is important because even the best plans do not always work out, and the unexpected often happens.

Planning is especially important the first time a practitioner meets a family, such as during the first home visit in a home visiting program. When the practitioner and parent talk about the expectations of the program during the first home visit, it can go a long way toward establishing a good collaboration. Focusing on developmental parenting immediately in the first visit will set the stage for future visits. Getting fathers, siblings, and other family members involved, if possible, also requires good planning.

Problem solving is needed in certain situations more than others to support parents in their parenting roles. For example, when a family has a crisis of some sort or when situations are chaotic and full of distractions, practitioners are likely to need good problem-solving skills along with good planning. Working with parents of children with disabilities or with parents struggling with depression are other examples of situations where additional planning and problem-solving will be required to support parenting. In these situations, understanding and implementing a facilitative approach to support developmental parenting is especially important and could be key in making a difference in the parent–child relationship and later child outcomes.

Home visits often are structured differently depending on the timing of the visit and the situation in the home. Thus, a first home visit, a home visit in the middle of a crisis or chaotic circumstance, and an enjoyable visit with an engaged family may all proceed differently with different outcomes. A typical visit may never happen! Most visits have an element of surprise and challenge to them. Regardless of the chaos, crisis, enjoyment, or growth that is happening around each home visit, each one is an opportunity to support a parent in supporting his or her child. Children will continue to develop amidst all of the good and bad around them. Practitioners who help parents recognize this fact and continue to promote their children's security, curiosity, and communication in difficult circumstances can guide parents in providing important protection from negative influences in these situations.

FIRST VISIT

A lot happens during the first home visit. Luckily, much of what happens is expected and planned. The first home visit requires careful planning to get started right away to facilitate developmental parenting. First impressions about the program and how it works are important for setting into motion a regular process that focuses on parenting and emphasizes parent–child interaction. In addition to good planning, a practitioner may also need good problem-solving skills to navigate through this first visit if certain situations are occurring such as when unexpected visitors are present, a parent is depressed, the family is not interested in participating in the program, or a child has a severe disability. Typically, the goals of the first visit are to describe the services being provided with the accompanying expectations, plan for the next visit, and gather information about the child and family to aid in future planning.

The following is an example of a first visit.

Meeting with a Parent for the First Time

Melissa, a home visitor in a developmental parenting program, parks on the street and goes around back of the big old house divided into several apartments. She goes up the back stairs to a tiny but sunny apartment and knocks on the door with the apartment number for Jennie, the mother of Kaylee.

Melissa: Hi, are you Jennie?

Jennie: Yes?

Melissa: I'm Melissa Roberts, and I'm from the Developmental Parenting Program in Fairview County. May I come in?

Jennie: Oh, yes, I forgot. Okay, come on in. This is Kaylee.

Melissa: Hi Kaylee. How are you? I see you have a red block! How are you doing today, Jennie?

Jennie: Okay. You?

Melissa: I'm fine. Oh, the sun in here is lovely! It's cold outside but cozy in here. As I said on the phone when we made this appointment, this first meeting will be short. I'd like to meet with you for about a half an hour today, just to get started. We'll start our regular meetings next week.

Jennie: Okay. Do you need me to be here?

Melissa: Sure do. I mostly need to talk with you today, but I'll enjoy getting to know Kaylee, too. First, I'll explain about how the program works and get to know you and Kaylee a little better. Then, before I go, we can decide what we'll do next time and what time we'll have our regular meetings.

Jennie: Okay.

Melissa: The purpose of the Developmental Parenting Program is to help parents do more of the things that support their children's early development. So because most of what helps children develop is just interacting and talking with their parents, we'll plan most of the time for activities that you and Kaylee do together.

Jennie: Just me and her? You won't be teaching her?

Melissa: I might teach her something sometime, but that's really your job because you're her mom and her most important teacher. I'll be here to offer suggestions, give feedback, and answer questions you might have.

(continued)

(continued)

Jennie: I don't think I'll be good at teaching her much.

Melissa: You're already doing lots of things that are teaching Kaylee. Just in these few minutes I heard you say her name and saw you smile at her, and I see she's playing with a brightly colored toy you have here.

Jennie: My brother gave her that.

Melissa: And you've got it out here for her to play with. She seems to enjoy it. She's already put two of the little blocks through the holes. Oh, did you see her look at you as soon as she got that one in?

Jennie: Yeah, she's a proud one. It's good she plays with her toys so I can get something done.

Melissa: I can tell she likes it when you watch her do the things she's trying. Do you play together with her toys?

Jennie: Nah, she's just a baby; she can't share very good.

Melissa: Well, that's true. You're probably better at sharing than she is, but she might let you take a turn.

Jennie: Yeah, I tell her that when she plays with the bowls. When it's my turn, I put them back away.

Melissa: The what?

Jennie: The bowls. I have plastic bowls in the kitchen, you know, from cottage cheese and stuff? And she plays with them sometimes.

Melissa: Yeah, toddlers love kitchen stuff—bowls and pans.

Jennie: No, I don't let her play with my pans.

Melissa: What does she do with the bowls?

Jennie: She just plays. She puts them on the floor and then puts them together.

Melissa: Does she put the smaller ones inside the bigger ones?

Jennie: Yeah, she does that.

Melissa: That's cool. She compares the sizes and nests them.

Jennie: I guess.

Melissa: Does she ever stack them?

Jennie: I don't know, I haven't noticed.

Melissa: See if she'll try that. Those are great toys—unbreakable and replaceable. And those are the kinds of things you can do to help her development.

Jennie: Okay, so I'll share my bowls with you, Kaylee!

Melissa: That's great! So let me get back to describing the Developmental Parenting Program. The purpose of the program is to help you help your child's development. Every week you and I will plan something for Kaylee and you to do together the next week while I'm here. It can be something really simple, like rolling a ball back and forth, or helping Kaylee wash her hands. But we can start with something you already enjoy doing with her.

Jennie: And you just watch?

Melissa: I can play too, but it's my job also to give you ideas and feedback and answer questions you have about child development.

Jennie: Well, Kaylee can't wash her hands good; I do that for her.

Melissa: Well, there are a million other things we can do. What kinds of things do you like doing with Kaylee?

Jennie: We don't do much. We go down to the playground sometimes but she can't do much. She's too little.

Melissa: If you like going, we can do that for our visit and just see what we can find to do. The little things she does and things she looks at can all be ways for her to learn. Be thinking about things she's learning on the playground, and we'll talk about it when I'm here.

Jennie: Okay, that's okay. I like going outside. Sometimes this apartment just gets to me. We don't have to stay here for the home visit?

(continued)

(continued)

Melissa: We can go other places where you and Kaylee go.

Jennie: Cool.

Melissa: So let's figure out a good time to have our visits. Is Wednesday a good day, usually?

Jennie: Yeah, but she's getting sleepy now, so it would be better earlier.

Melissa: How can you tell she's sleepy?

Jennie: She's getting frustrated with her favorite toy. That's always the first sign.

Melissa: I like that you can tell that from her behavior. You're "reading" her signs.

Jennie: I guess so.

Melissa: Is there anyone else in your family who would like to join us on the home visits?

Jennie: Her daddy sometimes comes by in the mornings.

Melissa: Would you like to meet when he's here?

Jennie: Nah, I don't want to do that now. Maybe later.

Melissa: Okay, maybe later. Would 12:30 work for me to come on Wednesdays?

Jennie: Yeah, that's good.

Melissa: Great! Okay, well, that's all we need to do this week. Oh, I do have a few forms to fill out. . . .

It is important to discuss program expectations clearly, allowing enough time for clarifications, questions, and open discussions about what will happen during the visits. Trust is an important part of the relationship between the practitioner and parent, so stating up front what the expectations are and then sticking to what was agreed on is an important step in building a strong relationship. It is helpful to keep the number of expectations to a minimum, selecting the basic expectations and then discussing the roles of the practitioner and parent in meeting these expectations. When the basic expectations about these

Table 6.1.   Who does what? Expectations and roles in home visits

Sample expectation	Practitioner role	Parent role
Promote child's development.	Support parents in identifying and implementing strategies and activities.	Play, talk, listen, respond, encourage, and enjoy your child.
	Find out about family strengths, concerns, routines, and interests to provide meaningful support.	Ask questions. Actively participate in home visits. Actively participate in planning.
Participate in a set number of home visits per month.	Come to each home visit prepared to follow up with plans made from the last home visit. Reschedule with parent if conflict arises.	Participate in the home visits with your child. Let practitioner know ahead of time if you will not be able to attend the visit.

roles are clear, then a parent will be unlikely to expect the practitioner to be the child's teacher or the parent's counselor. Table 6.1 lists expectations and roles of facilitative home visits.

Parents will fulfill their expected roles to varying degrees. A mother struggling with depression may not actively participate in planning, but she needs to know that planning is important for her child as she and the home visitor work toward more active participation. Language barriers may make discussion difficult, but even limited discussions combined with observation of parent–child interactions can provide a lot of information about interests and routines useful for planning future activities and visits. When a practitioner establishes up front that the visits are about encouraging a child's development and that the practitioner's role is to support the parent in doing so, this will help frame reminders when, in future visits, the parent appears interested in socializing with the practitioner or making him- or herself unavailable to participate. The facilitative home visiting behaviors discussed previously in Chapter 4 are especially important during the first visit. For example, handing toys or materials to a parent to give to the child, involving other family members, and building on family activities and routines when planning future activities are all important for reinforcing the expectations with behavior.

SWITCHING TO A FACILITATIVE APPROACH WHEN IT'S NOT THE FIRST VISIT

Switching to a facilitative home visiting approach after a practitioner has been delivering services for a while using a different approach may take time to make the transition, but it is worth the effort. Changing the presentation of the visit to fully involve the parent may involve subtle changes such as simply handing the materials to the parent to try out with the child or involving the parent more in the planning of visits. When parents participate minimally during visits, the presentation of a change in approach may need to be more direct. For example, consider this conversation between the home visitor, Brenda, and a parent, Jennifer.

Jennifer [*calling from the kitchen*]: Come in. I have some dishes to finish up, but Braxton has been so excited to have you come today. I'll join you when I can.

Brenda: I'm looking forward to seeing what Braxton thinks of the musical instruments we talked about making. He'll enjoy making them with you, so I can wait for a few minutes until you are ready.

Jennifer: That's okay, you can go ahead.

Brenda: Well, at our last meeting at work we decided to wait until parents could join us before we started activities during our visits.

Jennifer [with a sigh]: Well, okay.

The mother's response lacks enthusiasm about the switch. As the new routine gets established, however, the expectations will change too, especially if the activities are enjoyable for the mother, and if the home visitor and mother plan the activities together.

Planning an activity for the next visit during the first visit may be challenging for several reasons. Planning may seem rushed if too much needs to be accomplished during this initial visit. Also, parents may not be comfortable making suggestions for future activities because the program is new to them, they are unsure of what to expect, or they are not yet comfortable in the practitioner–parent relationship. Building a relationship with parents takes time, but as the parents feel more comfortable and have more experience with home visits, they will become more active participants. Asking questions, offering suggestions, listening, and observing will help a practitioner gather information needed for planning for the next visit. Observing how the parent interacts with the child and asking general questions like, "What is a typical day like for Tabatha?" will help guide the practitioner in the planning process and provide a sense of both family strengths and possible concerns. Understanding and building on the strengths will improve the relevance and effectiveness of any strategies implemented to address the concerns.

Making sure that parents are involved during the first visit in planning for the next visit lays the groundwork for future involvement. When a practitioner explains a great activity for the next visit that the child will enjoy and that is appropriate for the skills he or she is learning, it lets the parent off the hook in what might be an uncomfortable situation, but it also establishes the practitioner as the director of the home visits, not the parent. If the practitioner helps a parent select something very simple that the family already does on their own, then it will do much more to facilitate developmental parenting than if the practitioner plans a developmental activity for the child without involving the parent in selecting and planning the activity.

As previously mentioned, family members other than just the mother and child should feel welcome to be present during the first home visit. Involving other family members such as fathers and siblings during this initial visit sends them a message that their participation is important to the child's development. If they are a part of the child's life but not present at the first visit, getting more information about them can make future planning easier. Grandparents, aunts, uncles, and other family members may also be actively involved in children's lives and should feel welcome during home visits. Grandparents may be especially important resources for young teenage parents who still live with their parents or in some cultures where it is customary to consult with an elder before making family decisions. Although it is often easier to simply schedule visits with the mother, or whichever parent is home the most, at least some of the visits should be scheduled to involve the other parent or significant family members and other children.

CRISIS VISIT

The best plans can go awry when a crisis hits a family. Some families are faced with a serious unpredictable crisis, while others go from crisis to crisis, especially those with few coping strategies. Children need to be cared for and responded to even if the parents don't feel capable, whatever the crisis situation and whatever the cause of the crisis. Young children, children with delays, and children with insecure attachments may be especially vulnerable to not having their emotional and physical needs met during a crisis because they may have difficulty expressing their needs to a parent who may be less attentive than usual. It is important to help the parent cope with the crisis and help the parent support the child within a facilitative home visiting framework that emphasizes developmental parenting.

The notion that parents should be helped out of the crisis first because they cannot "be there" for the child until they get things figured out is not considered good practice under a facilitative developmental parenting approach. Children's development does not wait for their caregivers' lives to get fixed. For young children, their parents may be the only resource they have available to them. The children are likely to be experiencing many of the stressors of the crisis either directly or indirectly through their parents' stressed behavior. Parents need to be available to meet their children's needs or to obtain resources to help meet these needs. In other words, development goes on regardless of family circumstances.

Sometimes it is necessary to walk a fine line between helping a parent cope and helping the parent support the child. Listening to the problem is a first step, but asking questions such as, "How do you think this situation is affecting Ellie?" or "Have you noticed any changes in Ashok since this happened?" are ways to bring the child into the conversation so that parenting can be supported. These kinds of questions can help the parent identify resources to help the child cope with a crisis.

Some beliefs and behaviors seem to help people overcome stressors and crises better than others. Being aware of these characteristics may make it easier to promote and encourage them throughout the program so that parents are better prepared when a crisis occurs. Some of these behaviors that build resilience were recommended at the web site for Primary Children's Medical Center in Salt Lake City (n.d.):

1. Ask others for help when you have problems instead of letting stress build up.

2. Make goals and work toward them, believing that you will accomplish them.

3. Think of stressors and challenges as temporary, with solutions.

4. Think of change as normal and expected.

5. Take action to solve problems that come up.

6. Build and maintain relationships with family and friends. Don't shut them out during difficult times.

7. Take time to relax and have fun.

8. Be optimistic.

Example of a Crisis Visit

Diana has just arrived for a regular home visit with Angie and her son, Luke, who is 2½ and has a significant language delay.

Diana: Hi Angie, how have things been going with you and Luke this past week?

Angie: Not so good. Brett moved out this week and if that wasn't bad enough already, Luke has been horrible this week. He hit his little sister, again! I put him in his room and he pulled all of his books out of his bookcase and then peed all over them! I don't know what to do with him! He is being just awful!

Diana: How do you feel about Brett moving out?

Angie: I knew it was coming, but it is still so hard.

Diana: How do you think Luke feels about his dad moving out?

Angie: I think he is pretty upset. Brett wasn't around a lot anyway, but Luke was always so excited to see him when he came home. They would play together.

Diana: Because Luke doesn't have a lot of words yet, it can be hard to figure out what he is thinking. Do you think that his behavior has anything to do with his dad leaving?

Angie: It probably does. He doesn't say much and he has been so angry this week, I guess I have been pretty angry this week, too. Anyway, I haven't really tried to explain much to him.

Diana: What do you think will happen if you explain things to him? Do you want to try?

Angie: Right now?

Diana: Sure, I'll hold the baby for you while you talk to him and be here if you need me.

Angie: What about making the bird feeders that we talked about doing?

(continued)

(continued)

> **Diana**: We can still make the bird feeders if we have time or I can leave the things I brought so you can make them later. Luke has always enjoyed making things with you. Now may be a time when he is trying to get more attention from you. He just hasn't figured out the best way to let you know.
>
> **Angie**: It will be easier when he can talk more. Sometimes I forget that he understands a lot more than he says.

CHAOS VISIT

Some visits seem so chaotic that it is hard to tell if anything was accomplished. Many of the factors that contribute to chaotic visits will work themselves out over time, improve with better planning, or decrease with greater flexibility. Just experiencing a few visits helps the practitioner and family have a general sense of a process or routine of how the home visits will go. Knowing a bit more of what to expect during a visit aids in the planning and preparation for future visits.

Planning and preparation are especially important for helping family members cope with a chaotic situation. Planning ahead of time with the family for what activities will occur helps reduce chaos because everyone knows what he or she will be doing. In addition, when a practitioner is better prepared to coordinate the home visit with a parent, the visit will go more smoothly in most circumstances. Preparation includes helping the parent plan activities everyone present can do, helping the parent adjust activities so that they are developmentally appropriate for the child, and bringing information and materials requested by the parent on previous visits. These aspects of preparation are ways to prepare for a visit so it will go more smoothly regardless of what is going on in the home.

Being flexible during the visit by making the best of the circumstances and adjusting activities to work better in the context of what is going on in the home may make the difference between a chaotic visit where nothing was accomplished and a chaotic visit where the mother was supported in her parenting within her current circumstances. Everyday life has many interruptions. The telephone rings, a neighbor stops by, a child brings a friend home, the furnace repair person finally shows up, a pet gets loose, the toilet overflows, and so forth. Helping a parent continue an activity with the child after an interruption will help him or her in other chaotic situations to continue interacting with the child.

Additional people in the home other than the parent (usually the mother) and the child who are the intended recipients of the home visit support sometimes make home visits feel chaotic. Although visitors who are simply attempting to socialize with the parent during the home visit may be a temporary concern, other people, such as the father or siblings, are usually a permanent part of a child's life, and should be considered a beneficial family resource rather than a distraction. Being flexible in how the visits will occur and planning for father and sibling involvement can change a chaotic visit into a dynamic, meaningful visit simply by optimizing the rich, interactive resources in the home. When siblings are involved in the home visit activities, they are less likely to vie for the parent's attention and disrupt the activities. Involving siblings in the learning activities of the home visits can benefit both younger and older children. The suggestions and support to encourage children's development provided in this context of the involvement of other family members will be more useful for parents to implement throughout the week than if only the one child were present, when that is not reality for the family.

OTHER CONCERNS ON HOME VISITS

Families may experience many different health, mental health, development, employment, and relationship concerns during the time they participate in a program. Parental depression and children's below age-level functioning are two such concerns that may create some uncertainty in facilitating developmental parenting.

Parent with Depression

Trying to support developmental parenting when a parent is depressed can be frustrating for a practitioner. The practitioner using a facilitative approach may find that nothing seems to work when a parent is depressed. Sometimes identifying strengths feels like a stretch, but working from the assumption discussed previously—that parents want what is best for their child—is a place to start. The following example of a home visit illustrates being attentive and watching for strengths during the planning time of a first home visit. The responses of this parent are typical of a parent who has some symptoms of depression.

This mother's lack of responsiveness is a concern but it is actually typical of a mother who is depressed. Lynne Murray and colleagues at the University of Cambridge reported in 1996 that mothers who were

Working with a Parent with Depression

This is Diana's first home visit with Rachel and her son Jake, who is 5 months old. Rachel has said little during the home visit and speaks in a monotone voice. She has just finished changing Jake's diaper and is sitting on the floor with Jake, who is lying on the floor in front of her.

Diana: Let's take a minute to figure out what you and Jake would like to do on our next visit. What kinds of things does Jake like to do?

Rachel: I don't know.

Diana: What kinds of things do you do during the day?

Rachel: Not much.

Diana: I'd like to plan something that you and Jake would enjoy. Can you think of something you might like to do with Jake?

Rachel: No, not really.

During this interaction Rachel and Jake have stayed in the same position. Jake has started kicking his leg so that it touches his mother's hand. After several kicks, Rachel turns her hand over and squeezes Jake's foot when he kicks his foot into her hand.

Diana: Jake keeps trying to touch you with his foot. When you squeeze his foot with your hand, his eyes brighten a bit and it looks like he is holding back a smile. He keeps kicking toward your hand again and again. It looks like he enjoys being close to you. I wonder if he might like his legs and feet massaged?

Rachel: He might.

Diana: We could do some massage next time or I could bring a front pack and we could take a walk. Maybe Jake would like to look around at things outside if he is close to you. Which do you think you and Jake might like to do next time?

Rachel: Maybe the massage would be good.

depressed were more negative and less responsive to their infants than nondepressed mothers. Furthermore, infants of the depressed mothers were less likely to be securely attached than the infants of the nondepressed mothers.

Making an appropriate mental health referral, in addition to supporting a depressed parent's parenting behavior, is important when a parent shows signs of depression. But meanwhile, the child still needs support for development. And the mother in the previous example needs help to provide it. By shifting her focus toward developmental parenting in very simple activities the mother already does, the practitioner makes it more possible for this mother to parent as well as she can. On future visits, the practitioner most likely will need to keep doing things to keep the mother focused on her child and take a somewhat directive role in keeping the mother interacting with her child. In the visits with this family, it will be especially important for the practitioner to involve other family members, if possible, to help support this mother.

Long-term parental depression can be devastating to children's development. Helping parents manage their depression through other resources and facilitating developmental parenting can help depressed parents continue to support their children's development. The following signs of depression are provided by Mental Health America at their web site listed in the references at the end of this book. If a parent has experienced several of these things for 2 weeks or longer, then the practitioner should help the parent get mental health support:

- Persistent sad, anxious, or "empty" mood

- Changes in sleep patterns

- Reduced appetite and weight loss, or increased appetite and weight gain

- Loss of pleasure and interest in once-enjoyable activities, including sex

- Restlessness, irritability

- Persistent physical symptoms that do not respond to treatment, such as chronic pain or digestive disorders

- Difficulty concentrating, remembering things, or making decisions

- Fatigue or loss of energy

- Feeling guilty, hopeless, or worthless

- Thoughts of suicide or death

Child with a Disability

Developmental parenting is important for every child, regardless of whether or not they are developing typically. For a child whose development is atypical, developmental parenting behaviors support the child's emerging skills regardless of the age at which these skills are emerging. Actually, the warmth, responsiveness, encouragement, and conversation behaviors that are important for parents with a child who is typically developing are especially important for a child with a disability.

In fact, Gerald Mahoney and Frida Perales at Case Western Reserve University reported an intervention in 2005 in which parents were taught how to be more responsive in interactions with children with developmental disabilities and disorders. When the parents became more responsive, the children's outcomes improved. Parents' encouragement and conversation are important for any child to promote learning and communication. These parenting behaviors can be incorporated into everyday family routines and activities involving fathers and siblings for any child at any level of development, whether typical or atypical.

Parenting a child with a disability, nevertheless, often creates additional stress for families. Difficulty communicating, health concerns, feeding problems, limited mobility, and negative behaviors are just some of the challenges associated with disabilities that create additional stress. These difficulties and behaviors may seem overwhelming to parents and to practitioners. Most parents are not well-versed in typical child development, so compounding all of the nuances of typical child development with the unique difficulties and behaviors associated with the disability can make parenting a child with a disability extremely difficult. Helping a parent solve problems about specific child behaviors and identifying additional resources are especially helpful when a child has a disability.

Practitioners who work together with other providers, such as those that offer early intervention programs for children with disabilities, can offer a more effective support system to families with children who have a disabilities, resulting in better outcomes. Helping parents understand how children communicate their needs and feelings when they cannot talk, for instance, can help reduce the frustration for both the parents and the children. For children with disabilities, collaborating with staff from early intervention programs can be helpful so parents do not receive conflicting information and recommendations.

CONCLUSION

Putting it all into practice takes practice. The ideas and guidelines in this chapter were written to help practitioners get started at facilitating developmental parenting from the very first meeting with a family and through times of crisis or chaos. The special concerns of a parent with depression or a child with a disability were also discussed. But, as this chapter points out, the unexpected can be expected. New challenges will arise. Put the *attitudes* of the ABCs into practice by remaining responsive and flexible as you look for family strengths in every situation. Put the *behaviors* into practice by keeping the emphasis on parenting that supports child development and the focus on parent–child interaction, especially when parents are distracted by other problems. Put the *content* into practice by helping parents figure out what information they need and want at the time to support their children's development the best they can. These are the basics of a developmental parenting program that will help practitioners use the program's strategies to reach the program's goals.

7

Curricula and Activity Resources

Many good curriculum resources that support child development are available, but few are designed to support developmental parenting. Selecting curricula that are easy to understand, easy to use, appropriate for the home environment, and appropriate for a range of ages makes it much easier to support parents in their role of supporting their children's development. Although few curricula exist that meet all four of these criteria, many good curricula exist that can be adapted, as a whole or in part, to facilitate developmental parenting. Thus, this chapter focuses on ways to evaluate, adapt, and use existing curricula within a developmental parenting framework and not on reviewing the many curricula available.

Good curricula are family friendly. This means they have several characteristics that make them appropriate to use with a wide range of parents in diverse families with children of various ages. First, family friendly curricula are easy to understand. The language of a curriculum should be simple and straightforward so that practitioners and parents can use it together for planning good developmental learning activities for children. Materials with jargon and technical terms are not appropriate for most families. Furthermore, some families in developmental parenting programs have had negative school experiences in the past and may not have a positive reaction to "academic" writing. Some parents have limited literacy skills and find long, wordy explanations tedious and difficult to read. The best curriculum resources to help parents plan activities to support their children's development will have clear illustrations with short descriptions of child behavior or developmental learning activities.

Second, family friendly curricula are easy to use. Curriculum guides that suggest elaborately prepared materials for a learning activity are not family friendly. A curriculum is family friendly if it offers multiple suggestions for activities that are easy to plan, easy to prepare, easy to do, and easy to clean up. Those are the kinds of activities that are likely to be used again by the family. A one-time-only activity is not likely to be appropriate for facilitating developmental parenting because it has little usefulness over time.

Third, family friendly curricula are appropriate for home environments. Some curriculum activities may work well in child care or early education settings but are not appropriate for home environments. For example, messy art activities may not be appropriate in many homes, particularly if the family wants to do the home visits in their living room. Toys with many small pieces are unlikely to be appropriate if the practitioner brings the toys to the home with pieces that could be lost under furniture during the visit or that might pose a choking hazard to young children. Some curriculum activities require more space than some homes have. Materials used for activities in child care centers or preschools are often not available in grocery stores or other stores where families shop. Activities that use such materials are not likely to be useful for parents in the future when they do not have access to materials provided by a child development program.

Fourth, family friendly curricula are appropriate for a range of ages. A useful curriculum activity can involve the older children in the home. Curricula activities that are restricted to a narrow age range are not likely to be useful to parents over time. Facilitative practitioners include curricula activities that parents can use in the future.

QUESTIONS TO GUIDE
SELECTION OF CURRICULUM TOOLS

The following questions are helpful in guiding the effective selection of curriculum tools.

- Is it easy to understand?

- Is it easy to use?

- Will it work well in families' homes?

- Is it appropriate for the child's development?

- Can it be adapted for children of other ages?

- Is it flexible enough to adapt to different family strengths and needs?

- Will it promote attachment security, playful exploration, or communication?

- Will it be interesting to the family?

A curriculum has not been developed for the specific needs and strengths of every family that a practitioner serves. It would be impossible to predict the development of each child in any given family and the changing family, neighborhood, and community circumstances surrounding each child and influencing the child's development. Each child's developmental pattern and each family's resources and needs will influence development in slightly different ways. Working with parents requires flexibility, creativity, and extensive knowledge on the part of the practitioner in order to support parents in their role of supporting their children's development. Thus, being adaptable and thinking about adjusting for a parent's goals for a child and the parent's strengths in working with the child is a more useful approach than selecting a curriculum that requires a rigid series of lessons and activities. A useful curriculum is a resource for ideas, not an instruction manual.

Unfortunately, many curricula focus only on children's developmental progress and do little to support parents in their role of supporting their children's development. Good curricula that describe typical development in the various developmental domains and provide engaging activities to encourage children to develop new skills can be adapted to use with parents to facilitate developmental parenting. With an understanding of the facilitative attitudes, behaviors, and content described previously, program staff can adapt most good curriculum resources for early development to facilitate developmental parenting.

SELECT WHICH CURRICULUM TO USE WHEN

Guide your selection of appropriate curricula and activities with information from developmental assessments, observations of parent–child interactions, and discussions with parents. Several different curricula are available to support the broad-based foundational domains of early development, which include secure attachment, playful exploration, and communication skills. Although more than one curriculum resource can be combined in useful ways, too many can become cumbersome. Trying to juggle several different curricula or sticking to just one curriculum may make it hard to think through the needs and interests of each parent and child. Using a strictly outlined curriculum, especially one that focuses solely on children's development, can make it difficult to facilitate developmental parenting.

Supporting parents through everyday interactions can be powerful for many parents, especially those with multiple risk factors. Focusing more heavily on the parent–child relationship may be especially important when their relationship faces several challenges. Parent–child relationships are especially challenging when a mother is depressed, detached, or nonresponsive to the child, or when a transition is coming up or occurring such as a parental separation, a move to a different home, or the birth of a new sibling. Parent–child relationships can also be challenging when the child is pushing for more autonomy, such as when he or she is beginning to walk or demanding to have a say in what goes on. At these times, it is especially important to help the parent support the development of the child's attachment security. At other times, it may be easy to support the parent–child relationship as part of promoting playful exploration and communication skills.

Many curricula aim to promote typical developmental milestones through specific activities. Although useful for promoting developmental skills, sometimes these activities seem contrived and do not naturally flow from everyday parent–child activities, interests, and interactions. Sifting through these activities with an emphasis on playful exploration will naturally take into account children's developmental progress, child and parent interests, and the parent–child relationship. Many activities viewed through this lens will not seem appropriate for encouraging developmental parenting. Sometimes it can be hard to move beyond our training or materials that focus on single skill acquisition through a drill-type approach. For example, encouraging communication skills has a long history of both drill- and conversation-based strategies from curricula and from the field of speech-language pathology.

Open-ended activities that can be adapted to a variety of ages of children and a variety of family situations make the most sense in home visits, where the purpose is to help parents promote their children's development as part of their everyday activities. Open-ended, interactive activities that promote several different aspects of development such as nature walks, cooking, art, or block play are more likely to be appropriate for developmental parenting than narrow, practice-oriented activities such as naming colors or counting.

With many resources available, selecting the most appropriate tools for the families served may seem overwhelming. It may be easy to rely on well-developed strategies to promote language and communication that do not necessarily build on the rich family context or parent–child relationship. It can be challenging to work on communication skills in a home environment where little parent–child conversation occurs. It is likely to be more useful to identify activities that will facilitate the parent–child conversations and that can be used throughout the day than to use prescribed practice activities for children. Select activities that promote parent–child communication, build on the parent–child relationship, and encourage playful exploration. Activities that are fun and interesting to children and parents help engage families in meaningful activities that are likely to be continued after the program is over.

ADAPT CURRICULUM
ACTIVITIES TO SUPPORT PARENTING

To support developmental parenting for each individual family, even the best, most appropriate curriculum tools need to be adapted to the needs and interests of each child. Adaptations do not need to be complicated. For example, a typical skill to teach a 2-year-old is basic color identification. Often, children are asked to name colors or to sort colored shapes. Many different games and activities have been created to teach children to identify colors, but few of these activities also promote the foundational domains of attachment security, playful exploration, and communication skills. Before selecting an activity to help a child name colors, it is helpful to ask, "Why is this important?" Asking yourself about the purpose of an activity will help frame the activity in a broader context. For example, "Why will knowing the names of colors be helpful for this child and the family?" One reason why knowing the names of colors is useful is so that one is able to describe the world and make requests more precise. (Some days, only the pink shirt will do.) Incorporating a goal of learning colors into a broader activity such as art, cooking, or making a book, will help develop communication skills in a context in which naming colors is supported, but so is playful exploration and positive parent–child interaction. Open-ended art activities can easily follow the parent's and child's interests, involve other family members, and encourage development of fine motor as well as other skills across a large age range. Experimenting with different colors and combinations of colors while creating a masterpiece of art, a delicious snack, or a special book provides great opportunities for exploring while having fun and talking about many different things related to colors.

As a child and parent work together on a project such as one of the ones described, a facilitative practitioner encourages the parent to be specific in his or her praise such as describing task persistence, what the child is doing, and attributes of the final project as well as asking how the child feels about the result or what the child likes best. These parenting behaviors will not only promote communication skills but also attachment security. The parent's descriptions and questions provide the child with much more information and affirmation than statements such as "Good job" or "Good girl." Although it may seem easier and more direct to teach colors through a structured matching or naming task, the benefits pale in comparison with those described previously and are likely to be limited to basic color labels and not much else.

In addition to reflecting on the purpose of the activity to pull back to the broader picture, "What if?" and "Why not?" questions would also be useful to encourage the flexibility and creative thinking needed to individualize activities to promote developmental parenting. Against a backdrop of teaching a child his or her colors but reframed as a goal for parenting, practitioners can begin to think through different "what-ifs," such as, "What if we went for a walk?" "What if we started a collection?" or "What if I asked Mom when she noticed or enjoyed colors the most and used her answers to guide an activity?" Thinking through the "why-nots" may also help a practitioner effectively adapt curricula and activities by helping identify needs or potential barriers. For example, reflecting on questions such as "Why doesn't Susie know any of the colors yet?" or "Why doesn't Mom allow art materials in the house?" or "Why isn't Mom engaged during the home visits?" can aid in the adaptation of the curriculum activities used in a developmental parenting program by helping a practitioner think through things that aren't going smoothly and to identify hurdles that may need more attention.

Providing a comprehensive list of available curricula or recommendations supporting any one curriculum is not the purpose of this chapter. The best curriculum for one program may not be the best for another program. Thinking through the program's theory of change and identifying the strengths and needs of the families served will determine which curricula are the best fit for a developmental parenting framework. Table 7.1 illustrates how several different activities from published curricula can be adapted or incorporated into home visits following the principles of developmental parenting described previously. These available curriculum resources include the *Hawaii Early Learning Profile* (HELP), developed by Setsu Furano and colleagues in 2005; *Beautiful Beginnings: A Developmental Curriculum for Infants and Toddlers,* developed by Helen Raikes and Jane Whitmer in 2006; *Parents as Teachers Born to Learn,* developed by the Parents as Teachers National Center in 1999; and the *Creative Curriculum for Early Childhood,* developed by Diane Dodge and colleagues in 1999. These examples of commonly used curricula are not meant to be exhaustive, but are meant to stimulate ideas to help early childhood practitioners translate commonly used curricula activities in ways that will involve the parent and promote developmental parenting.

Curriculum tools are an important resource for content in a developmental parenting program. Bringing content into the home visits that is meaningful and relevant to a family increases the likelihood that

Table 7.1. Specific curricula activities in a developmental parenting framework

Curriculum	Activity	Target age range	Emphasize parent–child interaction	Build on family strengths	Address broad foundations of development	Adapt to older or younger children or siblings
Beautiful Beginnings: A Developmental Curriculum for Infants and Toddlers (Raikes, H.H., & Whitmer, J.M., 2006)	Playing with Things in Containers	6–12 months	Ask parent about objects and containers that child likes and those that would be novel. Ask parent what child does when he is frustrated and can't get something out. Talk about strategies to help child figure it out.	Help parent pull together objects and containers in the home that child could practice with. Identify times of the day and materials that would allow child to practice these skills when parent is busy with other tasks.	Encourage parents to use a wide variety of objects and containers to encourage exploration. Encourage parents to support communication by talking about objects as the child explores. Help parents observe child cues of frustration and help develop problem-solving strategies when child gets stuck to help strengthen their relationship.	Involve older siblings by having them help find objects and containers and then cut small holes in containers. Use puzzles with older children to help develop more advanced problem-solving skills.

(continued)

Table 7.1. (continued)

Curriculum	Activity	Target age range	Emphasize parent-child interaction	Build on family strengths	Address broad foundations of development	Adapt to older or younger children or siblings
Creative Curriculum for Early Childhood (Dodge, D.T., Colker, L.J., & Heroman, C., 1999)	Art Center	3- to 5-year olds	Encourage discussion about how the child feels about the product. Discuss ways art can communicate feelings.	Use materials that the family has available inside or outside. Encourage art activities that focus on family interests.	Use a variety of materials to encourage exploration. Encourage conversation during the art project about the materials being used, what is being created, or what the creation may represent.	Have enough art materials available for siblings to be involved. Have the art project be open-ended and not a recreation of a specific product. This allows children of different ages and abilities to be actively involved.
Hawaii Early Learning Profile (HELP; Furano, S., O'Reilly, K.A., Hosaka, C.M., Inatsuka, T.T., et al., 2005)	Take turns telling the story on different pages in a storybook.	30–36 months	Have the story telling turn-taking be between parent and child. Reinforce parent and child for responding and attending to each other.	Use books in the home. Create a book with the family. Visit the library to check out a book on a topic that the child is interested in.	Support relationship and communication skills by encouraging both parent and child to respond to each other's part as they tell a story. Encourage parents to elaborate on ideas, places, and things from the story.	Have the siblings take a turn telling about a page of the story or be the audience and ask questions about the story. Encourage story telling appropriate for the child's development (e.g., single words and gestures for toddlers, elaboration, and detail for preschoolers.

Source	Activity	Age			
Parents as Teachers Born to Learn (Parents as Teachers National Center, Inc., 1999)	Pocket Folder Matching Game	27 months	Ask the parent what things the child is interested in ahead of time and then help parents find newspapers, magazines, or stickers that would have pictures that follow along with the interest. Hand all materials to the parent to help the child create the game by gluing sets of pictures on note cards to be matched. Encourage the parent to follow the child's lead in talking about what is the same in the pictures.	Use materials that are available in the home. Encourage parent to involve child in other classifying and sorting opportunities throughout the day such as putting groceries away or sorting laundry.	Ask about child interests and discuss similarities to encourage general communication skills as well as specific vocabulary related to classifying. Ask the parent about child interests to send a message that the parent knows the child and you respect the parent's expertise in setting up the activity. These messages support the parent–child relationship. Extend this activity to classifying other objects in the child's world and encourage playful exploration.	Write the names of family members on cards and have older preschoolers match the names.

they will be engaged in the activity and will continue to engage in similar activities with their child. The content of home visits is important, but the delivery process for the content may be even more important for supporting developmental parenting.

Activities that are fun are likely to be repeated. Incorporating relevant content into everyday routines and activities that children enjoy will promote playful exploration. Keeping the emphasis for content on mutual enjoyment and playful exploration as much as possible taps into the power of play. Although some parents may think children need more than "just play" to learn what they need to know, play is actually one of the main ways children learn. Table 7.2 includes insights on play that show how play has been valued for centuries as part of development and life.

Even with a long history of developmental theories and research that emphasizes the value of play, practitioners and parents can get caught up in building isolated skills and forget how enjoyable skill building can be when it occurs during play. Some curricula activities are easier than others to incorporate into play. Often it is not what skills are being encouraged so much as how the skills are being encouraged. A learning activity can be experienced by the child as drill-like or play-like depending on how it is set up. A developmental parenting framework follows family interests, involves parents in decision-making, facilitates parent–child interactions, and emphasizes child exploration and communication outcomes. This framework helps ensure that activities selected from a curriculum are incorporated into playful interactions and family activities that engage both the parent and child.

Table 7.2. Insights on play

What has been said about play	Who said it when
"Life must be lived as play."	Plato, Greek philosopher (427–347 BCE)
"Whoever wants to understand much must play much."	Gottfried Benn, German physician (1886–1956)
"Play is the only way the highest intelligence of humankind can unfold."	Joseph Chilton Pearce, contemporary American scholar (1926–)
"Play is the highest form of research."	Albert Einstein, German-American physicist (1879–1945)
"A child loves his play, not because it's easy, but because it is hard."	Benjamin Spock, American pediatrician (1903–1998)
"Children need the freedom and time to play. Play is not a luxury. Play is a necessity."	Kay Redfield Jamison, contemporary American professor of psychiatry (1946–)
"In play a child always behaves above his average age, above his daily behavior. In play it is as though he were a head taller than himself."	Lev Vygotsky, Russian psychologist (1896–1934)

CONCLUSION

Curricula appropriate for a developmental parenting program should be easy to understand, easy to use, appropriate for the home environment, and appropriate for a range of ages. While few curricula exist that meet all of these criteria, many existing curricula can be adapted to support parents in their role of supporting their children's development. Selecting activities from curricula to promote communication, build on the parent–child relationship, and encourage playful exploration will help align the existing curriculum with the goals of a developmental parenting program. In addition, selecting activities that are interesting to children and parents will help engage families in meaningful activities that are likely to be continued after the program is over.

8

Assessment and Outcome Measures

How can early childhood practitioners help parents notice and anticipate their children's development? One way is to help them assess
their children's current developmental skills. Practitioners are often expected to do assessments of children's development as part of their job,
and by involving parents in the process they can facilitate developmental parenting. It may also be useful to assess changes in parenting behaviors that promote children's early development. Assessments can be
used in two ways: first, to individualize services to each parent and
child, and second, to track outcomes of the program.

Conducting assessments and measuring outcomes are common
components of home visiting programs. Many programs are required
or encouraged to measure progress toward specific child and family
outcomes that have been identified by the stakeholders of the program.
In addressing these outcomes, some assessments might be mandatory,
while others can be selected by the practitioner to use when needed.
Whichever the case, what is assessed, how the assessments are conducted, and what is done with the information gained from the assessments are all influenced by a program's goals and strategies. Whether
explicitly stated in a logic model or implicitly assumed, the program's
goals and strategies are part of its theory of change and influence the
kinds of assessments the program uses with children and parents.
Many good assessment tools are available, but not all are appropriate
for a developmental parenting program. The same criteria that were
applied to curriculum resources are just as appropriate for assessment

resources. In order to be useful in promoting developmental parenting, it is important to select assessment tools that are easy to understand, easy to use, appropriate for the home environment, and appropriate for a range of ages. These are the same criteria that were applied to curriculum resources and they are just as appropriate for assessment resources. The following questions will guide practitioners in selecting an appropriate "family friendly" assessment tool:

- Is it easy to understand?

- Is it easy to use?

- Will it work well in families' homes?

- Is it appropriate for the child's development?

- Can it be adapted for children of other ages?

ASSESSMENT

By assessing development and progress toward program goals, a developmental parenting program will get important information to guide home visits. What and how assessments are conducted should reflect the underlying vision of the developmental parenting program. For programs that aim to support parenting, assessments should include parents. Child development and parenting behaviors are two key assessment areas for programs emphasizing developmental parenting based on our theory of change.

A key intervention strategy to facilitate developmental parenting is to involve parents in the assessment of their children's development. Involving parents in child development assessments supports warm, responsive, encouraging, and communicative parenting. Parent observation of a child's current developmental skills and behaviors will help the parent anticipate the child's developmental progress. Parent involvement in a developmental assessment helps the parent become more knowledgeable about the child's development and also a better observer of the child's play and activities. Assessing parenting behaviors in the context of parent–child interaction is useful for both the parent and the practitioner. Reviewing this information with a parent helps the parent to better understand parenting behaviors and strategies that are likely influencing the child's behaviors and development. This information also allows the practitioner to see parent strengths and areas in need of additional support, both of which will help when working with the family.

Using Developmental Assessments Meaningfully

The ideal child assessment to use in a developmental parenting program is one that can be conducted by a parent with support from a practitioner. In a developmental parenting program, the practitioner serves as a facilitator to guide the parent on how to observe and score behaviors of interest. The parent ideally leads in setting up situations to observe behaviors or in answering questions. For a variety of reasons, however, only a few assessment tools lend themselves to this approach. Appropriate training, unbiased administration, and efficiency are just a few of the requirements for most assessments that make parent involvement in assessments difficult. Nevertheless, it is much easier to involve parents if practitioners select assessment tools that are easy to use and understand and appropriate for a range of ages rather than tools with rigid administration standards that require extensive training. Often, an easy-to-use assessment tool is designed for paraprofessional or developmental screening use. Sometimes a program is required to use more than a screening tool, but parent involvement should be part of any child development assessment in a developmental parenting program.

Many assessments can be adapted to involve parents. When using an assessment tool to make placement decisions or any other clinical decision, the administration protocol must be followed in the standardized manner. However, it is appropriate to ask parents, both formally and informally, to provide additional information about their children's skills. Informal information may involve questions about how well the children's performance on the assessment reflected what the parents observe on a daily basis. Formal information may be collected from assessments that rely on parent report. Most assessments have not been developed with diverse cultural groups in mind, making it even more important to include parents in their children's assessments to ensure that any culture-specific assessment items are discussed in broader terms applicable to all children's skills.

For many programs, ongoing monitoring of development is conducted with screening instruments or criterion-based instruments instead of formal, standardized assessment instruments, thus making the involvement of parents much easier. Table 8.1 shows examples of several assessment tools that can incorporate strategies to involve parents. *Ages & Stages Questionnaires® (ASQ): A Parent-Completed, Child-Monitoring System*, developed by Jane Squires, LaWanda Potter, and Diane Bricker in 1995 and revised by Bricker & Squires in 1999, and The Ounce Scale, developed by Samuel Meisels and colleagues in 2003, are briefly summarized in the table and described in more detail later. Other examples

Table 8.1. Examples of child assessment tools that incorporate strategies to involve parents

Measure	Age range	Developmental areas	Type	Parent involvement
Ages and Stages Questionnaires® (ASQ): A Parent-Completed, Child Monitoring System (2nd ed.) (Bricker, D. & Squires, J., 1999; Paul H. Brookes Publishing Co.)	4–60 months	Communication Gross motor Fine motor Problem solving Personal–social	Screening	Administration is structured for parent report. Scoring summary is easy to generate and discuss with parents.
Denver Developmental Screening Tool-II (DDST; Frankenburg, W.K., Dodds, J., Archer, P., et al., 1996; Denver Developmental Materials Inc.)	1 month–6 years	Fine motor Adaptive Gross motor Personal–social Language	Screening	Parent report can be used for several of the personal–social and language items. Scoring summary is easy to generate and discuss with parents.
Hawaii Early Learning Profile (HELP) Strands (Parks, S. 1992; Vort Corporation)	Birth–6 years	Cognitive Language Gross motor Fine motor Social Self-help	Curriculum-based assessment	Parent is asked to assist in presenting some of the tasks. Includes play-based assessment guidelines making it easier for parents to see the relevance of the task. Includes a comprehensive, sequenced list of skills making it easy for parents to see what skills are likely to be developing next.
MacArthur-Bates Communicative Development Inventories (CDI; Fenson, Marchman, Thal, Dale, Reznick, & Bates, 2006; Paul H. Brookes Publishing Co.)	8–30 months	Language and communication skills	Screening	Assessment is based on parent report. Assessment items consist of common, everyday words making it easy for parents to understand the relevance between the test items and their everyday interactions with their children.

Assessment	Age range	Domains	Type	Parent involvement
The Ounce Scale (Meisels, S.J., Marsden, D.B., Dombro, A.L., Weston, D.R., & Jewkes, A.M., 2003; Pearson Assessments)	Birth–42 months	Personal connections Feelings about self Relationships with other children Understanding and communication Exploration and problem solving Movement and coordination	Authentic performance assessment	Parents participate in providing information and in completing an observation record, a family profile, and developmental profiles.
Transdisciplinary Play-Based Assessment (TPBA; Linder, T., 1993; Paul H. Brookes Publishing Co.)	Infancy–6 years	Cognitive Social-emotional Communication and language Sensorimotor	Diagnostic assessment	Parents are involved throughout the assessment. Involves activities in real-life settings making it easy to generalize support for child strengths and needs to activities in the home.

of measures included in Table 8.1 that encourage parent participation during developmental assessments are the Denver Developmental Screening Tool II (DDST), revised by William Frankenburg and colleagues in 1996; the Hawaii Early Learning Profile (HELP) Strands for children birth to 3 years old, developed by Stephanie Parks in 1992, and the HELP Strands for children 3 to 6 years old, developed by the Vort Corporation in 1995; the Transdisciplinary Play-Based Assessment (TPBA): A Functional Approach to Working with Young Children, revised by Toni Linder in 1993 and 2008; and the MacArthur-Bates Communicative Development Inventories (CDIs), developed by Larry Fenson and colleagues in 1992 and revised in 2008.

There are several key advantages to involving parents in assessing children's development. First, children are usually more comfortable with their parents than with anyone else, especially at younger ages, so they may be more willing to try an assessment task when asked by their parents.

Second, parents observe and interact with their children every day and can report on skills that they have seen their children do in the past as well as those that they have seen their children attempt to do, but may not be able to accomplish yet. This information can add to an actual assessment of a child's skills or replace it.

Third, participating in assessments can help parents understand development and the sequence of skills necessary to accomplish more sophisticated skills. For example, by being involved in a developmental assessment of a child, a parent can become more aware of the role of trunk control in learning to walk or the role of babbling in learning to speak. These kinds of experiences help parents become generally aware of what skills can be expected at what age and specifically, what skills are the next steps for their children. Although an understanding of general child development is helpful, even more important is that parents understand their own children's development. Helping parents become experts in their children's development can help increase their responsiveness and encouragement as they become aware of their children's current abilities and emerging skills.

Fourth and finally, involving parents in their children's developmental assessment reaffirms their roles as the experts in their children's development. When parents have this assessment information, they share a common core of information with practitioners. Developmental information should not be a secret held by an expert. We have seen many parents use the information from assessments to encourage and practice emerging skills with their children, resulting in observable developmental progress by their children. Some measures are particularly appropriate for using collaboratively with parents.

Examples of Family Friendly Assessment Tools

The ASQ is an example of an assessment tool that we have seen foster parent recognition of age-appropriate skills in such a way that leads to immediate skill improvements. This tool is one that involves parents, is easy to use and understand, and is appropriate across the range of development from infants through preschoolers. The ASQ was created as a screening instrument for identifying developmental delays, but it can also be used to track children's development. Parents are asked to rate their children's progress on a series of developmental skills in five areas: communication, gross motor, fine motor, problem solving, and personal–social. A questionnaire on the area of social-emotional development was also created to accompany the ASQ so as to provide a more complete picture of children's development.

The ASQ has different scoring forms (protocols) for different ages of children. Scoring forms are selected based on age, with one per month available for young children and one per few months for older children. The activities that parents are asked to respond to are easily observed, likely to occur at home, written in understandable terms (sixth-grade reading level), accompanied by illustrations and concrete examples, and selected for "cultural sensitivity" with adaptations provided when appropriate.

To score the ASQ questionnaire, practitioners convert parents' responses of "Yes," "Sometimes," or "Not yet," to points—10, 5, and 0, respectively—and total the points for each developmental area. These five area scores are compared with empirically derived cut-off points, which are shown as shaded and unshaded areas on a bar graph. This provides information on whether a child's skills are at age level. The presentation of the information on bar graphs makes it easy for parents to understand areas of strengths and areas of concerns regarding their children's development. The ASQ can be used with a wide variety of families because it is available in English, Spanish, French, and Korean. It is being translated into additional languages, as well, which will increase the usefulness of the instrument for practitioners serving families from many different cultures speaking many different languages.

Many existing curricula include criterion-referenced assessments to monitor children's developmental skills. It may seem expedient for an "expert" to quickly observe a child and mark the boxes on an assessment form indicating the skills the child is able to perform. Although this information may be useful to plan future activities and monitor the child's progress, it ignores the purpose of a developmental parenting program. Involving parents in eliciting the skills from their children and coaching parents in determining what level their children are able to do the skill will help parents understand their role in observing and supporting their children's development. Play-based assessments and curriculum-based assessments conducted around play tasks, as described previously, provide hands-on experiences for parents as they learn more about the link between assessment tasks and their children's everyday experiences.

How often should practitioners help parents assess their children's development? The frequency of developmental assessments depends on a program's theory of change and the type of assessment being used. However, from a developmental parenting perspective, assessing more often is better than assessing infrequently if the instrument is designed for monitoring and parents are partners in the assessment process. For example, involving parents in monthly ASQ assessment is reasonable, especially with infants and toddlers, because development progresses quickly during this time. Parents and practitioners are able to stay on top of children's development, parents learn what is expected at different age levels, and parents and practitioners then share a common framework for planning appropriate activities.

Examples of assessments focused on general areas of child development have been presented in this chapter because these types of assessments are important and most often linked to outcomes required by program funding agencies. But, what if your program's theory of change focuses on child outcomes that are not directly assessed in common assessment tools? Outcomes such as secure attachment and playful exploration, included in our theory of change for developmental parenting programs, are not usually included in commonly available assessment tools. Assessing these outcomes is sometimes less straightforward than assessing communication, but there are ways to gain information about them.

Attachment security is traditionally assessed in a laboratory observation with a series of parent–child separations, reunions, and interactions with a stranger or, alternatively, with a complex card-sorting task to describe a child's proximity-seeking behavior. Although strategies involving an elaborate laboratory situation or complicated tasks for parents are not reasonable for most programs and their families, proponents of other strategies suggest that questionnaires and informal observations can provide meaningful information about a child's attachment security.

Kim Chisholm MacLean, at St. Francis Xavier University in Nova Scotia, has developed a short rating scale based on a card-sorting measure (originally developed by Everett Waters at the Stony Brook University in New York in 1987). MacLean's short rating scale has been used reliably in an interview format with parents in research she published under the name of Chisholm in 1998. Items on the questionnaire describe attachment behaviors such as proximity seeking (*Child keeps track of your location when playing around the house and notices if you change rooms or activities*) and comforting (*When child is upset or frightened, he quickly stops crying and recovers when you hold him*). Scoring instructions are included on the questionnaire, making it easy to use.

Other strategies, such as observing parent–child interactions in a variety of settings (during floor play), brief separations (when the parent leaves the room), and stressful tasks (a doctor's appointment), all provide opportunities to observe a child's attachment behaviors and the parent's responsiveness to the child's needs, concerns, and interests. Writing notes about these observations can provide a record that can be discussed with the parent, expanded on, and reviewed from time to time.

Exploration and motivation to learn are outcomes that also can be assessed through a parent interview or observation strategies. Parent questionnaires such as the Infant–Toddler Social and Emotional Assessment (ITSEA) can be used to assess aspects of exploration and motivation to learn. The ITSEA was developed at Yale University by Alice Carter and Margaret Briggs-Gowan in 2005 to detect social-emotional and behavior problems and delays in the acquisition of competencies in children ages 1 to 4. The measure encourages parent observations of how a child behaves in different environments. The competence domain of the ITSEA includes compliance, attention, mastery motivation, imitation/play, empathy, and pro-social peer relations. The other subscales include items such as depression/withdrawal, activity/impulsivity, and general anxiety. Asking parents the questions from the ITSEA can help identify any red flag areas of concern as well as areas of competence showing appropriate progress in these important areas of development.

The Ounce Scale, developed by Sam Meisels and his colleagues at the Erikson Institute in Chicago in 2003, measures several developmental areas related to the foundational outcomes of developmental parenting. It includes the following subscales: personal connections (trust), feelings about self, relationships with other children, understanding and communication, exploration and problem solving, and movement and coordination. The Ounce Scale is based on observations of children in day-to-day environments. The measure is designed for parents to be actively involved in observing their children and to work collaboratively with practitioners to complete the measure. Together, they complete a family record of the assessment information that is unique to each parent and child and similar to a scrapbook of information. The information is then used to complete a developmental profile where the information from these other records is used to get an indicator of the child's development and progress over time. The Ounce Scale is notable in being a less structured, more natural, approach that lends itself to a developmental parenting program.

Sometimes simply watching children and taking notes can provide good information. Observing children in a play situation and taking notes about their behavior can provide information about their exploration and motivation to learn. Behaviors to observe include persistence (e.g., continued attempts to try to open a door), pride (e.g., smiling or positive statements like "I did it!"), physical avoidance (e.g., pushes puzzle pieces away), verbal avoidance (making statements like "I can't"), and shame (withdrawal from task or negative self-statements like "I'm no good at this"). This information can be collected at different times and kept in a notebook. A practitioner and parent can each provide comments on what they saw and what they thought about what they saw.

Child assessment information can support developmental parenting by increasing parents' awareness and knowledge of their children's development; their time interacting with their children; and their responsiveness to their children's cues, interests, and changes. Observing the same child behaviors periodically provides valuable information about the impact that parenting behaviors are having on children's security, exploration, and communication. The basic foundations of children's development are often more closely linked to parent–child interactions than more distal outcomes such as school readiness. Regular assessments, both formal and informal, can provide more immediate feedback to parents about their impact on children's development.

Assessing Parenting Behaviors

Parenting behaviors should be assessed for two reasons. First, by evaluating their own behaviors, parents are likely to learn more about the kinds of parenting behaviors that support their children's development. Second, by assessing changes in parenting behaviors, practitioners can monitor the success of a developmental parenting program.

The appropriateness and responsiveness of parents' behaviors are especially important in the areas of attachment security, playful exploration, and communication. Warm, responsive, encouraging, and communicative parenting behaviors support the foundational areas of early child development, but harsh or neglectful caregiving can inhibit or stunt a child's development. Many factors such as stress, depression, and marital conflict can negatively influence parenting. Referrals for mental health services certainly should be made when appropriate. Nevertheless, a facilitative practitioner will focus on helping parents promote their children's development even in difficult times. The actual parenting behavior is what is directly experienced by the child and observed by the practitioner. Thus, parenting assessments should focus on observable parent behaviors that are likely to influence child development.

The research literature is full of evidence documenting the importance of supportive parenting behaviors and a stimulating home environment for a child's early development. The scientific evidence for developmental parenting is shown in Table 1.1 in the first chapter of this book. Several parenting instruments and rating scales have been developed to assess these factors, but they often require extensive training on the part of an observer or an extensive interview with a parent. After scores are obtained on these instruments, it is often difficult for practitioners to use the scores to develop strategies to build on parenting strengths and address areas of need. These instruments do not, for the most part, meet the criteria at the beginning of this chapter of being easy to use and understand and useful in homes. Fortunately, some instruments have been developed that are easier to use.

One parenting measure that is easily administered in a home setting is the Parenting Interactions with Children: Checklist of Observations Linked to Outcomes (PICCOLO). The first author and her colleagues at Utah State University developed the PICCOLO measure based on ratings of parenting behavior in more than 4,000 videotaped observations of parent–child interactions available from the national Early Head Start Research and Evaluation Project. PICCOLO, available as of 2007, focuses on key parenting behaviors that promote attachment security, playful exploration, and communication. PICCOLO was created based on behaviors reported in the research literature as important for children's early development. Items were tested for how easy they were to observe and how well they predicted child outcomes in the domains of cognitive, language, and social development. The best items were kept in a short version with four domains of parenting: affection, responsiveness, encouragement, and teaching. Practitioners in several in-home parenting support programs tried out the PICCOLO measure with parents in their programs. The information from this measure is intended to be shared between a practitioner and parent in a strengths-based manner. Because all of the items are positive, the practitioner can begin by identifying positive behaviors that the parent is already doing consistently and asking when the parent can do them more often and what family activities offer opportunities to do them. By identifying activities in which the parent already does a behavior, the practitioner can find activities to suggest for the parent to do more often to support the child's development. The PICCOLO measure works particularly well in a developmental parenting framework.

The Home Observation Measure of the Environment (HOME) can be used to assess several aspects of the home environment that support a child's development. The HOME was developed by Bettye Caldwell and Bob Bradley at the University of Arkansas at Little Rock. The measure has been used for decades in early parenting intervention programs, but the version in current use was published in 1984. The HOME measures the quality and extent of stimulation available to a child in the home environment and includes subscales assessing organization of the environment, appropriate play materials, parental involvement, variety in daily stimulation, and avoidance of restriction and punishment. The HOME is administered by observation in the home and supplemented by a parent interview in the home. The parent can easily be involved in the observation with the practitioner.

Another example of a parent–child interaction rating scale is the Indicator of Parent–Child Interaction (IPCI) developed in 2006 by Kathleen Baggett, Judy Carta, and their colleagues at Juniper Gardens Children's Project in Kansas City. This scale was designed to track growth toward the general outcome of responsive interactions that promote positive social-emotional behaviors. The specific parent behaviors rated with this scale are the following: acceptance/warmth, descriptive language, follows child's lead, introduces/extends, stress-reducing strategies, criticisms/harsh voice, restrictions/intrusions, and rejects child's bid. In addition, several child behaviors are coded to provide the context for the parent behaviors and to better understand the interaction. The child behaviors that are rated with this scale are the following: positive feedback, sustained engagement, follow-through, overwhelmed by negative affect, external distress, and frozen/watchful/withdrawn. This rating scale requires training to be able to become a certified assessor. Once certified, however, a practitioner would be able to train others in the program as they complete the steps for certification. This instrument, although somewhat difficult to use because of the certification requirement, is quick to administer and provides useful information that can be shared with parents.

An easy alternative to more formal assessment is to videotape the parent and child doing something together. The videotape does not need to be long—a short video clip (10 to 15 minutes) provides a lot of rich information. The practitioner and parent can then use a systematic but simple way to record observations from the video clip, such as the See-Like-Add-Change-Plan Form (SLACP; see Figure 8.1). The practitioner then watches the videotape and completes the SLACP using the following steps: First, describe the behaviors observed between the par-

See-Like-Add-Change-Plan (SLACP) Form

What did you SEE (hear, learn, realize)?

_____

_____

_____

_____

What did you LIKE?

_____

_____

_____

_____

What would you ADD?

_____

_____

_____

_____

What would you CHANGE?

_____

_____

_____

_____

What are your PLANS? (continue on back as needed)

_____

_____

_____

_____

Figure 8.1. A blank See-Like-Add-Change-Plan (SLACP) Form.

ent and child ("See"). Second, write about the things the parent was doing that you liked ("Like"). Third, think about what the parent could have added to the interaction ("Add"). Fourth, after focusing on what was liked and what could be added, in terms of strength-based qualities, write about what could be different in the interaction ("Change"). Fifth and finally, use this information to plan for future visits ("Plan"). All of these steps can be done together with the parent, or the practitioner's observations can be discussed later with the parent. The parent–child observation with the SLACP should be done regularly. Keeping the information from the SLACP collected in a folder provides a record of parent–child interaction over time. Because the SLACP form can be used for a variety of purposes, we will discuss it again in Chapters 10 and 11.

CONCLUSION

Assessments are important tools for monitoring progress and providing intervention. The theory of change that guides a program should also guide the assessment process in order for the process to be relevant, meaningful, and effective. Involving a parent in all aspects of a child's assessments provides a more accurate picture to the parent of the child's development and more opportunities for the practitioner to encourage parent responsiveness and encouragement based on the parent's specific knowledge of the child's development. For developmental parenting programs, assessing parenting behaviors in addition to child development is critical for planning intervention strategies and monitoring individual progress toward desired outcomes.

9

Theories of Change for a Developmental Parenting Program

A good developmental parenting program needs a good theory of change. This chapter provides more detail and guidance for a developmental parenting program to develop a theory of change as a kind of logic model that identifies the goals of the program and the program's strategies for reaching those goals. Why does a practitioner working with parents need to know about theories of change? A program's theory of change, whether it is written down or just assumed, is what guides everything the program does. For the "front-line" staff members who work individually with families, knowing their program's theory of change makes it easier to do the job. By knowing exactly what strategies are recommended and what outcomes are intended, practitioners will have a clear vision of what to do and how to know if it is working.

Some programs have their goals and strategies written clearly in a document labeled "Theory of Change," some programs have a theory of change but call it something else, and some programs may think they do not have one in place but nevertheless, they have obvious goals and strategies. For a developmental parenting support program, a theory of change is particularly important because the approach is more complex than simply teaching children directly. Consider the following hypothetical conversation between a home visitor and a new acquaintance:

A Conversation with a Home Visitor

New acquaintance: What do you do for work?

Home visitor: I'm a home visitor for an infant–toddler program

New acquaintance: What's an infant–toddler program?

Home visitor: It's a program to help children develop better.

New acquaintance: So what do you do?

Home visitor: I visit families in their homes.

New acquaintance: Is that all?

Home visitor: Well, it's a complicated job. I visit all kinds of
        families, sometimes in bad neighborhoods and sometimes
        out in the middle of nowhere. Some families are doing
        okay or even pretty well, but some family members have
        serious problems getting or keeping a job or being
        depressed or fighting with each other or having a child
        with a disability or not having enough money for food.
        And every family is different, too. In the same week I
        might be working with a teen mom to make her
        crowded, one-room apartment safer for her crawling
        baby, with parents in a large family to have more
        conversations that get their 2–year-old talking, and with
        an anxious and depressed new mother to find moments
        to simply play with her baby. It can be pretty challenging.

New acquaintance: That's quite a lot to do. I thought you said
        you were just a visitor!

Although the term *home visitor* can be misleading, some of the alternative terms used in the field also lack clarity in their meaning. What do *family educators* educate about, and how do they educate families? *Child development specialists* must have specialized knowledge about the development of children, obviously, but what do they do with that knowledge? Why do any of these practitioners visit or educate or specialize? And what are they supposed to be doing when they do it? The answers to these kinds of questions are not in a practitioner's title but in the program's goals and strategies, in other words, in its *theory of change*.

WHAT IS A THEORY OF CHANGE?

Although theory of change has been discussed briefly throughout this book, this chapter delves into the concept more thoroughly. A theory of change is a series of clear statements or a diagrammed model of the program's *goals*—what changes the program is trying to make happen, and the program's *strategies*—what the program is doing to make those changes occur. A comprehensive theory of change also shows the *processes* of how the changes are expected to happen and what *additional factors* might help or hinder making those changes. For example, if an in-home program is focused exclusively on childhood nutrition, it might have goals for parents to serve nutritious food, for children to eat nutritious food, and for families to have positive mealtime experiences. The main strategies for the home visitor, then, could include helping parents plan nutritious meals and snacks, promote their children's good food choices, and prevent mealtime behavior problems. The processes could include the parents learning more about nutrition, acquiring more food preparation skills, and practicing more effective child behavior management. Additional factors could include family income, parent education, family culture, individual food preferences, and the developmental level of individual children. These components are the basic structure of a program's theory of change.

Theories of Change in Infant–Toddler Parenting Programs

Different models of in-home infant–toddler programs use different theories of change. In a child-focused model, goals typically promote better child development and strategies typically emphasize practitioner interactions with a child. In a parent-focused model, goals may aim toward greater self-sufficiency and well-being, and strategies typically emphasize case management and emotional support for the parent. Either of these program models may include providing child development or parenting information, but not as a primary emphasis.

In a parenting-focused program, end *goals* may include those similar to the previous program models but will typically emphasize goals of more parent awareness of development, more parenting behaviors that support development, and greater parent adaptability to children's ongoing development over time. The program *strategies* are likely to involve

1. Helping parents observe developmental changes in children's behavior

2. Planning activities together that will involve parent–child interaction

3.   Helping parents identify learning opportunities in family routines and events

4.   Encouraging specific parenting behaviors that support child development

5.   Providing more information about child development generally so parents know what to expect and how to support their children's development as the children get older

The suggested goals to increase parents' awareness, support, and adaptability to children's development are part of a theory of change targeted to promote developmental parenting. Increasing the components of developmental parenting can be considered as the *processes* that bridge the strategies and goals of the model as parents become more aware of their children's development, more supportive of their children's development, and more flexible in adapting to their children's continuing development. *Additional factors* that could hinder (or help) the process include the children's health and development; the parents' ages, experiences, education, employment, and mental health; the families' household environments, social support networks and access to community resources; and the community's available resources.

All of the components of a theory of change may vary by program and may change over time within a program. The words and phrases used here for describing a possible theory of change make sense to the authors, but other words and phrases may be more meaningful for some practitioners working in the field or some administrators working with their program staff members to develop a theory of change. For a theory of change to be used in practical ways, it needs to make sense to the people using it. Keeping the ideas and language straightforward and simple will help practitioners use it. When the goals and strategies, in particular, are stated in clear language, the theory of change is likely to be more easily understood by parents who are participating in the program.

WHAT GOOD DOES A THEORY OF CHANGE DO FOR A PROGRAM?

Having a clearly articulated and explicitly stated theory of change benefits a parenting program in several ways. First, it makes practitioners more aware of the purpose and reasons for the program's strategies, including the general approach of working individually with families in their homes. From the theory of change, it should be clear why a parenting-focused model was selected and what kinds of techniques or specific strategies are expected to make the intended changes happen.

Second, it helps practitioners plan activities and select techniques and materials that are consistent with the goals and processes specified in the theory of change. Third and finally, when the unexpected happens, which can only be expected, the theory of change offers a clear guide to practitioners for problem solving "on their feet" when they are working in a family's home, often miles away from supervisors or other program support staff.

An intervention program is more likely to be successful if *everyone* working for the program understands how their services and activities fit with the program's theory of change. Programs develop strategies on the basis of their philosophy or theory about how to make changes in the lives of families and children. A written theory of change can be so valuable that if a program does not have a written theory of change, a practitioner may want to develop an individual one to discuss with a supervisor. The conversation may help both the practitioner and supervisor think about the best strategies for improving the practices by the practitioner and by the program in general.

At the very least, a theory of change specifies the outcomes expected and the activities believed to make those outcomes happen. A well-articulated theory of change also specifies what intermediate processes should occur or what the pathways are for change. In addition, a comprehensive theory of change specifies the additional factors that influence success or "what works best for whom." In other words, it includes what to do to get the outcomes hoped for and what assumptions are made about why that will work and what might get in the way. It specifies a theoretical model that includes outcomes, strategies, process pathways, and the additional factors that are often beyond our control, but may influence the effectiveness of the program. These components of a theory of change can guide problem solving when the program is not working well for a particular family or when the program is floundering because of funding changes, staff changes, or community changes. A review and revision of the theory of change will help a program adapt to change and remain responsive to family needs while still staying focused on the program's goals.

By stating the parts of a theory of change explicitly, a program also can better guide any evaluations to measure whether the program is succeeding at what it is trying to do and whether it is actually using the strategies it planned to use. In this way, the program can avoid the use of inappropriate outcome standards that focus more on children's developmental milestones simply because they are easily measured. Instead, the program can guide or design program evaluations to include measures of intended changes in parent–child interactions and parenting behaviors.

HOW DOES A PROGRAM
DEVELOP A THEORY OF CHANGE?

A worksheet to help programs develop their own theory of change is included in Figure 9.1. We presented the theory of change for this book in Chapter 2 and you can refer to that for ideas. We recommend, however, that each program develop its own theory of change using the ideas and words of the program staff members. As you develop your own theory of change, review the theory of change in Chapter 2 and discuss what you like and what could be added or changed.

To develop a theory of change, a program needs to specify the following:

1. Intended outcome *goals* for participants as a result of the program

2. Intended *strategies* for making those changes

3. Assumed *process*es by which the changes occur

4. *Additional factors* that may help or hinder the changes

See Figure 9.2 for a diagram illustrating these aspects of a theory of change.

The first question to ask to get thinking about the *goals* of a theory of change is this: "How will families who are in your program change?" It may be useful to think about how participants in the program will end up different from those who are not in the program. Practitioners typically can list multiple outcomes they believe will be changed by their program, including both parent and child outcomes. They may believe that the parents who are in the program, compared with those who are not, will become happier, more knowledgeable, less stressed, and more confident about themselves as parents. They may believe that as a result, the children in the program will be healthier, happier, more secure, and smarter. Because some outcomes are assumed but not necessarily talked about very much, it is important to consider a wide range of potential outcomes of a program. If the list of potential outcomes is initially long, it may be a useful strategy to discuss the most important outcomes to target. But it is more valuable to generate a longer list first and select the most important goals than to try to generate more thoughts about outcomes later.

The second question for identifying program *strategies* is this: "What exactly will the program do to make those changes happen?" This question is more difficult than the first one because it requires an examination of the links between program activities and the kinds of changes the program hopes to make in parents and children. By listing the activities already in place for the program, it becomes easier for practitioners to consider how each of those activities can be linked to particular outcomes for parents. For example, practitioners may believe that by providing information about children's cognitive development, parents will become more knowledgeable, and children will become smarter—or better developed cognitively. By specifying which program strategies or activities are expected to lead to which program outcomes or goals, practitioners are likely to become more aware of how to individualize their practices to the needs of each family. Parents who already have some knowledge may need only a little more, whereas parents who have very little knowledge may need quite a bit more basic information.

By listing the program goals first, practitioners may become aware of intended outcomes that are not well supported by program activities. Practitioners may become more aware of which activities are the most critical for making changes happen in families, but they may also discover gaps in their program's theory of change. For example, providing information about development to parents may increase parents' knowledge but not help them identify learning opportunities for their children. The parents may learn about development but still need help in applying that knowledge to support their children's development in their everyday lives. By considering the program's theory of change, it may then become apparent that more strategies are needed to help parents apply information about children's development.

The third question for identifying program *processes* is this: "How exactly will those activities make those changes happen?" This question is even more difficult. Practitioners can describe what they will do on home visits, the content of what they will teach parents, and the kinds of parent–child activities they will plan with parents. How these strategies will make changes happen may be less obvious. The process mechanism for more detailed or subtle strategies is likely even less clear. Practitioners typically have learned a lot about child development, infant and family health, social services, and how to do all of the paperwork. But they may not have a clear idea of the mechanisms of change. They know they are supposed to make home visits to parents and that parents and infants are supposed to be affected by the program, but they may not have considered exactly how the specific things they do on home visits will lead to specific program outcomes. Those who designed the program originally may have had a clear vision of the program, but those who have the responsibility for working directly with families need to see it just as clearly if they are to make the program work.

Finally, program staff members need to consider *additional factors* by answering this question: "For whom will the program work best and for whom might it not work as well?" The program needs to consider

Worksheet to Develop a Theory of Change

What are the main goals of your program?

_____

_____

Why do you believe the program CAN do that?

_____

_____

How do you expect the children in the program to be different from children not in the program. . .

at 1 year? _____

_____

at 2 years? _____

_____

at 3 years? _____

_____

How do you expect parents in the program to be different from parents not in the program . . .

after 1 year? _____

_____

after 2 years? _____

_____

after 3 years? _____

_____

Figure 9.1.   Worksheet to develop a theory of change.

How will your program make these changes happen for children?

_____

_____

How will your program make these changes happen for parents?

_____

_____

What will YOU do, in your job role, to make these changes happen?

_____

_____

_____

WHY do you think it will work? What will the PROCESS be for making changes happen?

_____

_____

_____

For WHOM (which families) will it work best? What ADDITIONAL FACTORS will help or hinder change?

_____

_____

_____

WHAT needs to happen in order make the program work best for everyone?

_____

_____

_____

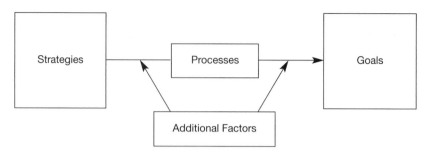

Figure 9.2.   Program theory of change.

factors that may help or hinder the process of change, either the impact of the program's strategies on the change processes or the impact of those processes on the program's goals. By discussing those things that may help parents get more out of the program, perhaps factors such as good parent mental health or a stable living situation, practitioners readily identify the opposite, the things that hinder parents getting something out of the program, such as a mother being depressed or having a history of negative interactions with her child. By identifying these factors, practitioners are prepared to consider ways of taking advantage of things that help and finding ways past the barriers presented by things that hinder. Programs often have their own words and phrases that describe their program. So when a program's staff members develop their own theory of change, it often has more meaning to them than a theory of change they adopt from another source. The theory of change shown in Figure 9.3 was developed by a program we worked with on a home visiting project.

Some programs may want to add other components to their theory of change. It may be helpful to examine and discuss the assumptions underlying the theory of change. What is the problem that this program is assuming can be solved? For example, a program may assume that parents simply lack information about child development. By basing their theory of change on that assumption, they would likely emphasize strategies for providing more information to parents. If the goals are not met as predicted, then one way to figure out why is to consider whether the underlying assumptions are correct. Perhaps parents do know a lot about child development but aren't using what they know for other reasons, such as family stress or difficult parent–child relationships. To use a theory of change in this way requires stating the often unstated assumptions as part of the written theory of change.

How will you know if the theory of change is a good theory? Good theories have evidence. Programs can identify ways to measure the

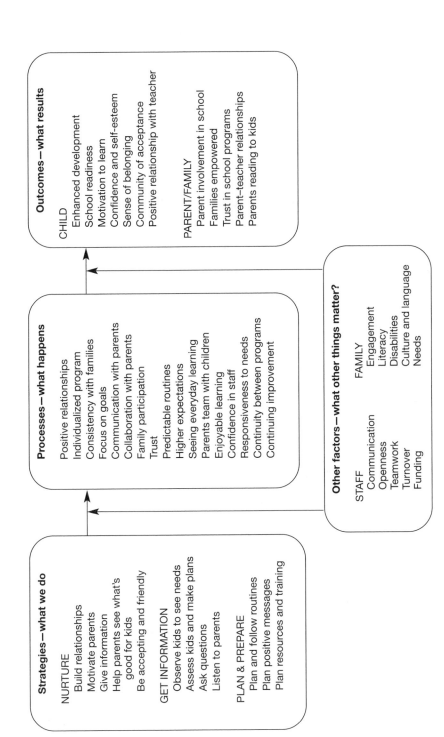

Strategies—what we do

NURTURE
Build relationships
Motivate parents
Give information
Help parents see what's
   good for kids
Be accepting and friendly

GET INFORMATION
Observe kids to see needs
Assess kids and make plans
Ask questions
Listen to parents

PLAN & PREPARE
Plan and follow routines
Plan positive messages
Plan resources and training

Processes—what happens

Positive relationships
Individualized program
Consistency with families
Focus on goals
Communication with parents
Collaboration with parents
Family participation
Trust
Predictable routines
Higher expectations
Seeing everyday learning
Parents team with children
Enjoyable learning
Confidence in staff
Responsiveness to needs
Continuity between programs
Continuing improvement

Outcomes—what results

CHILD
Enhanced development
School readiness
Motivation to learn
Confidence and self-esteem
Sense of belonging
Community of acceptance
Positive relationship with teacher

PARENT/FAMILY
Parent involvement in school
Families empowered
Trust in school programs
Parent–teacher relationships
Parents reading to kids

Other factors—what other things matter?

STAFF
Communication
Openness
Teamwork
Turnover
Funding

FAMILY
Engagement
Literacy
Disabilities
Culture and language
Needs

Figure 9.3.   Theory of change model developed for home visiting program.

goals, strategies, processes, and additional factors in their theory of change. Measuring goals is a standard part of tracking program outcomes, but many programs neglect to measure their strategies. Chapter 11, on evaluating and improving developmental parenting support programs, offers multiple ideas for measuring strategies. Information about additional factors such as parent age, education, and so forth, is usually available from application forms or other program records. Use these sources of information along with the theory of change to determine when and how a program has its intended impact and when and why it is not having its intended impact. See if the evidence supports the theory of change.

To use a theory of change for building and improving an effective program, those who put the program into practice need to read the theory of change regularly. This means it should be short and easy to read. A long series of dense paragraphs will not be read very often. A short series of clear statements or a diagram with key words is likely to be read more often. Sometimes a theory of change is diagrammed in different ways.

Figure 9.4 shows an example of a program's theory of change model that looks very different than the theory of change model for a developmental parenting support program shown in Chapter 2. Nevertheless, this diagram clearly implies a parenting support program and suggests particular strategies for making changes in parents and families.

Using a Theory of Change

By saying clearly, in writing, what is supposed to happen as a result of a program's activities and what exactly the practitioners are expected to do to make it happen, the program can use a theory of change model to guide its planning, practice, and problem solving. A theory of change that is filed away somewhere does not do much good. It needs to be out and available to be read frequently. A program's theory of change can inform staff training plans, indicate what resources practitioners need to do their jobs, guide budget allocations, and provide a framework for writing proposals for funding. A written theory of change can suggest supervision needs, targets for staff and program evaluations, and data needed as part of ongoing program documentation. When practitioners, families, or the program in general are struggling and getting off track, a written theory of change can help focus the discussion of ways to get back on track.

By defining the strategy in measurable terms, the program has provided a way to accurately measure, by direct observation, whether it is actually doing what it said it they would do. By identifying the intended

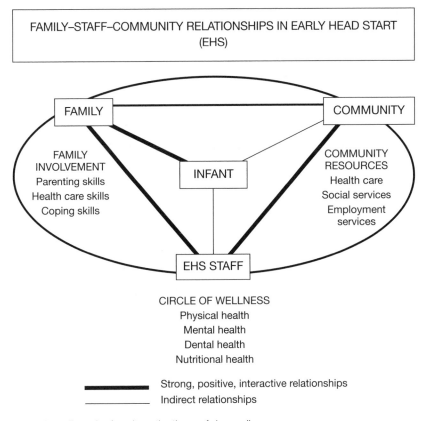

FAMILY–STAFF–COMMUNITY RELATIONSHIPS IN EARLY HEAD START
(EHS)

FAMILY

COMMUNITY

FAMILY
INVOLVEMENT
Parenting skills
Health care skills
Coping skills

INFANT

COMMUNITY
RESOURCES
Health care
Social services
Employment
services

EHS STAFF

CIRCLE OF WELLNESS
Physical health
Mental health
Dental health
Nutritional health

——————   Strong, positive, interactive relationships
——————   Indirect relationships

Figure 9.4.   Example of an alternative theory of change diagram.

strategies, practitioners can be guided in a self-evaluation of the effectiveness of the strategies they are using. Also, programs can get feedback from parents about how often particular strategies are used, how well those strategies are working, and which strategies parents prefer. For example, in our program partner with a primary goal of improving parent–child relationships, videotapes of home visits showed the strategies practitioners were using to improve parent–child interactions. By reviewing videotapes and reflecting on when the strategies were working and when they were not working, practitioners were better able to make changes toward a more effective program.

Revising a Theory of Change

After a theory of change is developed and written, it will need to be reviewed and revised regularly. We have revised our theory of change for developmental parenting programs several times as we considered our vision for developmental parenting programs and the words we wanted to use to describe our vision. Ongoing revisions to a theory of change reflect the ongoing development of a program as improvements and refinements are made. For example, one of our partner programs shifted from the first to the second year of the program from a primary strategy of mostly staff–parent discussion and relationship building toward an emphasis on more targeted intervention activities that required direct interactions between parents and their infants and toddlers. From the second to the third year, this program's strategies expanded toward getting fathers more involved and increasing family independence by helping both mothers and fathers plan the activities to do with their infants and toddlers both during home visits and between home visits.

A theory of change is not meant to be a final product. By regularly reviewing and revising a written "vision" of the program, the practitioners who work in a program can continue improving and fine-tuning their efforts to increase the quality of their program from year to year. As children and parents develop, so do programs. By being aware of their program's goals, strategies, processes, and additional factors that affect program outcomes, practitioners will continue to move forward on their own developmental path. For practitioners, regular review and self-assessment can provide feedback toward acquiring more of the attitudes, behaviors, and content for home visits that effectively facilitate developmental parenting.

CONCLUSION

As a written and graphic description of program goals and strategies, a theory of change model guides program planning, implementation, and evaluation. From the very beginning of the program, the process of developing a theory of change helps practitioners and other program staff to clarify the purpose and procedures of their program. Once the program is underway, these written goals and strategies provide guidance for practitioners who often must make good decisions during home visits miles away from their supervisors and program managers. The processes and additional factors described in the theory of change offer ideas for solving problems when the program is not effective for some families. Regular review and revision of the theory of change offers opportunities for making the goals more specific, the strategies more concrete, the processes better understood, and the additional factors better recognized. Finally, a program's theory of change provides a starting point for supervising practitioners and making program improvements over time.

10

Managing and Supervising a Developmental Parenting Program

In a Dilbert cartoon about supervision, the boss is reprimanding an employee, Alice, about her mistreatment of co-workers. The boss tells her a theory that by talking to her, her personality will be altered. Alice starts fuming and the boss comments, "If you feel something, it's just your DNA changing." Although the cartoon is a joke, it reflects a common perception that one can change a person's behavior just by talking to him or her. Those who are engaged in the process of supervision (or who are home visitors or have children) know it is not that simple. Supervision is a skill like any other. There are things that make it go well. There are things that make it not go well. When it goes well, program staff do their jobs well, the work atmosphere is pleasant, and work life is good. When it goes poorly, program staff turnover is high, people are stressed, and work life is not good. This chapter will provide some tools and suggestions to make supervision go well.

The focus of this chapter is on those who supervise, but understanding supervision is not just for supervisors. Supervision is about relationships in programs. Generally, this implies that those people with more experience are helping those with less experience. In a trusting program, an atmosphere should be maintained in which all staff members participate in the process regardless of their experience level. All program staff members, and not just supervisors, can benefit by understanding the supervision relationship.

The ideas in this chapter are based on an approach called *reflective supervision,* described in 1991 by Victor Bernstein and his colleagues.

The primary assumption behind reflective supervision is that it is a parallel process. *Parallel process* means that supervisors behave toward practitioners in the way that the supervisors would want the practitioners to behave with the parents with whom they work. The 1998 quote by Jeree Pawl and Maria St. John in a book by ZERO TO THREE, "Do unto others as you would have others do unto others," a slight twist on the Golden Rule, states the process simply.

> "Do unto others as you would have others do unto others."
>
> –Jeree Pawl and Maria St. John

Reflective supervision uses the techniques of facilitation that we have discussed throughout this book. The same techniques that are effective at facilitating developmental parenting can also be effective in facilitating effective practices by practitioners working with parents. If supervisors want practitioners to ask open-ended questions, then supervisors must ask open-ended questions. If supervisors want practitioners not to make assumptions about the beliefs behind parent behaviors, then supervisors must not make assumptions about the beliefs behind practitioners' behaviors. This principle is easy to describe but takes practice to do well.

MANAGEMENT VERSUS SUPERVISION

A supervisor in a focus group once said that "Management is paperwork, supervision is people-work." This is true to a point, but there is more to management than paperwork. One way to think about management versus supervision is to reflect on our approach to working with families. Children need both caregiving and nurturance. *Caregiving* is providing care for a child's physical needs (food, sleep, warmth) and environmental needs (a routine, a safe place to live). *Nurturance* is providing care for a child's emotional needs (affection, responsiveness) and mental health. A child can live with caregiving and not nurturance. But a child will only thrive if she or he has both caregiving *and* nurturance. This same framework applies to being a supervisor. Consider management as caregiving and supervision as nurturance. For program staff to thrive, they need good management, or caregiving of the structural support of the program, and also good supervision, or nurturance, of the staff members.

To begin, consider the perspectives of practitioners. In a focus group, practitioners were asked what supervisor supports are especially helpful. Certain themes emerged during their discussion that define a good supervisor as someone who does the following:

1. Listens willingly to the problem

2. Helps by serving as a mediator

3. Goes on home visits and offers input on what is and is not working well

4. Provides constant training to keep practitioner skills updated

5. Takes time in a crisis to offer solutions to the problem

6. Makes him- or herself available even when he or she is not at the office

7. Asks for the outcomes of a difficult home visit

8. Is flexible and dependable

9. Provides weekly meetings with all practitioners to discuss practices

10. Provides information in new areas

11. Provides materials for the practitioner to use as activities

12. Seeks ways to improve the program and better serve families

This list contains some things that would fall under the category of supervision and some that would fall under management, so some definitions may help. In the facilitative framework, management is what is set up to implement one's theory of change. Management ensures that the program requirements are met (e.g., number of visits, length of visits, paperwork requirements) and that quality is monitored. Management is making sure that program outcomes are measured. Management is making sure that practitioners have the links to community collaborators to refer parents as needed and to keep staff informed of what is available for families. Management is making sure that practitioners do the things they need to in order for their programs to survive.

Supervision is the process of helping practitioners stay focused on the program's theory of change. It is the use of continuous process improvement (discussed in the next section); it is setting up a feedback loop by which supervisors know that practitioners are doing what they should be doing. It is doing all of this while maintaining positive relationships. It is the process of making training part of the supervision process. It is how training, support, and problem solving are blended into every meeting with program staff members. Supervision emphasizes strengths, not only within the families being served but also within the practitioners. It is the process of allowing practitioners, not the supervisors, to solve the problem. Supervision is what helps people thrive in the workplace.

Management

Many aspects of management are basic to the running of any program: designing the right qualifications to look for in the practitioners hired, the number of times practitioners must meet with families in a given time period, and how long these visits must last. An effective supervisor knows what types of information are needed in order for the program to stay funded. He or she knows what types of paperwork must be completed and what times of year to keep the program's doors open.

A reflective supervision framework needs to include management activities such as the following:

1. A practitioner needs a regular place and time to meet with the supervisor. Supervision needs structure.

2. A practitioner needs multiple opportunities to have access to the supervisor. Some of these opportunities will happen in regular meetings, but a practitioner needs to know that he or she can come to the supervisor with concerns or problems as they arise. This is not to imply that a supervisor always needs an open-door policy, but structure that supports access is needed.

3. A supervisor needs to have efficient, supportive, and stimulating meetings to be effective. A practitioner's time should be respected, just as a supervisor would want his or her time respected. Meetings scheduled for a certain time should start and end on time. An agenda helps keep the meeting on track. Everyone at the meeting needs to participate.

4. Practitioners and supervisors need to work together in a respectful, positive, and facilitative atmosphere. Practitioners need to share ideas. Supervisors need to help solve problems with the group. The focus needs to be on strengths.

5. The program needs feedback. There must be a mechanism for frequent feedback on the strategies and processes in the program's theory of change. For example, in some programs the supervisor goes on a home visit with each practitioner twice per year, and practitioners videotape one home visit every other month for review in a staff meeting. Program expectations need to be clear about how supervisors will monitor the program's strategies and processes.

6. Families and staff need to know what the program does. Families must be made aware from the first program contact that the program is focused on developmental parenting (and whatever else practitioners may do as part of their theory of change). Parents

need to know how often videotaping will occur. Parents need to have a basic understanding of the program's theory of change so they know what to expect. If a practitioner describes the theory of change to a parent, then both the practitioner and the parent know what to expect. Some programs offer parents more services than they can deliver to get them in the door. This is unfair to the parents and the program staff. Decide on the theory of change and follow through with it. Evaluations of unsuccessful programs found that the expectations of the parents, the program staff, and the supervisors didn't match up. Parents thought the program did one thing, the staff another, and the supervisors thought something else was going on. Clarity and consistency across levels is needed for success.

7. Families need respect. There must be an attitude of respect for the family, for the family's culture, and for the family's privacy. This same attitude of respect must apply to program staff as well.

8. The program staff members need to have positive attitudes focused on improvement. We worked with some programs that had different levels of success. An independent evaluator interviewed staff from the different programs. The staff of less successful programs felt that the families were difficult or lacking in some way, and that the program's job was to keep families from falling further behind. The successful programs saw the parents as people who had skills and that their goal was to get them to be all they could be. Attitude does make a difference.

9. The program needs to develop ways to recognize and celebrate good work. This is more than sending gratuitous "Good work" messages quarterly. A real emphasis and celebration of high-quality work needs to be established.

Supervision

As part of a project focused on using strengths-based approaches to home visiting, the third author was invited to observe a supervision session. The supervisor, who had many years of experience, told us how she always used a strengths-based approach. One home visitor described a family with which she was having difficulty. After she described her session, the supervisor went on to tell her that families from this ethnic group were "all like that." The supervisor told the home visitor how she needed to go in and take charge, and gave her ideas for doing so. Another home visitor spoke next and talked about a family of the same ethnic group with whom she was having success, but she talked about what was working for her. The supervisor told her that her approach was wrong and told her some of the things she needed to do. The home visitors sat quietly for the remainder of the meeting and only answered questions from the supervisor. Not surprisingly, this program had a very high staff turnover rate.

It is hard to see the strengths in the observation just described. In a 1992 book on supervision, Emily Fenichel identified three characteristics of successful supervision. Supervision must be

1. *Regular*: The time for it needs to be respected.

2. *Reflective*: Supervision needs to provide a chance for practitioners to reflect on what is happening in their work with families and children.

3. *Collaborative*: Supervisors must foster partnerships based on mutual trust between all parties including practitioners, other staff members, and the supervisors themselves. The supervisor in the example just described may have been regular but was not being reflective or collaborative.

Some of our ideas about supervision overlap with our ideas about management. The distinction becomes clearer when one again considers management as caregiving and supervision as nurturance. Caregiving does overlap with nurturance. These concepts are not mutually exclusive. Changing an infant's diapers is a caregiving activity that can be all business or it can include nurturance activities of talking with the infant, massaging the infant, and playing with the infant. Nurturance is the harder, but more important, task.

We frequently serve families who come to us with difficulties. It is sometimes hard not to feel the stress the family feels. It can be hard to walk out the door and not worry about what will happen to the family after we leave. Practitioners need nurturance to continue to focus on parent–child relationships and to be able to support developmental parenting in the face of very real and very stressful life events.

One way to think about supervision as nurturance is to consider the mutual competence perspective. Mutual competence is discussed in Chapter 2 on building a facilitative developmental parenting program, but this chapter reinforces some of the key points of the theory as it applies to supervision. Mutual competence is defined by interactions that enable both the parent and the child to feel secure, valued, understood, successful, and happy—the parent and child enjoy learning together. A practitioner demonstrates mutual competence when he or she engages in interactions with a parent in which both practioner and parent feel valued, understood, successful, and happy, and the practitioner can observe the parent and child interacting in the same way—the practitioner and parent enjoy learning together.

Mutual competence is a parallel process. Supervision is a mutual-competence process, taken one step away from the practitioner–parent process, itself a step away from the parent–child process. The supervisor and practitioner want a mutually competent relationship so that the practitioner can do his or her job well, which, in turn, results in the parent and child having more successful interactions. This is the parallel process in practice. A mutual-competence perspective has several key components in the supervisor–practitioner relationship. Both the practitioner and supervisor should benefit from their interactions. A need of both is met. The practitioner needs support to implement the program's theory of change. The supervisor wants to see the theory of change implemented well.

The supervisory relationship needs to be pleasant. This does not mean that we are recommending avoiding difficult topics. Similar to how a parent needs to work with a child even when the child is being difficult, the practitioner sometimes needs to discuss difficult topics with the parent. The supervisor needs to do the same with the practitioner when necessary. However, this discussion needs to occur in an atmosphere of mutual trust and mutual respect.

Key Components of Mutual Competence in Reflective Supervision

• The staff person and supervisor both benefit from their interactions.
 –Mutual needs are met.

• The supervisory relationship is generally pleasant.
 –Mutual trust and mutual respect are established.

• Supervisory interactions are effective based on
 –Clear communication
 –Good manners
 –Respect for time
 –Mutually defined outcomes

Finally, supervisory interactions need to be effective. There needs to be clear communication, good manners, and respect for time in supervisor–practitioner interactions. Some of these responsibilities fall under the area of management, but some are based on communication between both parties. Both the supervisor and practitioner need to identify outcomes they are trying to meet in their interactions with each other.

The end goal of establishing mutually competent relationships is that parents and children make progress. The process is getting the program's theory of change to happen in a way that helps everyone work well. When this comes together, the program will be successful.

What Are Supervisory Behaviors? Supervision can be viewed as a position of power. There is a hierarchy in most organizations, and a supervisor typically has more power than a practitioner. A supervisor must be aware of this discrepancy. In our model, the supervisor must be a nurturer. This reflects the power discrepancy between parents and children, but within the developmental parenting model, parents should be encouraged to use their strengths to build strengths in their children. Similarly, supervisors should nurture the strengths in practitioners in their programs so that the practioners are better at facilitating developmental parenting with parents. Supervisors want to improve practitioners' self-confidence in doing their work so that they can increase the self-confidence of parents in doing the work of parenting.

Question:

What kind of communication and behavior is helpful between supervisor and program staff?

Answer:

Any communication or behavior that makes the program staff feel secure, valued, and successful.

There are three primary steps that lead to good reflective supervision practice.

Step 1: Establish the theory of change as the basic set of assumptions about how the program works. Earlier in this book, we discussed developing a program's theory of change. The theory of change represents basic assumptions about what a program does and how all program staff should act in their jobs. Everyone needs to be clear on what the theory of change is from the very beginning. This includes practitioners, supervisors, other staff, administrators, and parents. Initially this may be expressed in words, but it should become clearly expressed in the practices of those who work for the program.

Step 2: Establish a shared approach to communication. The approach to communication is the same as the one discussed throughout this book. Practitioners know the families better than the supervisor. Practitioners are the experts on the families. A supervisor's role is to make them more efficient experts through reflective listening. Here are some of the key communication approaches for supervisors to use.

1. Really listen to those being supervised regardless of agreement or disagreement. Sometimes supervisors will need to allow disagreements and then wait to see how the process develops and collect information about outcomes.

2. Never make assumptions about a practitioner's underlying reasons for what he or she is doing. Ask questions to get at the practitioner's beliefs about the practice.

3. Establish an atmosphere of experimentation. Allow practitioners to make mistakes and to learn from mistakes.

4. Ask about what worked, what did not work, and what the differences between these strategies were. This can be one of the most powerful communication techniques that supervisors use.

5. Don't solve problems. Solving problems establishes the supervisor as the expert; this is not an effective supervisory role. A supervisor once told me, "I really like asking questions so that the change for strategies or behavior comes from them instead of me." Change is always more meaningful when it comes from within.

6. Use these simple but powerful techniques regularly. If supervisors can use them regularly, practitioners will also use them regularly with parents.

Step 3: Ensure accountability. The things for which a supervisor is accountable come from the program's theory of change. Accountability is not something based only on information about the progress being made by the parent or child. There also needs to be accountability for the processes used by the practitioner and the supervisor. If a practitioner does not do what the theory of change indicates and the child does not make gains, then these are some of the accountability indicators. Accountability is discussed in more detail in Chapter 11.

Steps in the Supervisory Process   Victor Bernstein and colleagues, in 2001, identified steps for the supervisory session, and these
are adapted for use in this developmental parenting model. His steps
were designed for use in a supervisory session between a supervisor
and one staff person. Some programs may have several practitioners in
a supervisory session. This can be a powerful way to share perspectives
and maintain the theory of change. Practitioners can learn from each
other. However, a supportive environment is required. Practitioners
must be comfortable sharing successes and failures. The role of the supervisor takes on added importance in setting this tone. The final decision on how supervision will occur is part of management. Regardless,
even in a group setting a supervisor can only work on one family situation at a time. These steps can help guide the process.

Step 1: Let the practitioner describe how a session with a family went. This is a
time for listening to the practitioner's perceptions.

*Step 2: Ask the practitioner to discuss the session by focusing on the behaviors
that happened.* Bernstein talks about this as playing a "home movie."
The supervisor can encourage the practitioner to "play the movie" by
describing the actual behaviors. This is not the time to make assumptions but to ask for information on why the practitioner or parent may
have done certain things. If the practitioner makes assumptions
about the parent's behavior, then the supervisor can mention it. Try
to base the discussion on observed behavior, not assumptions.

Step 3: Find out what worked. Now is the time to ask about what worked
and what did not. Have the practitioner reflect on the differences between these. What was happening when the session was working
versus when it was not? Emphasize the positive. The main focus
needs to be on strengths. Supervisors and practitioners need to look
at what *did not* work only to better clarify what *did* work.

Step 4: Engage in reflective listening. Check to see if the message was heard
correctly. Restate what was heard to the practitioner. Let the practitioner correct the message as needed. Bernstein identifies three types
of statements that help the process. A supervisor can make statements that *normalize* by describing a similar experience that happened to the supervisor. A supervisor can *appreciate* by describing
those things seen as working effectively. A supervisor can *rotate* by offering a different perspective on what may be occurring. A supervisor can also use combinations of these three types of statements.

Step 5: Ask the practitioner to identify the next steps to be followed. This is part
of accountability. This is where the supervisor and the practitioner
plan for the next session the practitioner will have with the family.

Step 6: Ask the practitioner for feedback on today's supervision. When the supervisor gets some feedback on what worked and what did not, this gives him or her the opportunity to see what works best for this practitioner.

Step 7: Follow up at the next supervisory session. Follow up with the practitioner at his or her next supervisory session to see if the plan discussed was implemented. The family may not need to be discussed in detail, but the conversation should set a tone for accountability.

Each of these steps is part of a process that supervisors should repeat regularly. Practitioners can expect this each time they get together with a supervisor. Each step is important and needs to be followed. Sometimes the supervisor may want to skip a step, but this can be counterproductive. Supervisors sometimes want to skip Step 6, regarding asking for feedback on the supervision, but this step provides an opportunity for role change and demonstrates respect for the practitioner's opinion. The follow-up in Step 7 can sometimes be difficult, but a supervisor should be sure to revisit the plan to demonstrate that he or she thought the plan was important and is interested in the outcome. Each step is important to the supervisory process.

If multiple staff members participate in this process, then they must all be aware of the process and how it proceeds. Other staff members can ask questions and engage in reflective listening along with the practitioners. They can also be helpful during the planning step. To include other staff members, everyone in the supervisory session must demonstrate mutual respect and trust.

Video: A Powerful Tool

The most powerful tool for supervision is the video camera. Video as a tool can be used at many levels. Chapter 7 discusses videotaping parents as a way to observe parent–child interaction and provide feedback using the SLACP form. Similarly, practitioners can videotape their interactions with parents and children on home visits. This can be watched as part of the supervisory process. Supervisors can also videotape a supervisory session to observe their own supervisory skills. Video can be a powerful tool for evaluating parent–child interaction, practitioner–family interaction, or supervisor–practitioner interaction.

For supervision purposes, it is best if a practitioner videotapes him- or herself interacting with a parent and child. The video camera can be set up to record the entire home visit, or the practitioner can select a particular time during the home visit to record. What should be recorded depends on the program's theory of change and approach to supervision. The supervisor can identify with the practitioner which part of a session with a family will be videotaped. The supervisor can ask the practitioner to videotape easy and difficult sessions or ones that are just average. Practitioners can rotate through their case loads. Videos can be reviewed individually or in a group setting with other practitioners. There are many options. The supervisor needs to see what works for the program, the practitioner being supervised, and the supervisor him- or herself.

Typically, people are very interested in their own behavior and that of people they know, especially when it is on video. Watching video-taped observations is more effective that just discussing home visits and much more effective than simulated videos purchased for training. Supervisors realize its strengths when they start to use this technique.

Some people initially resist using video as a tool, however. People worry initially about how they will look both physically and behaviorally. As long as the video is used within a reflective framework, people will become comfortable with it and even enjoy it. Just as with any expectation, the use of video with parents and practitioners needs to be made explicit from the start. Parents need to know when they enter the program. Practitioners need to know when they are hired. Making expectations explicit is part of the reflective process.

A framework we have found useful for reviewing videotapes is the SLACP form (See-Like-Add-Change-Plan)—which we discussed earlier in the book. Chapter 8 includes a blank SLACP form. As a reminder, the form asks what was *seen*, what was *liked*, what could be *added*, what could be *changed*, and finally, the *plan* for improvements. Doing the SLACP immediately after watching the video is effective because it serves as a guide for discussion. When multiple staff members are involved in supervision, then everyone would complete the SLACP.

The process after completing the SLACP form includes following the seven steps previously discussed, then incorporating whatever modification each program needs. During group supervision meetings we have found it helpful to go through the *See* and *Like* portions of the SLACP as part of Steps 2 and 3. The *Add* and *Change* responses are useful during reflective listening in Step 4, and the *Plan* is helpful for the planning process in Step 5.

Sustaining the Theory of Change   An experienced supervisor once said, "If we don't constantly talk about things, we fall back into old patterns." The supervisory process is important to sustain a theory of change, but there are things that can keep the theory of change alive in both more senior and newer staff people. Continuous training is one activity. In addition to supervising current cases, supervisors often need to help practitioners learn new things. The field is constantly changing. In this model, training needs to be a mutually identified activity and not a mandated one. Ask practitioners to identify areas in which they would like more information. Perhaps they want to know more about helping parents work on children's language skills or to learn more strategies for increasing responsive parenting. The impact of cultural background on parenting may be a concern. The topics are endless. Supervisors can identify topics that they have read about and suggest these. Let practitioners modify the ideas. Of course, there will be times when practitioners need more directive training—for example, if a new outcome measure is required for practitioners to use—but most training should be collaboratively identified.

Supervisors will need to identify people in the community who can provide training using reflective approaches. These people may come from colleges or from other programs. The program's own staff people may have expertise in certain areas. If consultants who work this way are not available, then it may be better to identify materials for program self-study. Pick staff members to lead topics that are of specific interest to them. (Be sure to give them work time to prepare.) Be flexible and get help as needed.

The key to learning is engagement. Practitioners need to be engaged in the process—talking, discussing, using their experience to identify examples, and applying new ideas to current families. Identify the frequency of training and what resources the program can provide for training. Continuous training lets program staff members discuss their theory of change as it relates to new topics. It allows program staff to grow in knowledge and as a team. There are other ways to sustain a program's theory of change. A simple activity is to have practitioners occasionally observe other practitioners working with parents on home visits or in other settings. These peer observations provide opportunities for practitioners to talk with each other about what they did and how it relates to the program's theory of change. Practitioners also can talk about their experiences in group supervision meetings and use the supervisory steps with each other.

Identifying mentors, especially for practitioners, can be a helpful training activity. A mentor should be a practitioner or another staff member who has experience with the program's theory of change. The mentor can occasionally accompany the new practitioner on a home visit. As the new practitioner becomes more familiar with the program, the mentor can be a familiar person to talk with when the supervisor is not available. Mentoring can help the mentor and new practitioner grow. The supervisor will need to discuss the mentoring experience with the mentor. Mentoring can be stressful, and the staff mentor will need to learn how to act as a peer supervisor. This can add to the supervisor's work but it has many benefits.

Another strategy can be used if a program has established community partnerships with other programs serving families. The programs can exchange home visit observations: A practitioner from one program can visit some families with a practitioner in the other program, and then practitioners from the second program can do the same in return. This provides rich opportunities to discuss theories of change and the similarities and differences between the approaches of the two programs.

What Works and What Does Not

Information needs to be regularly collected on child and parent outcomes, on practitioner behavior during sessions with families, and on supervisor behavior during supervisory sessions. Specific measures will be identified as part of a program's theory of change. This information needs to be shared and discussed regularly with practitioners to determine what effects the program is having. Supervisors and practitioners can use this information to refine practice and the program's theory of change. Simple measures such as the SLACP with videotaping will keep program staff focused on the daily activities of the program.

In a focus group with practitioners from different programs we asked what they liked as part of supervision and training. Here are some of the practices they found effective

1. Discussing new things

2. Getting everyone in the group talking and brainstorming solutions

3. Getting new information

4. Sharing ideas of what works

5. Reflecting critically on practice

6. Using the SLACP

7. Having a casual atmosphere

8. Having the supervisor ask questions that make us think

9. Using videotapes

Supervising the Supervisor

Just as practitioners need help to work effectively with families, supervisors may occasionally need someone to help them reflect on their supervisory practice. This is not easy. Administrators in a program may or may not be up to the task. Even if there are other supervisory colleagues in the same community, they may not share the same theory of change. Supervisors need to identify ways to get the help they need. Perhaps the program can provide supervisors with regular times with a mental health professional to discuss supervision issues. Supervisors need to find ways to protect their own mental health and to keep supervision skills focused.

Another approach is based on videos of supervisory sessions. Supervisors can self-evaluate or work with a senior staff person or an experienced administrator to review videotapes. By using the SLACP after observing videos of supervisory sessions, supervisors can learn much about their own practices. As with many of the ideas presented, supervisors need to find out what works given individual circumstances. Regardless of what resources are available, supervisors need to find a way to get support and feedback on their supervisory skills.

CONCLUSION

Management and supervision are essential supports for a developmental parenting program. They are part of any effective program and cannot be ignored. Key aspects of management and supervision have been discussed in this chapter. These are not unbending rules but rather, they are guidelines for supervisors and their programs. The aspects of management and supervision that have been discussed are powerful tools for implementing an effective developmental parenting program. Some will fit better than others as a program develops its own culture. Remember the question, "What kind of management and supervision is best for the program?" This question can only be answered, "Any management and supervision that makes the staff feel secure, valued, and successful." Then supervision will be facilitative, and the program will be successful.

11

Evaluating and Improving a Developmental Parenting Program

How do you know if a developmental parenting program is working? How do you know if the attitudes, behaviors, and content are actually facilitating developmental parenting? If outcome assessments show that parents in the program are better than parents not in the program at supporting their children's development, then it must be working. If the children in the program are developing better than children not in the program, then it is likely that the program is working. But if parents and children in the program are not any different than other parents and children, how will you know why not? And long before it is time to assess the final outcomes of the program, how will you know if it is working? How will you know if the attitudes, behaviors, and content are anything like what are being described in this book?

Developmental parenting programs involve working with parents, typically during home visits to families' homes. Evaluating the quality or effectiveness of a developmental parenting program often depends on what information is available about the home visits. Because home visiting happens in families' homes, however, home visits often are observed only by the families and the practitioners, not by anyone else. Documenting and recording what happens during each home visit, if this is done at all, is often left to the practitioner. As a result, many researchers have referred to home visiting as a "black box" because there is so little objective information available about what happens during home visits—what practitioners actually do, about what, and with whom. As a result, there is often little information available about the process, content, or interactions involved when practitioners deliver developmental parenting programs to families in their homes.

Many research studies have tested child or family outcomes from home visiting programs and have described program intentions in terms of what is supposed to happen during the program's home visits. Few studies, however, have reported data on what actually happened during the home visits, what strategies were used, what content was included, or even who was there. Practitioners themselves sometimes comment that "It's different in the real world," and more challenging than their supervisors may realize to provide the ideal home visit described in program materials. Information about the process, content, and quality of home visits can be useful for researchers, but it is even more valuable for the programs and practitioners themselves.

INFORMATION FOR PRACTITIONERS

When practitioners get feedback about how they are doing, they can use the information to build their skills. For practitioners, detailed information about their home visits can help them figure out if what they are doing is what they are supposed to be doing! Working with parents in their homes is not an easy job, and not one that most practitioners have seen many other people doing. New classroom teachers benefit from years of experience as students in classrooms with a range of teachers, and they can reflect on the teachers they learned from, were inspired by, or simply enjoyed. Few practitioners have ever had a home visit. Classroom teachers often learn many of their teaching skills by working alongside another teacher, but practitioners rarely have the opportunity to work as student-practitioners on a home-visiting team.

Practitioners can develop their skills by having information about the quality of their home visits. How can a practitioner get that information? One powerful way is by videotaping a home visit and watching it later. A less powerful but still helpful alternative is to have a supervisor or another practitioner observe a home visit, take notes, use rating scales, or talk about it later. Reviewing a video or an observer's description of the home visit is a powerful way for the practitioner to acquire and improve his or her skills. In many cases, it is the only way. Practitioners in the same program can benefit from comparing home visits made by different practitioners with different families. They can use the information to improve their skills and their home visits. Using videos was discussed in Chapters 8 and 10. The information in this chapter builds on what was discussed in these earlier chapters.

INFORMATION FOR PROGRAMS

Programs can improve by getting information about how effectively their services are delivered. For a program that uses home visiting to deliver services, information about what happens during the home visits helps everyone figure out if the program that was originally planned is the program that is truly happening. If a program's goal is to help parents support early language development, for example, then it is important to know if the interactions occurring and information provided during the home visits are helping parents do that. If not, what is getting in the way? To evaluate and improve the effectiveness of a home visiting program, it is essential to know what is actually happening when practitioners meet with families in their homes.

Information about what happens during home visits helps programs engage in a process of *continuous program improvement*. This is the accountability discussed in Chapter 10. A program that uses this process regularly gets information and systematically uses the information to evaluate and improve the program. The information is used in a continuous feedback loop to evaluate the program, make improvements, evaluate again, make more improvements, and so forth. Such a program keeps track of progress toward program goals and makes adjustments to make it more likely that the program will achieve those goals. When practitioners and their supervisors work together on continuous program improvement, the process of program evaluation becomes part of ongoing, supportive supervision and training. Using information about home visits to improve the program makes it more possible to reach program goals for all enrolled families.

Getting Information about Home Visits

Information about a program's home visits is available from several sources:

1. Practitioner records (lesson plans, visit documentation, self-evaluation of visits)

2. Parent report (satisfaction ratings, informal feedback)

3. Direct observation (live or videorecorded)

Each of these sources of information has advantages and disadvantages, but the combination of all of them provides the most complete picture of what actually happens on a program's home visits.

Home visit records are often used for planning and documenting service delivery. If these records are maintained and accurate, then they can provide useful information. Their disadvantage, however, is that they are of little use if they just sit in a filing cabinet. Compiling information across many home visits, which can be done by family members or by practitioner (or both), can reveal patterns of in-home service delivery and parent participation that may not otherwise be obvious.

Practitioner self-evaluations and parent satisfaction ratings are often biased by feelings about the parent–practitioner relationship, but even so, they offer information about the subjective sense of quality of home visits from the perspective of the people involved in them. The use of rating scales or checklists that can be added up offer a quantifiable measure of the quality of home visits, even if subjective.

Direct observation is less subjective and can be the most valuable measure of the home visit process. Someone other than the parent or practitioner can observe a home visit and use a systematic way of recording the quality of the visit. This more objective information can offer a rich source of data to evaluate and improve in-home parenting programs. If the observations are videotaped, then this information becomes more detailed and is also available at any time for additional observations, reflection, evaluation, and training for improving practitioner skills program-wide.

Each of these sources of information provides different types of information—from simple records of the quantity of home visits to rich, complex observations of all of the strategies used in home visits. These measures vary in terms of depth, objectivity, and necessary resources, but they can be used as outcome measures to guide continuous program improvement. Each of these sources will be discussed further.

Various measurement approaches can be represented by a pyramid that has as its base broad, easy, inexpensive measures and at its top in-depth, selective, time-intensive measures. Simple information about the number of home visits to each family, the topics discussed, and the activities planned is available in the paperwork of most programs. Videos of home visits are much harder to get but are the best information resources to have. What this means is that there is a "layer cake" of measurement alternatives (see Figure 11.1).

Program Documentation   The "paperwork" involved in any service program is often seen by practitioners as a burden they must bear as part of the opportunity to do meaningful work. This "burden" of paperwork is actually, however, a wonderful opportunity for making the work even more meaningful. For example, many in-home programs require practitioners to record what they plan to do during home visits on forms and to record afterward, often on other forms, what they actually did during the home visits. The completed forms are typ-

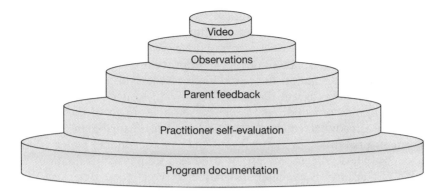

Figure 11.1.   Layer cake of measurement alternatives. At the base are measures easy to use but limited in depth of information; at the top are more difficult-to-obtain measures but which have richer information regarding process.

ically turned in to a supervisor who looks them over and then files them away. As a result, this valuable source of information is often under-used for improving practitioner skills and program services.

A program's documentation forms provide useful information about how often home visits occur, how long they last, what information is provided, what activities occur, what strategies and materials are used, which family members participate, and so forth. Practitioners and their supervisors can see from this information which families are getting the most services. They can also see which types and amounts of services seem to work best with which families and whether the services match the original design of the program. For example, a program may aim to promote parenting skills, but individual practitioners may plan most of the in-home activities for children to learn colors, shapes, and numbers, without planning strategies to help parents be more aware or supportive of their children's development. This discrepancy would help identify ways to improve the program.

Sometimes a program's service delivery is guided by the format of the program's forms more than supervisors realize. For example, a home visit documentation form could include places to indicate which family members participate in each activity. This information would help practitioners be more aware of which activities engage more of the family together and would regularly remind practitioners to involve more family members when possible. Similarly, having a place to record the materials used for each activity can guide practitioners to help parents learn to use materials they already have in their homes to support their children's development.

Practitioner Self-Evaluation   Practitioners who deliver in-home parenting support services are often quite aware of what is working and what is not. By documenting their awareness of effective and ineffective strategies, practitioners can improve their own skills, but by sharing that information they help improve the skills of other practitioners in their program. Programs may want to develop their own forms to guide practitioners in regular self-assessment of their work. We have already talked about the See-Like-Add-Change-Plan (SLACP) Form as a parenting assessment tool and as a practitioner supervision tool. The SLACP Form can also be used as a simple self-evaluation. A copy of the form is available in Chapter 8. Practitioners can use the form to describe what they see, hear, or feel during the visit; what they like about the home visit that went well or was effective; what they would change about the home visit to include other strategies or activities to improve the home visit process; and how they plan to improve their approach or strategies to be more effective.

By focusing first on the objective and positive aspects of the home visit, a practitioner is better able to consider improvements in the form of additions or changes that would make it even better. By ending with a plan, the practitioner is more likely to make the improvements based on this self-evaluation. These forms are completed by the practitioner and can be reviewed as program records. They can also be used for supervision purposes, as was discussed in Chapter 10.

Parent Feedback   Parents can provide valuable information for evaluating and improving developmental parenting programs. Parents can be thought of as the "customers" of a parenting support program. As such, they can report their "customer satisfaction." Parents enroll in such programs with certain expectations and hopes. If those expectations and hopes are met, then they are likely to be satisfied with the program. If, however, their expectations and hopes are not met, then they are likely to be dissatisfied. Expectations and hopes can be established during recruitment and may or may not match well with the program design. Nevertheless, by asking parents about their satisfaction with various aspects of the program, program staff can learn more about where they may be able to make program improvements.

A parent satisfaction questionnaire, Parent Satisfaction with the Home Visitor and Home Visits, is included in Appendix A of this book. Programs may want to develop their own survey to use that asks parents to give their opinions about specific things in a particular program. Parents also can be guided through a parent version of a SLACP Form that asks about their experience of home visits.

Observation and Videotaped Observation Imagine a classroom-based intervention in which the classroom activities are never observed by anyone other than the teacher and students. It may be difficult to imagine, yet there are home visits that are rarely observed by anyone except the practitioner and family. A parent may be reluctant to have more than one person in the home. A practitioner may be concerned that a fragile relationship with the family will be even more stressful by having an observer present during a home visit. Nevertheless, information from observations of home visits is essential for evaluating the effectiveness of a home visiting program. Observations are valuable for evaluating and improving home visiting programs, but they are also extremely valuable for training and supervising practitioners. For that reason, we strongly recommend the regular videotaping of home visits so that the observations can be repeated and reviewed. This process was discussed in detail in Chapters 8 and 10.

Although practitioners and families are sometimes reluctant to have home visits videotaped, the value of the videos for program improvement and staff development make it worth every effort to videotape regularly. The following tips may help programs increase the amount of home visit observation and videotaping:

1. Develop a clear program policy about how often home visits will be supervised, observed, and videotaped.

2. Let parents know when they apply to the program that home visits will be observed and videotaped from time to time and how often these things will happen.

3. Let practitioners know when they are hired that home visits will be observed and videotaped and how often these things will happen.

4. Let practitioners and families know well in advance when observation or videotaping visits will be scheduled.

5. Allow observation and videotaping visits to be rescheduled if needed.

6. Allow videotaping to be paused if needed.

7. Assure parents that the appearance of their family and home is not what is being observed, just the interactions with the practitioners and what the practitioners are doing.

8. Establish a supportive training and supervision approach that reassures practitioners that observation and feedback is not intended to judge them but to help them develop skills.

9.   Get signed permission from parents before using home visit videos
     to train other practitioners.

Videotaping is not always easy. Small, compact, easy-to-use video
equipment is now widely available at a reasonable cost, which makes
it somewhat easier. Nevertheless, conditions in family homes are not
always conducive to videotaping an observation of a home visit. See
the sidebar on videotaping tips for more recommendations for making
useful video recordings.

Videotaping Tips

- Use a tripod. It keeps the camera still and allows videotaping
  without a third person needed to operate the equipment,
  which sometimes helps families feel more comfortable.

- Don't point the camera at a window or bright space; it will
  make the people in the video look like they are just shadows
  in the dark.

- Include enough of people's faces and hands to tell what is
  going on.

- Focus in on the people who are actively engaged in the
  activities.

- Avoid noisy places, at least for visits being videotaped.

- Bring forms for parents to sign giving permission to use the
  videotapes for supervision and training.

Videos of home visits can also be viewed together with parents.
Sometimes when a parent or child was not fully engaged in the home
visit or when the interactions have been difficult or tense, it is useful to
watch together and look for the moments that went well and talk about
them with the parent. Once again, the SLACP process and form can be
used together with parents to evaluate home visits and plan new approaches that may work better with individual families.

Rating Videotaped Observations   What information can be gained
by observing a home visit? Actually, almost any information a program
wants or needs can be obtained from a home visit observation. System-

atic rating scales can be used to score the processes and strategies that the program intends to use. These ratings then provide detailed evaluations and suggestions for improvement. For example, if a program is focusing on helping parents support children's language development, then program staff may want to develop a scale to rate how effectively practitioners actually help parents support children's language development during home visits. Practitioners and supervisors can work together to describe what the behaviors look like for each point on a rating scale. For example, a low rating of *1* could mean that a practitioner didn't mention the child's language development at all, and a high rating of *5* could mean that the practitioner pointed out the child's language, observed and described how the parent responded to the child's language, and made suggestions to encourage additional ways for the parent to support the child's language practice.

The Home Visit Rating Scales (HOVRS) was originally developed by the authors and their colleagues at Utah State University, revised in 2006, and is included in Appendix B of this book. These scales have been used reliably, with observers showing inter-rater agreement over 85% (*kappa* > .75), and have been used to provide feedback to practitioners and supervisors for program improvement in several different in-home parenting support programs. The HOVRS includes seven rating scales, four for the actual home visit process and three for the engagement and interaction of parents and children during home visits. High scores on the home visit process scales, reflecting high-quality home visits, were correlated with positive outcomes for parents and children in a sample of families from two Early Head Start programs.

If program staff want to develop their own rating scales, then the following sequence is suggested. It is recommended that the new rating scales be developed collaboratively with the practioners. First, identify the primary goals of the program. Second, identify the strategies for meeting those goals. Third, describe what a practitioner's behavior looks like when those strategies are being used and are working well. This description is the starting point for the *high* end of the rating scale, so make the description as observable as possible. Fourth, describe how it looks when those strategies are not being used or are not working well. This description is the starting point for the *low* end of the rating scale and also needs to be as observable as possible. Finally, describe the points in between. Only one in-between point is needed, but some practitioners want more in-between ratings to be possible. When two different people give the same ratings to the same videotaped observation, then the rating scales are objective enough to use effectively for continuous program improvement.

Using the Information

All of this information can help guide and promote continuous improvements in developmental parenting programs using a facilitative approach. Information about how program services are delivered to each family is useful to the program staff members, parents in the program, or program evaluators. Any of these groups can review the goals of the program and use the information to assess progress toward those goals and make suggestions for continuous program improvement. Outside evaluators can use the information for a formal program evaluation, but practitioners and supervisors working in the program can use the information regularly and frequently for their discussions, work committees, and parent meetings. The information can also be used for planning for the program in general and for individual parent families in particular.

Regular program staff discussions about these sources of information are perhaps the most essential component of ongoing continuous program improvement. When these discussions are frequent and concerns are brought up right away, then practitioners can work together to generate and consider problem-solving strategies while problems are still small. A program's goals and strategies, as part of its theory of change, can guide these discussions and help practitioners make adjustments to their practices so that they clearly reflect the vision of the program. When practitioners use the information themselves to evaluate their programs, in contrast to feeling that the information is being used to evaluate *them,* they will be more likely to trust and be committed to the process of continuous program improvement.

CONCLUSION

To build and improve a developmental parenting program, practitioners and their supervisors need information about what actually happens when practitioners work with parents. There are several sources of information ranging from the limited information available on completed forms to document the services to the rich, detailed information available in videotaped observations of home visits. By reviewing this information regularly, discussing it, and generating ideas in response to it, practitioners and their supervisors can keep improving their programs overall and the individual programs as they are provided to each family. Like children, parents, and practitioners, programs also develop. To be effective at promoting the development of a program, the program's staff members need to be aware of the program's development, value it, support it, and change along with it.

12

Voices of Experience

A program is only as effective as the people who deliver the services. As they strive to deliver services that make a difference for children and their families, practitioners often face barriers, many of which seem overwhelming. Although the theoretical framework behind developmental parenting is sound and makes good sense, the realities of the day-to-day experiences of practitioners may make implementing the principles difficult.

This chapter summarizes the findings from several focus groups with practitioners from diverse programs to give a voice to their needs, struggles, solutions, and suggestions. We hope that by sharing the negative as well as the positive, other practitioners—both those who make home visits and those who work with parents in other ways—will feel understood and gain insight to overcome some of their own barriers. It is also hoped that supervisors who read this chapter will develop strategies to provide much-needed support.

FOCUS GROUP PARTICIPANTS

Eighteen home visitors from four different programs attended a day-long workshop focusing on many of the key principles from this book. Following the presentation, they were asked a series of questions addressing their experiences with managing the details, solving the problems, and coping with the stress involved in being a home visitor. Of the 18 home visitors, the majority (12) had bachelor's degrees in social service areas, 1 had a master's degree in audiology, and 5 had some college or a Child Development Associate (CDA) credential. Their home visiting experience averaged about 6 years with a range from 1 month to 34 years.

When asked, "What is the hardest thing about home visiting?" more than one third of the home visitors indicated that getting families to keep their appointments was the most difficult aspect of home visiting that they encountered. Other responses included getting families focused on the visit, keeping from becoming good friends with family members, finding out too many details about the families' lives, not getting too emotionally involved, achieving expectations of balancing program goals while addressing the needs of the families, staying motivated, coming up with new ideas, getting people to accept help when they need it, getting parents to interact with their children and not just the home visitors, and dealing with families that expect the home visitor to do everything for them.

The principles of developmental parenting discussed previously were established with many of these concerns in mind. Being able to engage families and keep the focus on parent–child interactions would alleviate most of the hardest things about home visiting listed previously. Unfortunately, this is often easier said than done. Our group of home visitors responded to several more questions about home visiting to add some context for understanding how to effectively support developmental parenting during home visits.

What Makes Home Visits Better?

The home visitors had many ideas about what makes home visits better. They identified several good tips for working with families. They also indicated during the focus groups that sometimes these tips are hard to implement with some families. (See the sidebar, Tips from Home Visitors.)

Tips from Home Visitors

- Establish a good relationship with parent.

- Accept the family.

- Develop trust.

- Be mindful of their problems.

- Get to know the family.

- Care.

- Be patient.

- Be on their level.

- Be flexible.

- Don't assume things work with all families.

- Make decisions only after you get to know families.

- Show empathy.

- Be open minded.

When asked, "What makes some home visits go better than others?" participants listed parent involvement as a key component. During the group discussion, an interesting interaction occurred between a home visitor who had been conducting home visits with primarily Caucasian families living in poverty for about 1 year (Jill) and a second home visitor who had been conducting home visits with primarily Hispanic families living in poverty for about 14 years (Marsha).

A Conversation Between Home Visitors

Jill: When parents want to be involved, some of my parents just sit there and when you ask them what they want to do, they won't say. They don't fill out [on the planning form] what they want to do. [It just goes better] when parents say what they want to do.

Marsha: Parents have ownership, an active role in making choices, although you have to . . . give them suggestions.

Jill: Yeah, you give them suggestions and make plans, bring something, and even though you both planned it they are still not interested.

Marsha: You always have to give them choices. If you give them three choices and say, "Choose one," then they will usually pick one and then the ball is in their court.

Parent involvement in planning the activities and participating in the activities goes a long way toward making home visits feel enjoyable and worthwhile—like you have accomplished something. The interaction just described between a newer home visitor and a somewhat seasoned home visitor illustrates the frustration that practitioners often experience with hard-to-engage families and offers a strategy for situations when planning with the family is not effective. Sometimes engaging families requires some astute observation skills to figure out what would be interesting to them and sometimes it just takes time to build the relationship before more open dialog can occur. As one fairly new home visitor put it, "If you have a good relationship with the parent, things go a lot better. One [of the mothers I work with] won't talk or open up so our visits are a lot more stressful because she won't talk. . . . You've got to have a good relationship with her and be able to talk to her."

Being prepared, being on time, having few social service concerns, planning the current visit based on the last visit, having good mental health as a home visitor, having a responsive parent, and feeling like you have accomplished something during the visit were additional comments that were made about what makes home visits go better. As one home visitor explained, "I know it makes it easier for me when I feel like I have accomplished something, when I have taught them something they didn't know."

What Makes Home Visits Harder?

The practitioners also identified several factors that made home visits difficult and several strategies to improve the home visits when these difficulties occurred. The factors that were raised that made home visits difficult were language barriers, all of the stressors associated with living in poverty, maternal depression and stress, lots of siblings or guests, a sick or sleepy child, lack of interest in the activity by the child, and parents who lose the focus of the purpose of the visit and want to vent or socialize. Several suggestions were made about what to do when parents lose the focus of the home visit. The following comments represent the range of responses.

- "Turn questions to the parent: What do you want from the program? What do you want for your child? How can we accomplish it?"

- "Redirect, keep trying."

- "Refocus, shift it back to child . . . have plenty of resources, know the family [well] enough to know what they need. If you build a relationship, they will let you know."

- "Set the tone from the beginning; from the start, let them know what is expected. I made a list of home visit expectations and I read it to them and had them sign it in the beginning. . . . For example, I told a person that if it is about having no heat, I will listen, but if that person is bragging about getting drunk, that is not part of my responsibility as a home visitor. It is part of our job to let them know."

Stressors and Coping

Home visiting can be a very stressful job. Difficult home visits are one source of stress for practitioners, but there are many other sources of stress. We asked our group of home visitors to discuss their stressors and their strategies for coping. Many of the stressors for home visitors were similar across programs and included homes that are dirty, families whose problems are such that helping them seems impossible, families who move often and are hard to locate, situations that don't feel safe, and neighborhoods that are difficult. Stressors that differed by program related to supervision and program expectations or mandates. These stressors were discussed with greater animation and frustration than the more general stressors listed previously. The following statements summarize some of the home visitors' frustrations and reflect the differing perceptions among the programs.

1. "Yeah, we haven't hit all the stressors: rigidity of management, [where we are told that] all of your families have to do this, [but] they don't all fit into that box. It doesn't work that way, there has to be more flexibility."

2. "We are lucky, we have flexibility."

3. "I have never in 7 years been to training on how to be a home visitor. This is the first training I have ever had."

4. "It's their families, our own families, politics of Head Start, schedules, our hours, getting all of our visits in. We hope for no shows because they count."

5. "They don't count for us. We always have to find them [or the visit doesn't count]."

6. "Ninety minutes is too long."

7. "There is more stress [when our home visits] are videotaped. My visits are different when they videotape than when they don't . . . I don't do things differently but [the parents] do."

8. "They need to build you up. Our boss is wonderful."

Only a few coping strategies were mentioned during these focus groups, to help deal with the stressors. The coping strategies mentioned were talking to a supervisor or co-worker, getting a social service worker to do a referral for additional support services, and remembering, "You do what you can and let the rest go." Discussing the stressors with co-workers was mentioned several times. One home visitor expressed, "How do we cope? This is a stress reliever being here today. It is nice that you guys are feeling the same way."

Table 12.1. When is supervision supportive?

Supervisors are supportive when they . . .	But not when they . . .
Provide information	Choose not to listen to us
Provide training or training opportunities	Lack trust
Follow through on the training by putting it into practice	Have never been on a home visit.
	Have unrealistic expectations
Meet with us once a week	Never have meetings
Look at reality; look at them [families] as real people	Make decisions without home visitor input

SUPERVISION: WHEN IT IS SUPPORTIVE, WHEN IT IS NOT

When asked, "What supervisor supports are especially helpful or would be helpful for you as you work with families on a daily basis?" the responses to this question from the home visitors were more negative than positive. Many home visitors' comments recognized the difficulties that their supervisors faced with so many demands on their time, but still expressed their frustration with inadequate support and training to accomplish their job. One fairly new home visitor expressed this concern: "We have huge turnover. . . . I have been here 15 months and I have been here the second longest. We can't meet their expectations so we have big turnover. It is really frustrating." A second home visitor added, "Your families suffer for that . . . ."

A home visitor from a different program provided a stark contrast to these comments about high turnover. She said, "I have families that I still have relationships with. I see their kids in middle school whose younger siblings I am working with now, and I still have a relationship with the older kids."

Other comments describing when supervision is supportive and when it is not are included in Table 12.1.

CONCLUSION

Our focus groups suggest that most home visitors have many different strategies in place to work with families in their homes; they are motivated and interested in learning new skills to better help the families they work with; and they are highly stressed, with many different demands from families and program policies/expectations wearing them down. Our discussion with these diverse practitioners has contributed to the identification of additional supports that would aid practitioners in better helping parents in their parenting roles. Ongoing training; opportunities to meet with each other; and efforts at building trusting, supportive relationships with their supervisors are all strategies that developmental parenting programs can use to help all practitioners be better prepared to address program goals, improve child outcomes, and avoid burnout.

13

Memories of Lessons Learned

I started out working with parents in their homes in my first job after graduating from college. During that first summer, I made weekly home visits to a few families with 3- and 4-year-olds who lived in small towns and farms in a western mountain valley. Although it was difficult, it was fun, mostly, and the families were nice to me and willing to teach me.

THE "BLASÉ" FAMILY

Every Thursday afternoon, I drove down to the south end of the valley on straight, two-lane rural roads through marshes and alfalfa fields to visit the "Blasé" family. Blasé wasn't their real last name, but it came to be what we called this family when the home visitors sat around discussing family problems at work. Of course, these were not our own family problems—although we said "my family" or "my mom" when we talked about them—but the problems of the families we visited or our own problems in visiting these families. The problem was that this family was not very enthusiastic about my home visits, at least this was true of the mother. She was friendly, seemed happy enough to see me, and greeted me nicely when I arrived for the weekly visit. But she wasn't into it—just "blasé" about the whole thing.

We sat together on the living room floor to do the activities, her three children and me. The children were enthusiastic. They climbed all over me, trying to get to the books, toys, and other colorful stuff in

---

The family stories in this chapter were contributed by the first author. Details have been changed to protect confidentiality.

my bag. I presented learning activities to the children while talking about child development to their mom. This is a common approach for home visitors, especially new ones. The mother sat nearby, usually on the sagging gray couch, and sometimes told me things about her life.

They were not "locals." Hoping for a better life, they had moved out to this mountain valley from a Midwestern city after answering a newspaper ad for a hired hand to help on a dairy farm. The owner of the dairy farm lived in a newer house on the farm and offered the old house as an incentive. It was indeed enticing: a three-bedroom house rent free, all the milk you can drink, and a small wage. Now they lived in an old worn-out house. The father of the family worked from before dawn until after dark every day, milking, feeding, and cleaning up after cows; repairing broken fences; and cutting alfalfa. They figured it was better than the life they had but they didn't realize that it would trap them outside of a small, isolated community far from a grocery store, a playground, or a movie theater, or that the very small wage would be too small for them to do much of anything anyway, or that even the quarter-mile between homes would be too far for children who were not already part of the community to make any friends.

I brought activities for the children to help them learn things that young children should be learning—such as colors and shapes—and usually the children would do the activities. I used household materials to make matching games, puzzles, and art supplies. But their mother didn't get involved in the activities. She didn't do the activities I suggested that they do together during the week either, and any materials I left would be lost by the next visit. And sometimes the children, even though they played with the things from my bag, seemed to stubbornly resist learning anything. Once I brought a clear plastic box of little items—a marble, a spool of thread, a bit of ribbon, a bottle top, lots of little things, all in just two colors—red and yellow—to help the 3-year-old name colors. He took them all out, kind of sorted them, mixed them up, and named them incorrectly whenever I asked. I coaxed, prompted, and rewarded every correct response with a cheer. He missed more and more. The 6-year-old wanted a turn to do this task that was too easy for her, and she did it all correctly; the 2-year-old took a try and did well for his age. The 3-year-old gathered the little red and yellow things and tossed them around the room. The mother looked out the window.

I made home visits to only three families a week because the program was just getting started. The other two families I visited were doing the activities during the visit, and even doing some of the things I suggested during the week. It was a new job, my first real job, and I didn't know what else to try with the Blasé family. I had really wanted

this job. I heard about the new "Home Start" program they were starting at Head Start when I volunteered there for a college course credit.
I applied for every opening they had, even a secretary position, because
I could type well and figured at least I would learn something that way.
They hired me to be one of three new home visitors—two 40–year-olds
who were experienced mothers with five children each and one 20-
year-old "hippie chick" with a college degree (me).

Our training had been simple. My supervisor said, "Go out there
and take Head Start into the homes, and keep track of what you are
doing on these forms." There were a lot of forms. We had forms for
keeping track of the hours we worked, the miles we drove to visit our
caseload of families (eventually around 12 families each), and the supplies we bought and needed to be reimbursed for. We had assessment
forms for showing how well the children did on the tests we gave at the
beginning of the year, family goal sheets for listing what we wanted
each family to get out of the program, lesson plans for outlining the activities and information of each home visit, referral forms for problems
we needed someone else to help with, and a "significant events" form
that was for recording things going on in the families that didn't get
recorded anywhere else. Most of my training was about how to fill out
forms. (That was more than 30 years ago, but home visiting programs
now have just as many forms. Whatever it is that home visitors are
doing in various home visiting programs, they are also filling out a lot
of forms.)

Every Friday, all of the families came to the Head Start center, con-
verted from an old abandoned school, for a get together. The kids were
together in the Head Start classroom (the kids in the Head Start part of
the program had Fridays off), and the parents, all mothers for the first
few years until a few fathers started coming too, were in the parent
room—another old schoolroom with adult-size tables and folding
chairs. The three family educators took turns being the head preschool
teacher on Friday mornings. We invited extension agents and other
people from the community to talk with the parents.

On Friday afternoons, we met with the program coordinators—an
education coordinator, a health coordinator, and a social services coordinator—and talked about the problems with "our families." The coordinators gave us ideas. When those didn't work, we all tried to think
of more ideas. Sometimes the coordinators had to coordinate something to help solve a family problem—for example, arranging a dental
appointment for a family who had never been to a dentist or arranging
a meeting with a social worker to help a family being evicted from their
rental house. But some problems didn't seem to need any coordinating; they needed something else that we couldn't figure out. The fam-

ily from the dairy farm, for example. It just wasn't working. When we talked about each family, one by one, updating each other, I would always sigh when I got to this one. This mother just had no enthusiasm at all. This was when the other home visitors started calling them the Blasé family.

One day I went to the Blasé home and everything was worse. It was a long drive down to that end of the valley but I arrived early, so I waited a few minutes in the car to be polite. When I went up to the house, the mother met me at the door and said they couldn't have a home visit. I said okay and tried to look pleasant and not take it personally even though I was too young not to. But I needed to use the bathroom and asked if I could. She let me in. I walked down the hall trying not to look surprised at the extraordinary disorder. The home had often been a little messy, but not ever anything like this—piles of stuff, mixtures of clothes, toys, dirty dishes, old food, bad smells—and the small bathroom had piles of stuff mixed with bathroom garbage and an overflowing potty chair. I used the bathroom, washed my hands, walked out, smiled, and said a quick hello and goodbye to everyone. I said I'd come back next week. I did, and she let me in. We sat in the kitchen instead of the living room (I don't remember why), and she told me it was just so hard to keep up. I said something lame like, "It's really hard when you get behind." She started talking about cooking vegetarian food, using whole grains, sort of hippie stuff in those days. I was interested. We ended up making whole-wheat biscuits with her kids.

On later home visits, she taught me how to use a tortilla press, gave me a recipe for green enchiladas, and invited me to stay for supper. I still tried to bring educational activities, and I still wrote lesson plans full of preschool activities for the children. It wasn't until later that I looked back on all that and learned something. By then the family wasn't in Home Start any more, but I stopped by to see them once after they had moved in closer to town. The Blasé mother had lost weight, she had plans for finding a job, the house looked good, and the kids played together happily. She said things started getting better when her husband quit the dairy farm, got another job, and they moved into town. She said she had been really depressed out there. I hadn't thought about depression. If I had, what would I have thought about it? We didn't have any services for that. She had been having a hard time. Now she was doing better. And the kids were, too. I was happy for them and grateful that they were doing better, even though my home visits probably had not helped much.

But after some reflection, I realized that I had learned some lessons from my year of home visits to the Blasé family. I learned that it takes a lot more than homemade games to get some parents to do the kinds of things with their kids that will help the children's development. I learned that good home visit activities are the ones families will do even when the home visitor isn't there, the things they would do anyway without any program at all. So it is just as well to get involved in what they are doing, like making biscuits or tortillas, than to try and get them involved in what the home visitor thinks they should be doing, like sorting red and yellow objects. I learned that whatever is going on inside the parent makes a difference in how home visits go because it makes a difference in how their lives go. And after my last visit to the Blasé family, I learned that when mothers and children are having a hard time, it's quite possible that the mother is feeling depressed.

THE FAMILY WHO RESCUED ME

By my second year as a home visitor, I was finally feeling okay about how well it was going. I had a full caseload of families, 12 of them, who lived all over the valley. I asked parents to help pick out the activities we would do on the home visits, got parents and children involved in interacting with each other, and used the activities to get mothers talking about their goals for their children and their own lives. "My moms" trusted me. And I kept my life mostly to myself. There were good reasons. This was a conservative area, but I was not a conservative person. I knew their personal stories, but it was unprofessional for me to share mine.

We made home visits to every family every week, but we took school holidays so we got a week off for the Christmas holidays. I was making visits the last week before Christmas and worked late finishing up an evening home visit to Nancy, a single mother who worked full time at the cheese factory. It was 3 days before Christmas and I was driving home out to the farmhouse I was living in way out in a tiny, windy town in the northeast corner of our mountain valley. I must have had some sort of stomach flu—I had to stop partway home to throw up.

I got home and got the coal heater going, threw up again, and collapsed in bed. The heater was a "Stoke-a-Matic"—meaning it was supposed to stoke automatically, adding more coal from the hopper as the fire went down but before it went out. What woke me up in the middle of the night was that it wasn't doing that—the usual familiar noises it made through the night as coal dropped into the firebox were missing, and the silence woke me. I got up and got the fire going again, but realized that the coal hopper was almost empty and there wasn't any more coal in the garbage can we used to haul coal in from the shed. Filling it meant going out to the shed, something I wasn't up to doing in the middle of the night, in December, sick and naked. I threw up again, went back to bed, and stayed under the thick covers until late the next morning. It was a sunny day and the house wasn't any colder, but it wasn't any warmer either. Moving slowly and carefully, I gathered up the bedcovers and went to check the stove. The last of the coal had burned up in the fire I started, and now there was nothing to burn. I got myself to the living room, wrapped in blankets, and sat there wondering what to do.

I was home alone because my boyfriend, the one who convinced me to move out to this farmhouse with him because the rent was cheap and we could raise goats and geese and have a big garden, was spending the holidays with his family in a tropical climate. I stayed home because I had to work, but now I had to think about how to solve the heating problem. I could barely stand up. I needed to feed the goats, the geese, the dog, and her litter of puppies. I concentrated on what it would take to get dressed to go out to take care of the animals and haul in the coal. But the thought of getting dressed was overwhelming. So I kept sitting there. The house was still cold and the animals were probably getting restless. My friends had all left town for Christmas, I was clear out in the middle of nowhere anyway, living a back-to-the-land life where I didn't even know my neighbors' last names. (How do you look up "Max with the pig farm" in the phone book?)

The phone rang and it was Nancy, the mom I'd just made a visit to the evening before. Did I leave my bag there or something? She wanted to come out to see me. She and her two young children had made Christmas gifts for me that she wanted to deliver. I explained that I was sick, that the house was cold because the fire went out, that I just couldn't handle it that day. And she said, ignoring my protests, "We'll be out in a while and we'll help." She brought chicken soup, she brought handmade gifts from her children and hand-crocheted mittens from her, and she brought her boyfriend who fed the animals, hauled the coal, and started the fire again. And I was so grateful. I was the one who was supposed to be providing services. I was the one bringing handouts and materials and activities and intervention techniques to her house every week. I was the one helping her figure out how to get her life together. And she was the one who cheerfully and unquestioningly rescued me from mine. I survived, I recovered, and I slept the rest of that day and all night and into the next morning until I felt well enough to take care of the animals again before driving to my parents' house for Christmas.

I learned that these relationships were real ones. I had gotten to know "my" families well. Whether it was talking with a young mother about her child's behavior problems, helping a single working mother figure out how to plan enjoyable evening time with her three young children, or offering some understanding to a mother frustrated by her husband's frequent bouts of unemployment, I had been allowed into their lives. For good reasons, I had not allowed them into mine. I had maintained a professional detachment that helped me stay focused on the whole reason for the home visits, helping children learn, and also helped me cope with the sad stories of families in poverty, the occasional referral for abuse, homes with little heat but strong smells. But my detachment had gotten in the way here and I had to learn something new. This mother who had so generously come to my aid had started out suspicious of me. She hid her coffee pot before each home visit because many people in her community were of a religion that forbids coffee. Our visits were in the evening because she worked full time at a factory, and one time I yawned and said I hadn't had my coffee. From then on she made coffee every week. Her coffee was strong and kept me awake on Tuesday nights, but I kept drinking it. I felt like I had to. It was about trust. And it went both ways. To earn their trust, I needed to trust them. Even more important, I needed to be willing to learn from them in order to be able to teach them anything.

MRS. G

I learned valuable lessons from the mom who was probably the most different from me of all the moms I worked with as a home visitor. Mrs. G was a Mormon mother of 10 children who lived in a small town in northern Utah. I am grateful that I knew her. Every week for a year we met in her warm living room with her youngest child, Sam, and sometimes one of the older children. Every week we planned activities to help Sam's development. By then our program had come up with the idea to use home visits to help parents plan their own activities to help their children's development, but in this case it was a little hard. Mrs. G was in our program because Sam had Down syndrome.

Head Start serves children with disabilities along with children from low-income families; in fact, each program is required to have at least 10% of the children with a documented disability, so Sam qualified. Back then, it was a relatively new rule. Having children with disabilities in the classroom made sense to me because the program had a disabilities specialist who could help in the classroom. But assigning me to make home visits to a family with a child who had a disability didn't make sense because I had no idea what to do, especially with this family.

Mrs. G. told me frankly on our very first visit that she only stopped having children when Sam was born because Down syndrome is linked to the mother's age. She said—she actually *said* this—that when she packed up all her maternity clothes it felt like she was being put out to pasture. I went home disturbed by the thought, "She felt like an animal who had only been meant for breeding, and was now useless?" and I was convinced that this would be too hard, probably impossible, to work with someone so different from me. Oh yes, and my training was in child development, not special education, so how could I possibly help with her child who had Down syndrome? Mrs. G actually had lots of ideas, but I felt like I needed more help. The disabilities specialist at Head Start shook his head when I went to him. "Hopeless case," he said, "unrealistic expectations." So much for help.

But it turned out that the visits were fun. They were fun because this family was fun. Every week I learned more—about Mrs. G, about Sam, about what a loving family can do. It wasn't simple—it wasn't just a matter of finding activities for a child with Down syndrome, it was a matter of finding something just right for Sam, helping him have fun while trying something new, celebrating with his mom every time he learned a little something new. My visits to Sam and Mrs. G became the highlight of my week. Sam was delightful, and Mrs. G was generous with her thoughts and ideas.

I learned a lot from Mrs. G about families and parenting. I learned that having fun is really important and that having fun together as a family builds love. Mrs. G told me she believed in giving children a lot of love, she didn't think spanking helped much, and she always sent her children to the stairway for "time-out." She also shared lessons about life more generally. She told me to wallpaper a room with my boyfriend—then I'd know if I should marry him. She told me she was always completely sure of her husband's love for her—that it was the most important thing to know.

When the year ended, she gave me a little doll—a doll that looked a little bit like Sam—so that whenever I saw it, I would be reminded of him. I kept it in my dresser drawer for many years, until one of my own children mistakenly thought it was just an old doll and took it out to play with it and it got lost. I can still see it though. I can still see Sam's sweet, delighted face when I came to the door, his joyful, laughing face when playing with an older sister or brother, his look of confidence when we would find a simple puzzle or game or some other learning activity he could be successful at. I was blessed to share Mrs. G's delight in Sam, her delight in finding ways for him to play and to learn, and her joy in being his mom. I have never forgotten either one of them.

I learned that it only mattered a little bit how many things could be checked off on a developmental checklist. I learned that home visiting could best help children by sharing with parents the delight of seeing children discover their world and themselves. I learned that we were all learning together. Any idea learned in one home could be a good idea to share another time with someone else.

Other Moms

I have many other memories of my years as a home visitor. I remember a mother whose husband couldn't tie his shoes because he had worn only cowboy boots his whole life. She worried about her children and made sure they could tie their shoes well. I remember a mother who only pretended to read all of the handouts I brought every week with suggested learning activities to do during the week, recipes for inexpensive nutritious meals and snacks, outlines of developmental milestones in every domain, and safety pamphlets from the gas company. She always looked attentively at the handouts, and it was a long time before I figured out that she couldn't read and didn't know what they said, but I could tell she was embarrassed so I started just telling her everything they said.

Some of them tried so hard, loved their children so much, and apologized with embarrassment at not finishing their "homework" of activities I had suggested they do during the week between visits. Others loved their children just as much, but didn't do as much. One mother was already teaching her young children how to play the piano. She routinely stretched their minds—asking her 3-year-old, "Do you want your sandwich cut straight or diagonally, into rectangles or triangles?" She had been majoring in child development in college, but got married, started a family right away, was on her way to having many children and enjoying them very much. She would have done fine without me—she just wanted her children to be able to go on the field trips. And she seemed to have a secret pleasure—talking with me, adult-to-adult, intellectually, about child development and psychology theories, a topic she was deeply interested in.

There were lots of different kinds of families and a lot of different ways to work with them. One day, a consultant from Washington, D.C., was explaining that to us. She asked us what our program was for. Well, it was for helping children get a "head start" so they'd be ready for school. And our jobs were to educate families so children would learn more. "Okay," she said, "that's it over there"—she pointed across the room to an imaginary family with a child ready for school. Okay. She walked over to the imaginary family. Then she walked back across the room, sat down and took off her shoes and socks, and walked back to the imaginary family. Next, she walked back and tiptoed over to the "family," came back and got down on her hands and knees and started to crawl, looked up at our confused faces, and laughed and stood up. "I'm showing you that there are many ways to get there."

CONCLUSION

It seems like all of these events happened during the same year, but they didn't. I made home visits for 9 years. Sometimes I had a lot of families. Sometimes I had only a few and did other jobs—such as training other home visitors at other programs. I learned a lot, perhaps more than any of the families I visited learned. I had been away from that job a little over a year when I had a baby of my own. All "my moms" had trained me well. By the time she was 2, my little girl knew all about cutting sandwiches diagonally, spending time on the steps for time-out, and having fun with Mom.

Beyond the lessons for one practitioner, these stories of families in a home visiting parenting program illustrate several general points we have been trying to make in this book. Each of these families had unique strengths that the practitioner at first did not recognize. Each of the families also faced unique challenges in their lives while they were trying to support the development of their young children. Finally, the strategies that were eventually effective in facilitating developmental parenting with these families were different from the strategies the program and practitioner were already using. What it took to help these parents support their children's development was the facilitative attitudes we describe: responsiveness to each family's individual strengths, flexibility in the choice of strategies to use with each family, and acceptance of each family's unique situation. Those attitudes are critical for anyone trying to work with parents to promote developmental parenting. Practitioners who have these attitudes will be better prepared to use the strategic behaviors and content tools we have presented that are effective when working with parents.

Developmental parenting is facilitated best when practitioners use lessons such as those learned from the experiences described in this last chapter. First, "show-and-tell" approaches, in which a practitioner shows a parent what to do and then tells the parent to do it, do not work well with most parents. They are particularly ineffective with parents who are stressed, depressed, or overwhelmed with their life situation. Building on family strengths requires that a practitioner notices a parent's skills or interests and helps the parent use those skills or interests to engage their children in interactions in which the parent can be warm, responsive, encouraging, and conversational. Parents are certainly less likely to be able to show these developmental parenting behaviors when they are doing something assigned by a practitioner who thought up the activity than when they are doing an activity they already enjoy.

Second, facilitating developmental parenting is easier in the context of a positive relationship between the parent and the practitioner. Mutual competence, as we have described it in this book, refers to a parallel process in which mutually competent relationships are built not only between parents and children but also between practitioners and parents and between supervisors and practitioners. These other mutually competent relationships also include the kinds of behaviors we describe as developmental parenting: warmth, responsiveness, encouragement, and conversation. Effective practitioners connect in real ways with the families they serve, showing warmth to each family member, responding to each family's unique qualities, encouraging parents and families to try new things, and having conversations about children's development in the context of everyday family life. They also, sometimes, share their real selves as individuals who are also learning and developing.

Third, developmental parenting can be facilitated by learning together with parents and sharing interest and delight in their children's development. An expert-learner model, in which the practitioner is the expert and the parent is the learner, is unlikely to be effective with many families. It is especially unlikely to be effective with families who have had any negative past experiences with other experts. Parents usually know their own children and their own families better than any expert does. Recognizing parents' expertise about their own children is fundamental to effectively facilitating developmental parenting. Going a step beyond that recognition requires a sense of partnership and cooperation that is more readily established when the planning is shared and the success is enjoyed together.

Finally, there are many ways to get there. We have presented basic approaches, suggested specific strategies, and provided concrete examples of facilitating developmental parenting. We have also provided examples of the developmental parenting behaviors that support children's early development. The examples in this book are not, however, the only parenting behaviors that support development or the only approaches and strategies that facilitate developmental parenting. Every practitioner working with families is likely to discover new ways to facilitate parents' warmth, responsiveness, encouragement, and conversation to support the development of their young children. Discovering effective new ways to facilitate developmental parenting is more likely if those who work with parents recognize and build on family strengths and develop positive relationships with families and are willing to learn together with families.

References

Administration for Children, Youth, & Families. (2002). *Making a difference in the lives of infants and toddlers and their families: The impacts of Early Head Start.* Washington, DC: Department of Health and Human Services.

Arnold, D.H., Ortiz, C., Curry, J.C., Stowe, R.M., Goldstein, N.E., Fisher, P.H., Zeljo, A., & Yershova, K. (1999). Promoting academic success and preventing disruptive behavior disorders through community partnership. *Journal of Community Psychology, 27,* 589–598.

Azmitia, M., & Hesser, J. (1993). Why siblings are important agents of cognitive development: A comparison of siblings and peers. *Child Development, 64*(2), 430–444.

Baggett, J.J., Carta, J.J., & Horn, E.M. (2006). *Indicator of Parent-Child Interaction (IPCI).* Unpublished Measure. Juniper Gardens Children's Project. University of Kansas.

Bakeman, R., & Adamson, L.B. (1984). Coordinating attention to people and objects in mother–infant and peer-infant interaction. *Child Development, 55,* 1278–1289.

Baldwin, D. (1991). Infants' contribution to the achievement of joint reference. *Child Development, 62,* 875–890.

Barnard, K.E., Morisset, C.E., Spieker, S. (1993). Preventive interventions: Enhancing parent–infant relationships. In C.H. Zeanah (Ed.), *Handbook of infant mental health* (pp. 386–399). New York: Guilford Press.

Baumwell, L., Tamis-LeMonda, C.S., & Bornstein, M.H. (1997). Maternal verbal sensitivity and child language comprehension. *Infant Behavior and Development, 20,* 247–258.

Belsky, J., & Most, R.K. (1981). From exploration to play: A cross-sectional study of infant free-play behavior. *Developmental Psychology, 17,* 630–639.

Bernstein, V.J., Campbell, S., & Akers, A. (2001). Caring for the caregivers: Supporting the well-being of at-risk parents and children through supporting the well-being of the programs that serve them. In J.N. Hughes, A.M. La Greca, & J.C. Conole (Eds.), *Handbook of psychological services for children and adolescents* (pp. 107–132). New York: Oxford University Press.

193

Bernstein, V.J., Hans, S.L., & Percansky, C. (1991). Advocating for the young children in need through strengthening the parent–child relationships. *Journal of Clinical Child Psychology, 20*, 28–41.

Bloom, L. (1998). Language development and emotional expression. *Pediatrics, 102*, 1272–1277.

Booth, C.L., Rose-Krasnor, L., McKinnon, J., & Rubin, K.H. (1994). Predicting social adjustment in middle childhood: The role of preschool attachment security and maternal style. *Social Development, 3*(3), 189–204.

Bornstein, M.H., Haynes, O.M., O'Reilly, A.W., & Painter, K.M. (1996). Solitary and collaborative pretense play in early childhood: Sources of individual variation in the development of representational competence. *Child Development, 67*, 2910–2929.

Bornstein, M.H., Haynes, M.O., & Painter, K.M. (1998). Sources of child vocabulary competence: A multivariate model. *Journal of Child Language, 25*, 367–393.

Bornstein, M.H., & Tamis-LeMonda, C.S. (1989). Maternal responsiveness and cognitive development in children. *New Directions in Child Development, 43*, 49–61.

Bornstein, M.H., Tamis-LeMonda, C.S., Tal, J., Ludemann, P., Toda, S., Rahn, C.W., et al. (1992). Maternal responsiveness to infants in three societies: The United States, France, and Japan. *Child Development, 63*(4), 808–821.

Bricker, D., & Squires, J. (with Mounts, L., Potter, L., Nickel, R., Twombly, E., & Farrell, J.). (1999). *Ages & Stages Questionnaires® (ASQ): A parent-completed, child-monitoring system* (2nd ed.). Baltimore: Paul H. Brookes Publishing Co.

Bronfenbrenner, U. (1979). Toward an experimental ecology of human development. *American Psychologist, 32*, 513–531.

Bronfenbrenner, U. (1986). Ecology of the family: A context for human development: Research perspectives. *Developmental Psychology, 22*, 723–742.

Brorson, K. (2005). The culture of a home visit in early intervention. *Journal of Early Childhood Research, 3*, 51–76.

Caldwell, B.M., & Bradley, R.H. (1984). *Home Observation for Measurement of the Environment (HOME)*. Little Rock: University of Arkansas.

Caldwell, C., Green, A., & Billingsley, A. (1994). Family support in black churches: A new look at old functions. In S.L. Kagan & B. Weissbourd (Eds.), *Putting families first: America's family support movement and the challenge of change* (pp. 137–160). San Francisco: Jossey-Bass.

Carter, A.S., & Briggs-Gowan, M. (2005). *The Infant-Toddler Social and Emotional Assessment* (ITSEA). San Antonio, TX: Pearson Education.

Carton, J.S, & Carton, E.E.R. (1998). Nonverbal maternal warmth and children's locus of control of reinforcement. *Journal of Nonverbal Behavior, 22*, 77–86.

Caspi, A., Moffitt, T.E., Morgan, J., Rutter, M., Taylor, A., Arseneault, L., Tully, L., Jacobs, C., Kim-Cohen, J., & Polo-Tomas, M. (2004). Maternal expressed emotion predicts children's antisocial behavior problems: Using monozygotic-twin differences to identify environmental effects on behavioral development. *Developmental Psychology, 40*, 149–161.

Catts, H.W., Fey, M.E., Zhang, X., & Tomblin, J.B. (1999). Language basis of reading and reading disabilities: Evidence from a longitudinal investigation. *Scientific Studies of Reading, 3,* 331–361.

Charman, T., Baron-Cohen, S., Swettenham, J., Baird, G., Cox, A., & Drew, A. (2001). Testing joint attention, imitation, and play as infancy precursors to language and theory of mind. *Cognitive Development, 15,* 481–498.

Chisholm, K. (1998). A three-year follow-up of attachment and indiscriminant friendliness in children adopted from Romanian orphanages. *Child Development, 69,* 1092–1106

Cowan, P., Powell, D., & Cowan, C. (1998). Parenting interventions: A family systems perspective. In I. Sigel & A. Renninger (Eds.), *Handbook of child psychology* (4th ed.): *Vol. 4: Child psychology in practice* (pp. 3–72). New York: Wiley.

Culp, A.M., Hubbs-Tait, L., Culp, R.E., & Starost, H.-J. (2001). Maternal parenting characteristics and school involvement: Predictors of kindergarten cognitive competence among Head Start children. *Journal of Research in Childhood Education, 15,* 5–17.

Daro, D., & Harding, K.A. (1999). Healthy Families America: Using research to enhance practice. *Future of Children, 9,* 152–176.

Daro, D., Jones, E., & McCurdy, K. (1993). Preventing child abuse: An evaluation of services to high-risk families. Philadelphia: The William Penn Foundation.

Daro, D., & McCurdy, K. (1994). Preventing child abuse and neglect: Programmatic interventions. *Child Welfare, 73,* 405–430.

David, T., Gouch, K., Powell, S. and Abbott, L. (2003). *Birth to three matters: A review of the literature.* London: Department for Education and Skills.

Davidov, M., & Grusec, J.E. (2006). Untangling the links of parental responsiveness to distress and warmth to child outcomes. *Child Development, 77*(1), 44–58.

De Wolff, M.S., & van Ijzendoorn, M.H. (1997). Sensitivity and attachment: A meta-analysis on parental antecedents of infant attachment. *Child Development, 68,* 571–591.

DeTemple, J.M. (1999, April). *Home and school predictors of sixth grade vocabulary and reading skills of children from low-income families.* Poster presented at the Biennial Meeting of the Society for Research in Child Development, Albuquerque, NM.

Dickinson, D.K., McCabe, A., Anastasopoulos, L., Peisner-Feinberg, E.S., & Poe, M.D. (2003). The comprehensive language approach to early literacy: The interrelationships among vocabulary, phonological sensitivity, and print knowledge among preschool-aged children. *Journal of Educational Psychology, 95,* 465–481.

Dickinson, D.K., & Tabors, P.O. (1991). Early literacy: Linkages between home, school, and literacy achievement at age five. *Journal of Research in Childhood Education, 6,* 30–46.

Dickinson, D.K., & Tabors, P.O. (Eds.). (2001). *Beginning language with literacy: Young children learning at home and school.* Baltimore: Paul H. Brookes Publishing Co.

Dickinson, D.K., Wolf, A., Abbott-Shim, M., Bryant, D., Lambert, R., & Peisner-Feinberg, E. (1999, April). *Phonemic awareness in Head Start children: Relationship to language and literacy and parenting variables.* Poster presented at the Biennial Meeting of the Society for Research in Child Development, Albuquerque, N.M.

Diener, M.L., Nievar, M.A., & Wright, C. (2003). Attachment security among mothers and their young children living in poverty: Associations with maternal, child, and contextual characteristics. *Merrill-Palmer Quarterly, 49,* 154–182.

Dodge, D.T., Colker, L.J., & Heroman, C. (1999). *The Creative Curriculum for Early Childhood.* Washington, DC: Teaching Strategies, Inc.

Dodici, B.J., Draper, D.C., & Peterson, C.A. (2003). Early parent–child interactions and early literacy development. *Topics in Early Childhood Special Education, 23,* 124–136.

Donnelly, A.C. (1992). Healthy Families America. *Children Today, 21,* 25–28.

Downey, D.B., & Condron, D.J. (2004). Playing well with others in kindergarten: The benefits of siblings at home. *Journal of Marriage and Family, 66,* 333–350.

Duggan, A.K., McFarlane, E.C., Windham, A.M., Rohde, C.A., Salkever, D.S., Fuddy, L., et al. (1999). Evaluation of Hawaii's Healthy Start Program. *The Future of Children, 9,* 66–90.

Dunham, P., & Dunham, R. (1992). Lexical development during middle infancy: A mutually driven infant–caregiver process. *Developmental Psychology, 28,* 414–420.

Dunst, C.J., Bruder, M.B., Trivette, C.M., & Hamby, D.W. (2006). Everyday activity settings, natural learning environments, and early intervention practices. *Journal of Policy and Practice in Intellectual Disabilities 3*(1), 3–10.

Dunst, C.J., Trivette, C.M., & Hamby, D. (2006, October). *Characteristics and consequences of help-giving practices in contrasting human services programs.* Presented at the Division for Early Childhood (CEC) Conference. Little Rock, AR: Division of Early Childhood (DEC).

Easterbrooks, M.A., Biesecker, G., & Lyons-Ruth, K.A. (2000). Infancy predictors of emotional availability in middle childhood: The role of attachment and maternal depression. *Attachment and Human Development, 2,* 170–187.

Emde, R.N., Korfmacher, J., & Kubicek, L.F. (2000). Toward a theory of early relationship-based intervention. In J.D. Osofsky & H.E. Fitzgerald (Eds.), *WAIMH handbook of infant mental health. Vol. Two. Early intervention, evaluation, and assessment* (pp. 3–32). New York: Wiley.

Estrada, P., Arsenio, W.F., Hess, R.D., & Holloway, S.D. (1987). Affective quality of the mother-child relationships: Longitudinal consequences for children's school relevant cognitive functioning. *Developmental Psychology, 23,* 210–215.

Feldman, R., Greenbaum, C.W., Mayes, L.C., & Erlich, S.H. (1997). Change in mother–infant interactive behavior: Relation to change in the mother, the infant, and the social context. *Infant Behavior and Development, 20,* 151–163.

Fenichel, E. (1992). *Learning through supervision and mentorship to support the development of infants, toddlers and their families: A source book.* Arlington, VA: ZERO TO THREE.

Fenson, L., Dale, P.S., Reznick, J.S., Thal, D., Bates, E., Hartung, J.P., et al. (1992). *MacArthur-Bates Communicative Development Inventories (CDIs)*. Baltimore: Paul H. Brookes Publishing Co.

Fenson, L., Marchman, V.A., Thal, D.J., Dale, P.S., Reznick, J.S., & Bates, E. (2006). *MacArthur-Bates Communicative Development Inventories (CDIs)* (2nd ed.). Baltimore: Paul H. Brookes Publishing Co.

Fewell, R.R., & Deutscher, B. (2002). Attention deficit hyperactivity disorder in very young children: Early signs and interventions. *Infants and Young Children, 14*, 24–32.

Field, T. (1998). Maternal depression effects on infants and early intervention. *Preventative Medicine, 27*, 200–203.

Frankenburg, W.K., Dodds, J., Archer, P., et al. (1996). *The DENVER II Technical Manual*. Denver, CO: Denver Developmental Materials Inc.

Furano, S., O'Reilly, K.A., Hosaka, C.M., Inatsuka, T.T., Allman, T.L., & Zeisloft, B. (2005). *Hawaii Early Learning Profile (HELP) Activity Guide*. Palo Alto, California: VORT.

Gardner, F., Ward, S., Burton, J., & Wilson, C. (2003). The role of mother–child joint play in the early development of children's conduct problems: A longitudinal observational study. *Social Development, 12*, 361–378.

Goldberg, S. (1977). Social competency in infancy: A model of parent–infant interaction. *Merrill-Palmer Quarterly, 23*, 163–177

Goldfield, B.A. (1987). The contributions of child and caregiver to referential and expressive language. *Applied Psycholinguistics, 8*, 267–280.

Gomby, D.S., Culross, P.L., & Behrman, R.E. (1999). Home visiting: Recent program evaluations—analysis and recommendations. *The Future of Children, 3*, 4–26.

Grossman, K., Grossman, K.E., Fremmer-Bombik, K., Kindler, H., Scheuerer-Englisch, H., & Zimmermann, P. (2002). The uniqueness of the child–father attachment relationship: Fathers' sensitive and challenging play as a pivotal variable in a 16–year longitudinal study. *Social Development, 11*, 307–331.

Grusec, J.E., & Goodnow, J.J. (1994). Impact of parental discipline methods on child's internalization of values: A reconceptualization of current points of view. *Developmental Psychology, 30*, 4–19.

Guralnick, M. (Ed.). (1997). *The effectiveness of early intervention*. Baltimore: Paul H. Brookes Publishing Co.

Guralnick, M.J. (1989). Recent developments in early intervention efficacy research: Implications for family involvement in P.L. 99–457. *Topics in Early Childhood Special Education, 9*, 1–17.

Guralnick, M.J. (1997). Second-generation research in the field of intervention. In M.J. Guralnick (Ed.), *The effectiveness of early intervention* (pp. 3–22). Baltimore: Paul H. Brookes Publishing Co.

Guralnick M.J. (1998). Effectiveness of early intervention for vulnerable children: A developmental perspective. *American Journal on Mental Retardation, 102*, 319–345.

Gustafson, G.E., Green, J.A., & West, M.J. (1979). The infant's changing role in mother–infant games: The growth of social skills. *Infant Behavior and Development, 2*, 301–308.

Harnish, J.D., Dodge, K.A., & Valente, E. (1995). Mother–child interaction quality as a partial mediator of the roles of maternal depressive symptomatology and socioeconomic status in the development of child behavior problems. *Child Development, 66,* 739–753.

Harris, K.M., Furstenberg, F.F. Jr., & Marmer, J.K. (1998). Paternal involvement with adolescents in intact families: The influence of fathers over the life course. *Demography, 35*(2). 201–216.

Hart, B., & Risley, T.R. (1995). *Meaningful differences in the everyday experiences of young American children.* Baltimore: Paul H. Brookes Publishing Co.

Hebbeler, K., & Gerlach-Downie, S. (2002). Inside the black box of home visiting: A qualitative analysis of why intended outcomes were not achieved. *Early Childhood Research Quarterly, 17,* 28–51.

Hinshaw, S.P. (1992). Externalizing behavior problems and academic underachievement in childhood and adolescence: Causal relationships and underlying mechanisms. *Psychological Bulletin, 111,* 127–155.

Hrncir, E.J., Speller, G.M., & West, M. (1985). What are we testing? *Developmental Psychology, 21,* 226–232.

Hubbs-Tait, L., Culp, A.M., Culp, R.E., & Miller, C.E. (2002). Relation of maternal cognitive stimulation, emotional support, and intrusive behavior during Head Start to children's kindergarten cognitive abilities. *Child Development, 73,* 110–132.

Hunter, F.T., McCarthy, M.E., MacTurk, R.H., & Vietze, P. (1987). Infants' social-constructive interactions with mothers and fathers. *Developmental Psychology, 23,* 249–254.

Kelly, J.F., Morisset, C.E., Barnard, K.E., Hammond, M.A., & Booth, C.L. (1996). The influence of early mother–child interaction on preschool cognitive/linguistic outcomes in a high-social-risk group. *Infant Mental Health Journal, 17,* 310–321.

Kochanska, G. (1995). Children's temperament, mothers' discipline, and security of attachment: Multiple pathways of emerging internalization. *Child Development, 66,* 597–615.

Kochanska, G. (2001). Emotional development in children with different attachment histories: The first three years, *Child Development, 72,* 474–490.

Kuhl, P.K. (2000). A new view of language acquisition. *Proceedings of the National Academy of Science. 97,* 11850–11857.

Kuhl, P.K. (2004). Early language acquisition: Cracking the speech code. *Nature Reviews Neuroscience, 5,* 831–843.

Kupersmidt, J.B., & Coie, J.D. (1990). Preadolescent peer status, aggression, and school adjustment as predictors of externalizing problems in adolescence. *Child Development, 61,* 1350–1362.

Laasko, M., Poikkeus, A.M., Eklund, K., & Lyytinen, P. (1999). Social interactional behaviors and symbolic play competence as predictors of language development and their associations with maternal attention-directing strategies. *Infant Behavior and Development, 22,* 541–556.

Ladd, G.W., Birch, S.H., & Buhs, E.S. (1999). Children's social and scholastic lives in kindergarten: Related spheres of influence? *Child Development, 70,* 1373–1400.

Ladd, G.W., Kochenderfer, B.J., & Coleman, C.C. (1997). Classroom peer acceptance, friendship, and victimization: Distinct relational systems that contribute uniquely to children's school adjustment. *Child Development, 68,* 1181–1197.

Laibile, D.J., & Thompson, R.A. (2000). Mother–child discourse, attachment security, shared positive affect, and early conscience development. *Child Development, 71*(5), 1424–1440.

Landry, S.H., Garner, P.W., Swank, P.R., & Baldwin, C.D. (1996). Effects of maternal scaffolding during joint toy play with preterm and full-term infants. *Merrill-Palmer Quarterly, 42,* 177–199.

Lanzi, R., Terry, K., Guest, K., Cotton, J., & Ramey, C. (1999*). Home visiting with families at risk for child abuse and neglect: Review of programs, findings, best practices, and lessons learned from the field.* Birmingham: Civitan International Research Center, University of Alabama at Birmingham.

Lay, K., Waters, E., & Park, K.A. (1989). Maternal responsiveness and child compliance: The role of mood as a mediator. *Child Development, 60,* 1405–1411.

Layzer, J.I., Goodson, B.D., Bernstein, L., & Price, C.(2001). *National evaluation of family support programs: Volume A. The meta-analysis.* Cambridge, MA: Abt Associates.

Lee, E.J., Murry, V.M., Brody, G.H., & Parker, V. (2002). Maternal resources, parenting, and dietary patterns among rural African American children in single-parent families. *Public Health Nursing, 19,* 104–111.

Leseman, P.P.M., & de Jong, P.F. (1998). Home literacy: Opportunity, instruction, cooperation, and social-emotional quality predicting early reading achievement. *Reading Research Quarterly, 33,* 294–318.

Leventhal, J.M. (1996). Twenty years later: We do know how to prevent child abuse and neglect. *Child Abuse and Neglect: The International Journal, 20,* 647–653.

Linder, T.W. (1993). *Transdisciplinary Play-Based Assessment.* Baltimore: Paul H. Brookes Publishing.

Linder, T. (2008). Transdisciplinary Play-Based Assessment (TPBA2), Second Edition. Baltimore: Paul H. Brookes Publishing Co.

Londerville, S., & Main, M., (1981). Security of attachment, compliance, and maternal training methods in the second year of life. *Developmental Psychology, 17,* 289–299.

Lyon, R.G. (1999, April). *Longitudinal studies of reading abilities: Biological and educational influences on development and persistence.* Paper presented at the Biennial Meeting of the Society for Research in Child Development, Albuquerque, N.M.

Lyon, R.G. (2002). Overview of reading and literacy research. In S. Patton & M. Holmes (Eds.), *The keys to literacy* (pp. 8–17). Washington, DC: Council for Basic Education.

MacDonald, K. (1992). Warmth as a developmental construct: An evolutionary analysis. *Child Development, 63,* 753–773.

MacLeod, J., & Nelson, G. (2003). A meta-analytic review of programs for the promotion of family wellness and the prevention of child maltreatment. In K. Kufeldt & B. McKenzie (Eds.), *Child welfare: Connecting research, policy, and practice* (pp. 133–145), Waterloo, Ontario, Canada: Wilfrid Laurier University Press.

Mahoney, G., Boyce, G.C., Fewell, R., Spiker, D., & Wheeden, C.A. (1998). The relationship of parent–child interaction to the effectiveness of early intervention services for at-risk children and children with disabilities. *Topics in Early Childhood Special Education, 18,* 5–17.

Mahoney, G., & Perales, F. (2005). Relationship-focused early intervention with children with pervasive developmental disorders and other disabilities: A comparative study. *Developmental and Behavioral Pediatrics, 26,* 77–85.

Meisels, S.J., Marsden, D.B., Dombro, A.L., Weston, D.R., & Jewkes, A.M. (2003). *The Ounce Scale.* Minneapolis, MN: Pearson Assessments.

McBride, S., & Peterson, C. (1997). Home-based intervention with families of children with disabilities: Who is doing what? *Topics in Early Childhood Special Education, 17,* 209–233.

McClelland, M.M., Morrison, F.J., & Holmes, D.L. (2000). Children at risk for early academic problems: The role of learning-related social skills. *Early Childhood Research Quarterly, 15,* 307–329.

Mental Health America. (n.d.). Factsheet: Signs of depression checklist. Retrieved February 28, 2008, from http://www.nmha.org/go/information/get-info/depression/signs-of-depression-checklist

Moran, P., Ghate, D., & Van der Merwe, A. (2004). *What works in parenting support? A review of the international evidence* (Research Report No. 574). Annesley, Nottingham, UK: Policy Research Bureau, Department for Education and Skills.

Mullan, H.K., Furstenberg, F.F., & Marmer, J.K. (1998). Paternal involvement with adolescents in intact families: The influence of fathers over the life course. *Demography, 35,* 201–216.

Mundy, P., Kasari, C., & Sigman, M. (1992). Nonverbal communication, affective sharing, and intersubjectivity. *Infant Behavior and Development, 15,* 377–381.

Murray, L., Fiori-Cowley, A., Hooper, R., & Cooper, P. (1996). The impact of postnatal depression and associated diversity on early mother-infant interactions and later infant outcomes. *Child Development, 67,* 2512–2526.

National Association of Child Care Resource and Referral Agencies. (2006). *Is this the right place for my child? Research-based indicators of high-quality childcare?* Retrieved October 2, 2007, from http://www.naccrra.org/docs/parent/38IndicatorsChecklist.pdf

Neuman, S.B., & Dickinson, D.K. (Eds.). (2001). *Handbook of early literacy research.* New York: Guilford Press.

Newland, L.A., Roggman, L.A., & Boyce, L.K. (2001). The development of social toy play and language in infancy. *Infant Behavior and Development, 24,* 1–25.

NICHD Early Child Care Research Network. (1999). Child care and mother–child interaction in the first three years of life. *Developmental Psychology, 35,* 1399–1413.

Nugent, J.K. (1991). Cultural and psychological influences on the father's role in infant development. *Journal of Marriage and the Family, 53,* 475–485.

Olds, D.L., & Kitzman, H. (1993). Review of research on home visiting for pregnant women and parents of young children. *The Future of Children, 3*, 53–92.

Oshima-Takane, Y., Goodz, E. & Derevensky, J. L. (1996) Birth order effects on early language development: Do secondborn children learn from overheard speech? *Child Development, 67*, 621–634.

Parents as Teachers National Center, Inc. (1999). *Born to Learn™ Curriculum Prenatal to 3 Years*. St. Louis, MO.

Parks, S. (1992). *Hawaii Early Learning Profile (HELP): Strands (0–3)*. Palo Alto, CA: Vort Corporation.

Pawl, J.H., & St. John, M. (1998). *How you are is as important as what you do . . . in making a positive difference for infants, toddlers, and their families*. Washington, DC: ZERO TO THREE.

Perez-Granados, D.R., & Callanan, M.A. (1997). Parents and siblings as early resources for young children in mexican-descent families. *Hispanic Journal of Behavioral Sciences, 19*(1), 3–33.

Petrill, S.A., & Deater-Deckard, K. (2004). Task orientation, parental warmth and SES account for a significant proportion of the shared environmental variance in general cognitive ability in early childhood: Evidence from a twin study. *Developmental Science, 7*, 25–32.

Pettit, G.S., Brown, E.G., Mize, J., & Lindsey, E. (1998). Mothers' and fathers' socializing behaviors in three contexts: Links with children's peer competence. *Merrill-Palmer Quarterly, 44*, 173–193.

Pfannenstiel, J., & Seltzer, D. (1989). New Parents as Teachers: Evaluation of an Early Parent Education Program. *Early Childhood Research Quarterly, 4*, 1–18.

Poe, M.D., Burchinal, M.R., & Roberts, J.E. (2004). Early language and the development of children's reading skills. *Journal of School Psychology, 42*, 315–332.

Primary Children's Medical Center. (n.d.). *Stress*. Retrieved April 1, 2007, from http://www.kidshealth.org/PageManager.jsp?dn=PrimaryChildrens&lic=5&article_set=20400&ca

Raikes, H., Green, B.L., Atwater, J., Kisker, E., Constantine, J., & Chazan-Cohen, R. (2006). Involvement in Early Head Start home visiting services: Demographic predictors and relations to child and parent outcomes. *Early Childhood Research Quarterly, 21*, 2–24.

Raikes, H.H., & Whitmer, J.M. (2006). *Beautiful Beginnings: A developmental curriculum for infants and toddlers*. Baltimore: Paul H. Brookes Publishing Co.

Raver, C.C., & Zigler, E.F. (1997). Social competence: An untapped dimension in evaluating Head Start's success. *Early Childhood Research Quarterly, 12*, 363–385.

Roberts, P. (1998). Fathers' time. In E.N. Junn & C.J. Boyatzis (Eds.), *Child growth and development, Annual editions, 98/99* (pp. 146–152). Guilford, CT: Dushkin.

Roggman, L.A., Boyce, L.K., Cook, G.A., & Christiansen, K. (2004). Playing with daddy: Social toy play, early head start, and developmental outcomes. *Fathering, 2*, 83–108.

Roggman, L.A., Boyce, L., Cook, G., & Jump, V. (2001). Inside home visits: A collaborative look at process and quality. *Early Childhood Research Quarterly, 16*, 53–71.

Roggman, L.A., Cook, G.A., & Jump, V.K. (2000, May 31). *Early Head Start Continuous Program Improvement: Final Report.* Logan, UT: Bear River Early Head Start.

Roggman, L.A., Cook, G.A., Jump, V., Boyce, L.K., & Innocenti, M.S. (2006). *Home Visit Rating Scales (HOVRS).* Unpublished manuscript, Utah State University, Logan, UT.

Roggman, L.A., Cook, G.A., Jump, V., Innocenti, M.S., Christiansen, K., (2007). *Parenting Interactions with Children: Checklist of Observations Linked to Outcomes (PICCOLO).* Unpublished manuscript, Utah State University, Logan, UT.

Roggman, L.A., Cook, G.A., Peterson, C., & Raikes, H. (2008). Who drops out of Early Head Start home visiting programs? *Early Education and Development, 19.*

Roggman, L.A., Hubbs-Tait, L., & Langlois, J.H. (1987). Social play and attachment: A study in construct validation. *Infant Behavior and Development, 10*, 233–237.

Rome-Flanders, T., Cossette, L., Ricard, M., & De'carie, T.G. (1995). Comprehension of rules and structures in mother-infant games: A longitudinal study of the first two years of life. *International Journal of Behavioral Development, 18*, 83–103.

Ross, H.S., & Kay, D.A. (1980). The origins of social games. In K. Rubin (Ed.), *New directions for child development: Children's play, 9* (pp. 17–32). San Francisco: Jossey-Bass.

Saxon, T.F., Colombo, J., Robinson, E.L., & Frick, J.E. (2000). Dyadic interaction profiles in infancy and preschool intelligence. *Journal of School Psychology, 38*, 9–25.

Sénéchal, M. (1997). The differential effect of storybook reading on preschoolers' acquisition of expressive and receptive vocabulary. *Journal of Child Language, 24*, 123–138.

Shonkoff, J.P., & Phillips, D.A. (2000). *From neurons to neighborhoods: The science of early childhood development.* Washington, DC: National Academies Press.

Slade, A. (1987). Quality of attachment and early symbolic play. *Developmental Psychology, 23*, 78–85.

Slaughter-Defoe, D.T. (1993). Home visiting with families in poverty: Introducing the concept of culture. *The Future of Children, 3*, 172–183.

Smith, L. (1995). *Healthy Families California: A review of standards and best practices in home visiting programs across California.* Sacramento, CA: California Consortium to Prevent Child Abuse.

Smith, K.E., Landry, S.H., Swank, P.R., Baldwin, C.D., Denson, S.E., & Wildin, S. (1996). The relation of medical risk and maternal stimulation with preterm infants' development of cognitive, language, and daily living skills. *Journal of Child Psychology and Psychiatry and Allied Disciplines, 37*, 855–864.

Snow, C.E. (1983). Literacy and language: Relationships during the preschool years. *Harvard Educational Review, 53*, 165–189.

Snow, C.E. (2001). *The centrality of language: A longitudinal study of language and literacy development in low-income children.* London: Institute of Education, University of London.

Snow, C.E., Burns, M.S., & Griffin, P. (1998). *Preventing reading difficulties in young children*. Washington, DC: National Academies Press.

Snow, C.E. and the RAND Reading Study Group. (2002). *Reading for understanding: Toward an R&D program in reading comprehension*. Santa Monica, CA: RAND.

Spencer, P.E., & Meadow-Orlans, K.P. (1996). Play, language, and maternal responsiveness: A longitudinal study of deaf and hearing infants. *Child Development, 67*, 3176–3191.

Sroufe, L.A. (1983). Infant-caregiver attachment and patterns of adaptation in preschool: The roots of maladaptation and competence. In N. M. Perlmutter (Ed.), *Minnesota symposia on Child Psychology: vol. 16, Developmental and policy concerning children with special needs* (pp. 41–83). Mahwah, NJ: Lawrence Erlbaum Associates.

Stern, D. (1977). *The first relationship*. Cambridge, MA: Harvard University Press.

Suess, G.J., Grossman, K.E., & Sroufe, L.A. (1992). Effects of infant attachment to mother and father on quality of adaptation in preschool: From dyadic to individual organization of self. *International Journal of Behavioral Development, 15*, 43–65.

Tamis-LeMonda, C.S., & Bornstein, M.H. (1989). Habituation and maternal encouragement of attention in infancy as predictors of toddler language, play, and representational competence. *Child Development, 60*, 738–751.

Tamis-LeMonda, C.S., & Bornstein, M.H. (1990). Language, play, and attention at one year. *Infant Behavior and Development, 13*, 85–98.

Tamis-LeMonda, C.S., & Bornstein, M.H. (1994). Specificity in mother-toddler language-play relations across the second year. *Developmental Psychology, 30*, 283–292.

Tamis-LeMonda, C.S., Bornstein, M.H., & Baumwell, L. (2001). Maternal responsiveness and children's achievement of language milestones. *Child Development 72*(3), 748–767.

Tamis-LeMonda, C.S., Cristofaro, T.N., Rodríguez, E.T., & Bornstein, M.H. (2005). Early language development: Social influences in the first years of life. In L. Balter & C.S. Tamis-LeMonda (Eds.), *Child Psychology: A Handbook of Contemporary Issues, 2*. Philadelphia: Taylor & Francis Group.

Tomasello, M. (1990). The role of joint attentional processes in early language development. *Language Sciences, 10*, 68–88.

Trivette, C.M., & Dunst, C.J. (1986). Proactive influences of support on children and their families. In H.G. Linger (Ed.), *Family strengths: Positive and preventive measures*. Lincoln: University of Nebraska Press.

van den Boom, D.C. (1994). The influence of temperament and mothering on attachment and exploration: an experimental manipulation of sensitive responsiveness among lower-class mothers with irritable infants. *Child Development, 65*, 1457–1477.

van den Boom D.C. (1995). Do first-year intervention effects endure? Follow-up during toddlerhood of a sample of Dutch irritable infants. *Child Development, 66*, 1798–1816

Vort Corporation. (1995). *HELP for preschoolers: Assessment strand*. Palo Alto, CA: Author.

Walker S.P., Chang S.M., Powell C.A., & Grantham-McGregor, S.M. (2006). Effects of early childhood psychosocial stimulation and nutritional supplementation on cognition and education in growth-stunted Jamaican children: prospective cohort study. *Lancet, 366,* 1756–1758.

Walker, S.P., Chang, S.M., Powell, C.A., Simonoff, E., & Grantham-McGregor, S.M. (2006). Effects of psychosocial stimulation and dietary supplementation in early childhood on psychosocial functioning in late adolescence: Follow-up of randomized controlled trial. *British Medical Journal, 333,* 472–480.

Warren, D.I. (1980). Support systems in different types of neighborhoods. In J. Garbarino, & S.H. Stocking (Eds.), *Protecting children from abuse and neglect* (pp. 61–93). San Francisco: Jossey-Bass.

Wasik, B.H., & Roberts, R.N. (1994). Survey of home visiting programs for abused and neglected children and their families. *Child Abuse and Neglect: The International Journal, 18,* 271–283.

Weiss, H.B. (1993). Home visits: Necessary but not sufficient. *The Future of Children, 3,* 113–139.

Wentzel, K.R., & Asher, S.R. (1995). The academic lives of neglected, rejected, popular, and controversial children. *Child Development, 66,* 756–763.

Weston, D.R., Ivins, B., Heffron, M.C., & Sweet, N. (1997). Formulating the centrality of relationships in early intervention: An organizational perspective. *Infants and Young Children, 9,* 1–12.

Woods, J., Kashinath, S., & Goldstein, H. (2004). Effects of embedding caregiver implemented teaching strategies in daily routines on children's communication outcomes. *Journal of Early Intervention, 26,* 175–193.

Yogman, M.W., Kindlon, D., & Earls, F. (1995). Father involvement and cognitive/behavioral outcomes of preterm infants. *Journal of the American Academy of Child and Adolescent Psychiatry, 34,* 58–66.

Youngblade, L.M., Park, K.A., & Belsky, J. (1993). Measurement of young children's close friendship: A comparison of two independent assessment systems and their associations with attachment security. *International Journal of Behavioral Development, 16,* 563–587.

ZERO TO THREE. (n.d.). *How can leaders promote infant mental health in their programs?* Retrieved February 20, 2006, from http://www.zerotothree.org/cpe/tip_2002_01.html. Author.

Parent Satisfaction with the Home Visitor and Home Visit

A Survey for Parents

Instructions: Ask parents, in an interview or written survey, how much they agree with each of the statements in the forms in Appendix A. Both the total score and individual items will provide information about how the family feels about the home visitor and the home visits. Discuss any area of concern.

Parent Satisfaction with the Home Visitor
A Survey for Parents

For each item, circle a number to indicate how much you disagree or agree with the statement about the practitioner who works with you.

MY HOME VISITOR...	Strongly Disagree	Somewhat Disagree	Neither Disagree/Agree	Somewhat Agree	Strongly Agree
1. Has a generally positive relationship with me	1	2	3	4	5
2. Is easy to talk with	1	2	3	4	5
3. Is supportive of me	1	2	3	4	5
4. Seems to know a lot about babies	1	2	3	4	5
5. Seems to know a lot about how to take care of babies	1	2	3	4	5
6. Seems to know a lot about our community	1	2	3	4	5
7. Is well organized and prepared for our visits	1	2	3	4	5
8. Appreciates the ways my family is unique	1	2	3	4	5
9. Respects and supports my religion and my culture	1	2	3	4	5
10. Is responsive to my needs	1	2	3	4	5
11. Is responsive to my baby's needs	1	2	3	4	5
12. Knows what my goals are	1	2	3	4	5
13. Plans things for our home visits that will help me reach my goals	1	2	3	4	5
14. Knows what my interests are	1	2	3	4	5
15. Plans things for our home visits that are interesting to me	1	2	3	4	5

Total score =

The total score equals the sum of all circled numerals. The highest possible score is 75. Higher scores indicate higher parent satisfaction with the home visitor. Specific items may show areas of concern.

Comments?

_____

_____

Parent Satisfaction with the Home Visits
A Survey for Parents

For each item, circle a number to indicate how much you disagree or agree with the statement about the practitioner who works with you.

MY HOME VISITS...	Strongly Disagree	Somewhat Disagree	Neither Disagree/ Agree	Somewhat Agree	Strongly Agree
1. Are a positive experience	1	2	3	4	5
2. Are enjoyable and fun	1	2	3	4	5
3. Give me a lot of information I need and want	1	2	3	4	5
4. Are planned in response to *my* family's needs and interests	1	2	3	4	5
5. Have changed as our needs have changed	1	2	3	4	5
6. Are planned well	1	2	3	4	5
7. Help me reach my goals	1	2	3	4	5
8. Are interesting to me	1	2	3	4	5
9. Involve both me and my home visitor working together	1	2	3	4	5
10. Help me solve my own problems	1	2	3	4	5
11. Help me make my own decisions	1	2	3	4	5
12. Get me playing with my baby more	1	2	3	4	5
13. Help me take better care of my baby	1	2	3	4	5
14. Help me make my baby feel happy and secure	1	2	3	4	5

Comments?

_____

_____

Total score =

The total score equals the sum of all circled numerals. The highest possible score is 70. Higher scores indicate higher parent satisfaction with the home visits. Specific items may show areas of concern.

Home Visit Rating Scales (HOVRS)

An Observation Tool for Practitioners and Supervisors

Home Visit Rating Scales (HOVRS)
An Observation Tool for Practitioners and Supervisors

Instructions:

The Home Visit Rating Scales (HOVRS) are designed for use by practitioners or their supervisors to assess the quality of home visits from direct observation. The measure includes seven rating scales:

Scales on Home Visit Process Quality

- Home Visitor Facilitation of Parent–Child Interaction

- Home Visitor Responsiveness to Family

- Home Visitor Relationship with Family

- Home Visitor Nonintrusiveness

Scales of Home Visit Effectiveness Quality

- Parent–Child Interaction During Home Visit

- Parent Engagement During Home Visit

- Child Engagement During Home Visit

Each scale lists indicators of different levels of quality for a particular home visit process. Observing either live or from video recordings, the observer checks each indicator item he or she observes. At the end of the observation, the observer decides on an overall rating, from 1 to 7, based on the pattern of items checked. For example, if most checked items are in the "Good" column, then the rating would most likely be a 5. If, however, items in the "Adequate" column are also checked, the overall rating would most likely be a 4. Similarly if most checked items were in the "Good" column, with a few items also checked in the "Excellent" column, then the rating would most likely be a 6.

Ratings from the first four scales may be summed to provide an index of process quality. Ratings from the last three scales may be summed to provide an index of effectiveness quality.

Home Visit Rating Scales (HOVRS), by Lori A. Roggman, Gina A. Cook, Vonda K. Jump Norman, Katie Christiansen, Lisa K. Boyce, & Mark S. Innocenti
In *Developmental Parenting: A Guide for Early Childhood Practitioners,* by Lori A. Roggman, Lisa K. Boyce, and Mark S. Innocenti.

Home Visitor Facilitation of Parent–Child Interaction

Inadequate 1	2	Adequate 3	4	Good 5	6	Excellent 7
Home visitor:						
☐ Rarely helps parent respond to child's cues for interaction		☐ Tries to facilitate interactions, even if not always effectively		☐ Facilitates some parent–child interactions		☐ Consistently facilitates parent–child interactions
☐ Ignores parent–child interactions		☐ Tells parent to interact with child		☐ Observes parent–child interactions and gives feedback		☐ Facilitates parent–child interactions that are rich and easy
☐ Interacts with either parent or child but not both		☐ Tells child to interact with parent		☐ Comments on child's cues for interaction		☐ Provides appropriate suggestions and encouragement for parent–child interactions
☐ Intrudes on ongoing parent–child interactions				☐ Prompts parent to engage in interaction with child		☐ Uses materials already in the home to promote parent–child interaction
				☐ Brings materials or activities to the home to promote parent–child interactions		

Overall rating =

Home Visit Rating Scales (HOVRS), by Lori A. Roggman, Gina A. Cook, Vonda K. Jump Norman, Katie Christiansen, Lisa K. Boyce, & Mark S. Innocenti
In *Developmental Parenting: A Guide for Early Childhood Practitioners*, by Lori A. Roggman, Lisa K. Boyce, and Mark S. Innocenti.

Home Visitor Responsiveness to Family

Inadequate 1	2	Adequate 3	4	Good 5	6	Excellent 7

Home visitor:

- ☐ Instructs family rather than sharing activities with family
- ☐ Does not plan well for the visit; forgets necessary materials
- ☐ Works primarily with child, showing parent what to do

- ☐ Responds to parent's input
- ☐ Suggests activities to parent to support child development
- ☐ Shares activities with parent and child
- ☐ Is prepared for activities of the home visit
- ☐ Models appropriately
- ☐ Provides information on child development

- ☐ Gets more information by asking questions
- ☐ Gets more information by observing parent and child
- ☐ Asks parent about goals
- ☐ Asks parent about activities for visits
- ☐ Comments on child's developmental level
- ☐ Gives developmental information relevant to this child

- ☐ Comments on family's strengths or positive interactions
- ☐ Follows parent and child's lead in activities
- ☐ Helps parent plan activities for visits
- ☐ Helps parent plan how to meet goals
- ☐ Gives developmental information relevant to activities

Overall rating =

Home Visit Rating Scales (HOVRS), by Lori A. Roggman, Gina A. Cook, Vonda K. Jump Norman, Katie Christiansen, Lisa K. Boyce, & Mark S. Innocenti.
In *Developmental Parenting: A Guide for Early Childhood Practitioners*, by Lori A. Roggman, Lisa K. Boyce, and Mark S. Innocenti.

Home Visitor Relationship with Family

Inadequate 1	2	Adequate 3	4	Good 5	6	Excellent 7

Home visitor:

Inadequate	Adequate	Good	Excellent
☐ Does not appear to enjoy being in the home	☐ Is engaged in the home visit	☐ Is warm and respectful of the parent	☐ Attempts to involve everyone in the room in activities
☐ Engages in little (or forced) conversation with family members	☐ Interacts sociably with child	☐ Is relaxed in interacting with both parent and child	☐ Obviously enjoys being in the home
☐ Is critical, condescending, or tense	☐ Interacts sociably with parent	☐ Is accepting of the family system	☐ Is sensitive to various situations that arise
☐ Seems distracted, detached, or bored	☐ Interacts with other family members	☐ Interacts with everyone present	☐ Shows interest in what is happening with the family
☐ Ignores family members other than parent and child			

Overall rating =

Home Visit Rating Scales (HOVRS), by Lori A. Roggman, Gina A. Cook, Vonda K. Jump Norman, Katie Christiansen, Lisa K. Boyce, & Mark S. Innocenti
In *Developmental Parenting: A Guide for Early Childhood Practitioners*, by Lori A. Roggman, Lisa K. Boyce, and Mark S. Innocenti.

Home Visitor Nonintrusiveness

	Inadequate		Adequate		Good		Excellent
	1	2	3	4	5	6	7

Home visitor:

Inadequate	Adequate	Good	Excellent
☐ Is intrusive or directive	☐ Makes suggestions and directions, but not excessively	☐ Usually facilitates but some faltering	☐ Consistently sits back when parent–child interaction is ongoing
☐ Overwhelms parent or child	☐ Hands materials to child instead of parent	☐ Occasionally hands toys or materials to child instead of parent	☐ Is consistently responsive to parent and child cues
☐ Often tells parent what to do	☐ Reinforces child before parent does	☐ Occasionally reinforces the child before the parent does even though parent shows ability to do it	☐ Is consistently responsive to parent ideas and interests
☐ Takes over activities	☐ Persists with activity too hard for parent and/or child	☐ Usually hands materials for child to parent instead of to child	☐ Consistently hands toys and other materials for child to parent instead of to child
☐ Plays with or teaches child him- or herself	☐ Persists with activity not interesting to parent or child		

Overall rating =

Parent–Child Interaction During Home Visit

	Inadequate 1	2	Adequate 3	4	Good 5	6	Excellent 7

Parent and Child:

☐ Interaction is minimal, negative, or nonresponsive

☐ Interaction disrupted by crisis

☐ Interaction not maintained due to child's noncompliance or temper tantrum

☐ Interaction occurs infrequently

☐ Interaction starts unengaged, but then they get involved in activities together on and off

☐ Interaction starts engaged, but then one of them becomes unengaged

☐ Interaction is sometimes positive, but less than half of the time

☐ Engage in eye contact fairly frequently

☐ Interact with some warmth

☐ Make positive physical contact

☐ Are in close physical contact during activities

☐ Parent occasionally allows child to take lead in activities

☐ Consistently are responsive to each other during the home visit

☐ Obviously enjoy each other's company and the time they spend together

☐ Interact with a great deal of warmth

☐ Parent consistently allows child to take lead in activities

Overall rating =

HOME VISIT RATING SCALES

Parent Engagement During Home Visit

	Inadequate 1	2	Adequate 3	4	Good 5	6	Excellent 7
Parent:							

Inadequate (1)
- ☐ Does not indicate interest in material or activities
- ☐ Does not initiate activities or conversations with child or home visitor
- ☐ Positions self away from home visitor and child
- ☐ Is distracted, disinterested, physically distant, or involved in another activity

Adequate (3)
- ☐ Is available for interaction with home visitor and child
- ☐ Occasionally participates in activities
- ☐ Is in proximity to home visitor and child during most of the visit
- ☐ Shows some interest in material or activities
- ☐ Answers questions but does not elaborate

Good (5)
- ☐ Appears interested in activities of home visit
- ☐ Initiates topics or asks questions
- ☐ Is an active participant with the child and home visitor

Excellent (7)
- ☐ Frequently initiates discussions on child's development or family
- ☐ Engages in play and learning activities with child during visits
- ☐ Asks questions or provides information related to discussion
- ☐ Stays in proximity to child and home visitor throughout visit
- ☐ Shows enjoyment of visit activities

Overall rating =

HOME VISIT RATING SCALES

Child Engagement During Home Visit

Inadequate 1	2	Adequate 3	4	Good 5	6	Excellent 7
Child:						
☐ Does not participate in home visit activities		☐ Is sometimes engaged in home visit activities		☐ Is frequently engaged in home visit activities		☐ Consistently and enthusiastically interacts with the parent and/or home visitor
☐ Does not interact with parent and/or home visitor		☐ Appears only somewhat interested in the home visit activities		☐ Frequently shows interested in the home visit activities		☐ Consistently and enthusiastically participates in home visit activities
☐ Cries when coaxed to participate in activities in the home visit		☐ Sometimes interacts with the parent and/or home visitor through body language, gaze, gestures, or vocalizations		☐ Frequently interacts with the parent and/or home visitor through body language, gaze, gestures, or vocalizations		☐ Tries to initiate activities or interactions during home visit
						☐ Consistently shows enjoyment that home visitor is in the home

Overall rating =

Index

Page numbers followed by *f* indicate figures; those followed by *t* indicate tables.